Information Eclipse

Books by Michael Fraase

As Author

Internet Tour Guide series

Rapid Reference series

Structured Publishing

Groupware for the Macintosh

MediaTracks

Macintosh Hypermedia

As Coauthor

Guide to the Macintosh Underground

Michael Fraase

Information Eclipse

Privacy and Access in America

Arts & Farces • Saint Paul

ARTS & FARCES
2021 Grand Avenue
Saint Paul, MN 55105 USA
www.farces.com

Library of Congress Catalog Card Number: 98-96455

ISBN: 1-892659-00-X

Printed in the United States of America.
First Edition 1999.

Cover concept, design, and production: MacLean & Tuminelly
Interior Design: ARTS & FARCES
Editing: Karen Caldwell Fraase

This book is printed on acid-free, recycled paper containing 20 percent post-consumer waste. ARTS & FARCES is committed to using high-quality recycled paper with the highest post-consumer waste content.

Table of Contents

Foreword

You ever get the feeling something is wrong but you can't put your finger on it? You know it has something to do with corporations, special interests, conglomerates, the law making process, the political system, arcane statutes, the changing nature of modern "media," and so forth. But it's so damned complex all you can evolve to think about it is a paranoid sounding set of prejudices based on disjunct groups of "factoids" that can't exactly explain or communicate your unease. If you try to talk about it, your scanty intuitions sound suspiciously like wild conspiracy theories. It's not that it was exactly planned this way, it's just that the fact base is so complex and inter-related not even the law makers know what might be a good action and what would be a poor one. They have political careers to attend to and little time to become experts on what amounts to a Ph.D. program in law and technology. Often enough, all they know for sure is that they don't want the kids having access to porn, because that stance is where the votes lie. But that particular red herring has next to nothing to do with the true power struggles for control of information flow. Not that it isn't a subject of grave concern, but it's essentially a way of diverting attention from the true issue of just who is to rule the world.

Wool covers the eyes of all except those who've devoted their professional lives to figuring the ins and outs of the emerging techno-monstrosity; of those tending to serve the special interests which profit from the confusion. The movers and shakers. *Information Eclipse* puts the mountain of facts and implications together and wises the marks. According to somebody's way of reckoning, that's probably subversive. Nothing is more dangerous to special interest groups than an enlightened public. The fact is, you must know what your rights are in order to exercise them. And you must know exactly which rights are being eroded, and how, in order to reclaim them.

Michael Fraase has written a textbook for the dispossessed. The system has the seeds of fairness planted in it, but you have to know where to spade and hoe. And spade you must. Your privacy and rights of access have been turned into a commodity which does not profit you. Wise up. Read this and begin to speak and act with accurate knowledge. Democracy is not a form of rule which favors the apathetic. Lift that rock in the garden and watch things scurry from the light.

Robert Hunter

PREFACE

The interests of government, corporations, and citizens are simultaneously orbiting each other and producing an information eclipse. This eclipse threatens to diminish two very important information rights we should all be enjoying:

- Access to information
- Personal privacy

These "twin" rights of access and privacy are, at the same time, eclipsing each other in spite of a tradition of a politically active citizenry.

Two hundred years ago, the only bureaucracy capable of amassing enough power to infringe upon individual rights was the federal government. America's founding fathers foresaw the dangers of a large, centralized bureaucracy overstepping its bounds and infringing the rights of citizens and intentionally built specific limits and restrictions into the founding documents.

Of course, that was two hundred years ago. Could our founding father's have foreseen multi-national corporate entities, often operating beyond the scope of single governments? Corporations have managed, somehow, to wrest the same rights—and in some cases even more rights—as those vested in the citizenry. Today, the majority of our laws are written largely to support and advance corporate interests.

Corporations first existed in the public interest, at the pleasure of the citizenry, and enjoyed no rights granted a citizen. They could be easily and swiftly dissolved when they were no longer useful. Building infrastructures—roads, bridges, ports, utilities, etc.—is still a compelling reason for the rise and use of corporations.

Currently, we have four main undulating, sometimes colliding, and certainly eclipsing interests competing for citizen awareness and participation:

- Diminishment of individual information rights by government
- Diminishment of individual information rights by corporate interests
- Diminishment of individual access to information by government
- Diminishment of individual access to information by corporations

Envision the two colliding information interests—information access and personal privacy—overlapped by the two eclipsing bodies—government and corporations—as a four-dimensional eclipse.

What do we do when such eclipses occur? In natural systems there are two ingrained responses to a threat: fight or flight. We can choose to either run away from the threat or stand our collective ground and fight. The appropriate response depends upon the specifics of the situation, of course.

Before we can make our fight or flight choice, though, we must clearly identify the threat. That's the purpose of this book; to serve as a sort of early-warning virtual canary in an informational coal mine. The need for citizen participation increases along with the recognition and realization that power does exist in limitations.

The United States Constitution both recognizes and has depended upon a system of checks and balances for each of its three branches of government. Knowing that ultimately each branch will, from time to time, test its powers, our Constitution honored the power inherent in limits by its very design.

No such system of checks and balances exists in the private sphere. Corporations have enjoyed a long run of virtually unchecked free reign in America. There are glimmers of hope that this corporate eclipse is beginning to wane in the form of public sentiment gradually turning against large corporate interests when they exist solely to provide wealth for their shareholders, without concern for their stakeholders.

Acknowledgments

One of the prevailing myths surrounding authors is that our words spring forth—fully formed—in isolation. It's a romantic, and sometimes even attractive, notion. But little is further from the truth. Even within a business as intentionally small as Arts & Farces, nothing happens in isolation.

I am grateful for the help I received during the course of writing this book from some truly remarkable individuals.

Very special thanks to my wife and business partner, Karen C. Fraase, for her editing, marketing, and promotion efforts. Not many people know that she edits and refines virtually everything I write before it ever goes out the door (or network router). Karen's patience and remarkable insight amazes me almost daily.

Robert Hunter kindly provided the time and attention necessary to craft an exceptional foreword.

Dana Bierma, Steve Bierma, Steve Bryan, Dan Kaufmann, Gwen Short, Andrea Tipple, and Griff Wigley all provided wonderfully useful suggestions during the early, formative stages of this project.

Nancy Tuminelly, Pam Scheunemann, and everyone else at MacLean & Tuminelly did a great job on the cover and helped refine the interior design.

Charly Herscovici, Succession René Magritte, graciously permitted and approved the use of *Le chef d'œuvre ou Les mystères de l'horizon* (The Masterpiece or the Mysteries of the Horizon) for the cover. Janet Hicks at The Artists Rights Society and Joanne Greenbaum at Art Resource, were very helpful in handling the license issues and reproduction rights, respectively, for the cover art.

And of course, thanks to you for purchasing this book.

CHAPTER

1

INFORMATION 101

Chances are, you feel the same way I do about the information economy. We've all become knowledge workers, yet we feel as if we know proportionately less about our world now than our parents did. We feel like we have less time for life's important things. We feel our collective attention spans growing shorter each year and we have an almost imperceptible, yet constantly nagging, feeling of dread that we're missing Something Important. Of course, we have learned to drive the latest wonder of the twentieth century—we know how to operate *computers*—but less knowledgeable we sometimes feel, nonetheless.

We are likely feeling this way due to a combination of factors and forces—some we control, and some we may not even know exist—that have combined to form the *information eclipse*.

An eclipse occurs when the orbit of a body causes the body to come between, surpass, or overshadow other bodies, normally within each other's view. An information eclipse occurs when two colliding information interests—information access and personal privacy—encroach upon each other. A four dimensional eclipse occurs when two additional overshadowing bodies—government and corporations—are added to the mix.

Most of us no longer make things with our hands. We create or manipulate symbols with our minds. The underlying source material for most of what we do in our personal and professional lives is information. Information is the coal, real estate, and machinery of our time, and it requires a new set of principles for intelligent observation and discussion.

The New Principles of Information

Before we can discuss privacy and other information rights and their impact on us individually and collectively, we need a foundation of some of the leading theories about information and a shared vocabulary. The remainder of this chapter is an attempt to provide such a foundation. If you're already familiar with contemporary information theory, feel free to skip ahead to the next chapter.

Information expands with usage. Stewart Brand, Global Business Network principal and former editor of the *Whole Earth Review*, is fond of saying "information wants to be free; information wants to be expensive." But what does that enigmatic paradox really mean?

If I give you a copy of the manuscript for this book on a disk, or publish the contents of this book on the Web, I still have my original, yet your copy is indistinguishable from my original. This type of information, because it has value over time, expands as it is used. Each time you share this book—or more importantly, information about this book—with a friend, the value of the book grows in a measurable way. On the other hand, some types of information—usually time-critical information like stock prices, weather forecasts, or a horse-racing tip—have little long-term value and therefore contract measurably with each use.

Information is compressible. In fact, information is the most useful when it is compressed or concentrated. Imagine getting my research notes and a series of uncompressed rough drafts instead of this integrated book. Compressed—or fully integrated—information is not resource intensive. Integrated information is efficient. The creation and manipulation of information is downright stingy in the use of energy and other physical resources, relative to manufacturing technologies and processes. Someday, probably very soon, you'll read books like this on small, light, book-like electronic devices with electronic ink, and the information will be even more highly refined, compressed, and integrated.

Information, by nature, is synergistic. The more we have the more we use (but we don't use it up). The more we use, the more uses for the information we discover. Its reminiscent of those newer elements on the chemistry chart that chemists managed to find *after* society had created a need for them.

Information is not scarce. Facts are so abundant we are bombarded with what appears to be crucially important information. That bombardment then becomes one of the critical factors in planning for uncertainty. The more we earn our livings from manipulating information, the more we will find it necessary to reduce information overloads. Information has become so plentiful that lots of very smart people have created very lucrative careers helping us manage it.

Information is transportable. Information is more transportable than just about anything else we can imagine. And it moves from here to there quicker than a blink of an eye. How much does a telephone number weigh? How long does it take to transmit? This intangible quality of information allows a virtual community, for instance, to exist in cyberspace free of geographic constraints.

As virtual communities become more and more common within business communities, *where* people locate geographically will become less of an issue. We will all decide where we want to live based on a set of personal criteria that matters to us and us alone. No longer will we be forced to relocate at the whim of the workplace. My wife and I immensely enjoy working from our home in Saint Paul, but we often find a need to work virtually with friends and colleagues in Baltimore, San Francisco, Silicon Valley, New York, Austin, Atlanta, Moscow, and a variety of other places.

Information wants to leak. As every schoolboy and political operative knows, it's exceptionally difficult to contain information. Like mercury, information tends to be highly malleable in some ways, yet very resistant to shape or constrain in other ways, always morphing to fit its container. The tendency of information to leak makes it extremely difficult to monopolize. Information's uncontrollable nature can make it tricky and, again like mercury, at times even dangerous to work with.

Information wants to be shared. In purely economic terms, information cannot be constrained by exchange transactions. Like water, information wants a dynamically fluid, sharing transaction, and seeks its own level. If I sell you my computer, you have it and I don't. But if I sell you the *information* contained within my computer, we both have it. As information is shared it gains velocity, picking up speed as it ricochets from receptive node to receptive node.

What Good is Information?

Information isn't much good at all, actually. But information is necessary to form knowledge, which can make information worth a great deal. Information, by its very nature, is continually displaced by new information; knowledge endures.

There are two limits to the growth of knowledge:

- *Time*. The time we need for interpreting, analyzing, and integrating information.
- *Capacity*. Our capacity to think in an integrated manner.

The most important economic development of our lifetime has been the replacement of the second-wave industrial economy with an economy based on information, ideas, and knowledge. Instead of creating wealth with muscle and sinew, as previous generations did in the industrial economy, we now create wealth by manipulating symbols; by converting information into knowledge.

CHANGING OF THE INFORMATION GUARD

Holding the belief that information—and the knowledge distilled from that information—is neutral, is a hazardous mistake. Information and knowledge are both based on underlying facts and assumptions. The facts have to come from somewhere, and assumptions are, by definition, invariably loaded with bias.

Agricultural and industrial economies were based on vertical hierarchies and control structures. Power was greatest at the top, where the population was also the smallest, and was determined by whomever controlled the physical resources, usually land and capital. Influence was wielded largely through secrecy.

In an information-rich environment, even basic notions of control change. Secrecy is usually abandoned simply because secrets are too hard—or too expensive—to keep. Openness becomes a compelling economic imperative in its own right, rather than a preference, and many businesses are already operating with this assumption.

As a brief example, consider Jack Stack's concept of open-book management outlined in his book, *The Great Game of Business*. In businesses bound to rusty industrial age thinking, no benefit could be found in revealing complete financial statements to all employees. It was unheard of. Enlightened businesses in the information economy, however, see immediate and measurable benefit in not only revealing complete financials but also teaching everyone involved how to read them and what they mean. "A business should be run," according to Stack, "like an aquarium, where *everybody* can see what's going on—what's going in, what's moving around, what's coming out."

In those earlier economies, one's position in the hierarchy was based on ownership. In an information-based society, the very concept of ownership changes drastically. When an idea or other piece of information is shared, it is intangible and not subject to an exchange-based economy. The creator doesn't lose possession of the information when it is shared it with a recipient, but he or she is no longer the sole "owner."

Even when information is paid for—as in the case of the purchase of a book—what's really being purchased is presentation and delivery of information, rarely the information itself.

Because information can really only be shared, rather than exchanged, current power structures throughout the culture will likely undergo significant change. Since information can be shared more equitably and is virtually infinite (and infinitely renewable), benefits are likely to spread across the populace rather than contribute to the further concentration of wealth. Natural restrictions—like affordability—on exchange-based information transactions will lead to a greater level of diversity within the culture as we make the shift to non-exchange-based transactions.

THE ECONOMICS OF INFORMATION

In agricultural and industrial economies, poverty was justified by shortages. When demand outstripped supply, prices went up and someone invariably went without. That's no longer an acceptable justification (if it ever was). Information isn't scarce and it's easily created and distributed. Information is plentiful, renewable, and nonpolluting; education is the keystone to building equitability in the information economy.

Access to information will become one of the most politicized issues in the coming years. Japan, for example, has already adapted its culture to the realities of access. An island with so little tillable soil and lacking in virtually all other natural resources, Japan bet heavily on its single greatest asset: its own people. The country has hit a few rough spots along the way, but is reasonably well positioned for the coming changes.

According to International Data Corporation, world consumption of information technology exceeded US$1 trillion per year in the 1980s. By the end of the 1990s, information technology consumption is expected to double to US$2 trillion each year. Not surprisingly, North Americans produce and consume roughly one-half of this total.

In the earlier agricultural and industrial economies, political power was wielded based on geography; you couldn't conquer what you couldn't reach. In an economy based on intangibles, relationships become more important than geographic proximity. Pyramidal organization charts—the kind enjoyed by most industrial-age corporations—are distortions of reality. The corporation of the future will look very different, becoming much more flat, or at least a less steeply pointed pyramid.

Information Dis-Ease

Even infrequent visits to a local bookstore would bear witness to the explosion in stress, self-help, and information "coping" titles of the last decade.

Richard Saul Wurman—best known as the progenitor of the TED conferences, author of *Information Anxiety*, and designer of the ACCESS *Guides*—identified a condition he coined as "information anxiety." Information anxiety refers to the state of increasing discontinuity between what we actually understand and what we think we should understand. We are being inundated with tremendous amounts of information, most of which is useless, some of which is useful, and little of which is really important. Only recently have we realized that most of our information anxiety problems are caused by failing to recognize the interconnections of various pieces of knowledge.

To get a handle on information dis-ease, it's helpful to inventory the various components of what we commonly refer to as *information*—the raw material most of us will work with for the foreseeable future. The core task performed by most information workers is actually a four-phase refinement process that could be referred to, somewhat facetiously, as the "getting of wisdom."

- *Data* can be recognized as that body of unassimilated observations and objective facts that make up the raw materials used by knowledge workers to create, or at least form, useful information.
- *Information* is nothing more (or less) than organized data. The data have usually been organized by someone else, however, and maintain a thin patina of objectivity.
- *Knowledge* is simply organized information. At this stage, information is organized and *internalized* by the individual. Knowledge is information that you

have managed to integrate with everything else you already know.

- *Wisdom* is fully-integrated knowledge—that which you "know in your bones"—bits of knowledge that have been made even more useful by the nature of their relationships to other bits of knowledge.

Our tools for turning the raw resource of information into knowledge haven't managed to keep up with the amount of information we are bombarded with on a daily basis. We become uncomfortable when we can't find what we need to know in a growing mountain of formless data. Anyone returning from a week's vacation to find a hundred or more messages demanding immediate attention, has experienced what Wurman identifies as information anxiety.

Unfortunately, that mountain of formless data continues to grow in an out-of-control manner. Imagine the repercussions of being inundated with more information on a daily basis—from a single information source—than our ancestors managed in their entire lifetimes. Wurman writes, "a weekday edition of the *New York Times* contains more information than the average person was likely to come across in a lifetime in seventeenth-century England."

Complex information is more easily understood when it is presented in a series of contiguous hierarchical layers, like the layers of an onion. The recipient of the information ideally should be able to peel away layer after layer of information, traveling deeper and deeper into the specifics of the body of information. This information layering helps us refocus ourselves in relation to the continual bombardment of information.

An entire new profession—that of the information architect—has formed around the need to make information more accessible, navigable, and manageable by its intended audience. The term "information architect" was coined by Wurman in 1976 but didn't come into common use until the advent of complex

Web sites in the late 1990s. Wurman, in his 1996 *Information Architects*, identifies a practitioner in the field as:

> "1) the individual who organizes the patterns inherent in data, making the complex clear. 2) a person who creates the structure or map of information which allows others to find their personal paths to knowledge. 3) the emerging 21st century professional occupation addressing the needs of the age focused upon clarity, human understanding, and the science of the organization of information."

Wurman offers a model for this onion-like layering of information. He calls his model the Five Rings, based on the degree of immediacy that various types of information have for us in our daily lives. According to Wurman, "the rings radiate out from the most personal information that is essential for our physical survival to the most abstract form of information that encompasses our personal myths, cultural development, and sociological perspective."

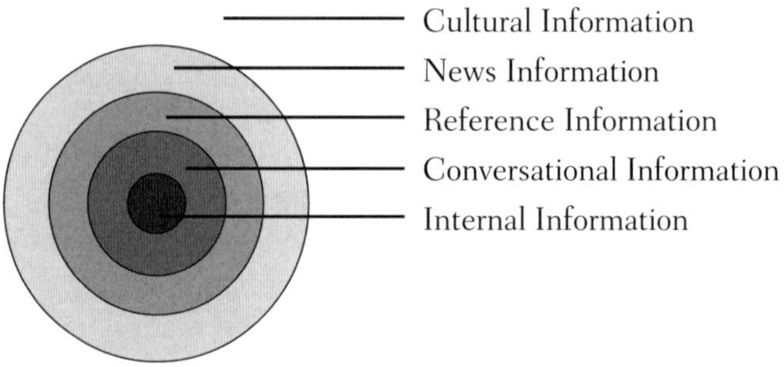

Figure 1-1: Richard Saul Wurman's Five Rings of Information Immediacy.

- *Cultural Information.* The outermost ring in Wurman's model is cultural information. This is our history, philosophy, and arts. It represents our attempts to understand our culture. This is where information accumulated from the other layers is combined to build the information set that determines our attitudes and our beliefs.

- *News Information*. Current events that have only a relatively minor impact on our daily lives comprise the news level. Most of the information we receive from the media falls into this category. When we learn the name of the political candidates in Peru, for example, it's news information. This type of information, while not impacting directly on our lives, influences us in more subtle ways including the shaping of our individual conception of the world around us.

- *Reference Information*. This layer is made up of information sources including textbooks, directories, encyclopedias, maps, dictionaries, and telephone books. We use reference information when we research a specific topic, such as the year Portugal declared its independence or the phone number of a local city council member.

- *Conversational Information*. Conversational information is comprised of all the verbal and written exchanges of information that we have with people around us. Wurman identifies this form of information as a main source and the one we most easily ignore. Conversational information can range from the banal ("What's your name?" What do you do for a living?") to the poignant ("What do you think about the proposed water referendum?"). Information in this layer is also the most easily controllable. This is the layer Wurman tells us that we should focus most intensely on if we are to gain greater control over our own information spaces.

- *Internal Information*. Internal information is defined as the collection of cerebral messages that

> enables our bodies to function. When we feel pain or hunger, for example, we are dealing with internal information. This is the type of information over which we have the least control but that affects us the most.

The Information Infrastructure

Computing and telecommunications tools have improved at an annual rate of about 25 percent since the early 1970s, according to International Data Corporation reports. An information infrastructure allows hundreds of millions of computers to communicate with each other in a few seconds. Typical paper-based business correspondence takes about five days. The computer assisted and accelerated compression of "information float" is having dramatic effects on the substance of all business and personal communications.

Computers can manipulate information much faster and more accurately than humans. Unlike humans, however, computers almost never understand the information they machinate. The emerging information infrastructure could easily be configured to place the burden of communicating and processing information on computers rather than humans.

In order for this to happen, computers must begin to "understand," at only the crudest level, the meaning of the information they process. Even though we are continually inundated with information, we often have only an intuitive hunch about its meaning and virtually no sense of its value. Until we understand the meaning and value inherent in the information, our machines won't either.

The emerging information infrastructure has several properties in common with well-established infrastructures like the telephone system, the electrical grid, the sewer system, community water service, and the national highway system:

- Wide availability
- Ease of use
- Multiple useful applications

To be successful and ubiquitous, the information infrastructure needs several basic capabilities: flexibility, speed, security, reliability, accessibility, and accountability.

Flexible information transport capability with varying levels of speed, security, and reliability are needed. The telephone infrastructure was designed to carry digital voice signals at a fixed speed of 64,000 bits per second (64 Kbps) with non-varying levels of security and reliability. Computers can transmit information at a wide range of speeds, depending on the information being delivered. Brief text messages require only a few *thousand* bits per second of speed, while high-resolution video requires tens of *millions* of bits per second capabilities.

Monetary transactions require high levels of security and reliability, but a digital photograph can tolerate a few lost bits here and there. The point is that we should have a wide selection of levels of speed, security, and reliability from which to choose, paying only for the level of service we want. Directories, regulations, census data, and other common resources must be available to everyone on an equal basis.

Vinton Cerf at MCI and Robert Kahn at the Corporation for National Research Initiatives (CNRI) have developed software programs they call Knowbots. Knowbots travel throughout a network, inspecting and understanding similar kinds of specific information without regard to language or form. Cerf articulated the concept of knowbots in a September 1991 *Scientific American* article:

> "Autonomous, interprogram communication is being explored today in an even more general form under the rubric of knowledge robots (Knowbot is a registered

> trademark of the Corporation for National Research Initiatives), programs that move from machine to machine, possibly cloning themselves. Knowbots support parallel computations at different sites. They communicate with one another, with various servers in the network, and with users. In the future, much computer communication could consist of the interactions of Knowbots dispatched to do our bidding in a global landscape of networked computing and information resources."

An information infrastructure with features like Knowbots could help us lead more productive and enjoyable lives in three basic ways:

1. Relieve us of many of the repetitive, boring, and unpleasant tasks related to retrieving, processing, and transmitting information.
2. Improve the way we do things now, both qualitatively and quantitatively.
3. Open a wide range of unexplored possibilities to all members of the society.

Such an information infrastructure would allow free enterprise to flourish, but not at the expense of the individual. Telephone companies could continue to lay down the physical media for the network and continue to bear a major portion of the responsibility of providing flexible information transport services, minimal common services, and access to shared resources.

Allowing telephone companies, or other centralized bodies, to have strict control over services or content would be shortsighted, however. Focusing on the work they do best—laying the pipe, not controlling the content that flows within—is putting a telephone company to its highest and best use.

As in all previous market economies, any number of goods and services could be bought and sold, and not all transactions would be monetary. Individuals, companies, and organizations that profit by providing services need to be accountable and held responsible for services that misbehave. If your rogue Knowbot, for example, picks a fight with my Knowbot and causes damage to my information space, you should be held accountable.

LIBRARIES IN A KNOWLEDGE ECONOMY

Libraries have been around at least since the sixth century when they shared the same physical space with publishing houses. Benedictine monks painstakingly produced exquisitely illustrated manuscripts. So transcendent were these illustrations that we call them "illuminated." The monks carefully guarded their work; in England's Hereford Cathedral, books were actually chained to the shelves. The monks collected books and guarded them for communal use, but the books were not allowed to circulate.

Modern libraries have traditionally broken the barriers between publishers and individuals by providing unprecedented access to books from various publishers. Libraries in a knowledge economy will break the barriers between each other. This is likely to drastically change the economics of publishing and subsequently, the dissemination of ideas.

Librarians—public or private—can no longer afford to have all the books and journals they feel they should have in their collections. An alarming cycle is occurring: rising prices of books and journals cause declining library circulations; declining circulations cause prices to rise even further. With the advent of a ubiquitous information infrastructure, this self-perpetuating cycle can be broken.

Providing a remote researcher with materials or saving text from paper decay causes librarians to spend much of their time duplicating text on paper. Since much of the duplicated text was originally created in electronic form, why not divorce paper from the process and reproduce content directly from the electronic version? The Library of Congress's head of technology, Joseph Price, estimates that some 80,000 items on the Library's shelves disintegrate each year to the point that the pages become so brittle as to be impossible to turn.

The Bibliothèque nationale de France (the French National Library) hopes to make electronic copies of 100,000 of the "canonical works of the 20th century" available.

The Boston Spa in Yorkshire's branch of the British Library locates hard-to-find journal articles and other documents. The library receives a CD-ROM containing digitized images of the journal articles from which it makes paper copies whenever needed. Basic library services are free. Boston Spa documents are supplied for the cost of photocopying and shipping when the service is provided to United Kingdom citizens. Providing documents to foreigners is run at a profit.

Copyright payments for photocopies in Britain are handled through the Copyright Licensing Agency (CLA); roughly equivalent to the Copyright Clearance Center in the United States. The CLA negotiates on behalf of publishers to set and collect copyright fees from high-volume photocopiers including libraries, universities, and corporations. Publishers so far have not given the CLA permission to negotiate electronic publication fees. In the United States, it is against the law for the Library of Congress to charge more than reproduction costs plus 10 percent for the documents it distributes.

If, in the future, we can get an electronic copy of anything we want from a library—free of charge—what role will bookstores have? On the other hand, if the libraries begin to charge for distribution of materials, how is a library differentiated from a printer, a publisher, or a bookstore? More importantly, what happens to the library's traditional role of making information available to those who cannot afford to purchase it? What will the impact be on writers?

Electronic card catalogs promise to enable enterprising authors to effectively become their own publishers. Amazon.com claims to be Earth's biggest bookstore. It's more accurate to think of Amazon.com as the Earth's most easily accessible electronic card catalog; a search engine for books.

A traditional publisher's power arises from the cost and difficulty surrounding the printing process, "barriers to entry" in business-speak. The "printing" process for electronic publishers is so simple as to be trivial, requiring only a few keystrokes. The distribution problem, long associated with print publishing, evaporates with the advent of the electronic card catalog.

FURTHER...

Like me you're probably still trying to get your arms around this whole big concept of "information" and everything it encompasses. This chapter offered a very brief overview of some of the leading theories about information and how it affects us. A very basic foundation has been laid so at least we can discuss information intelligently with a shared vocabulary. Information, and our relationship to it, carries a sometimes heavy burden of rights and responsibilities.

Chapter 2 investigates the basic information rights we enjoy as American citizens and provides a historical overview of information control in England and Colonial America. While Americans cannot to ignore the information policies—current or historical—of the rest of the world, I have, for the purposes of this book, necessarily limited the majority of my observations to American issues.

Resources

- Amazon.com: <www.amazon.com>
- Bibliothèque nationale de France (French National Library): <www.bnf.fr>
- Boston Spa Library: <www.leeds.gov.uk/library/branches/bs.html>
- Stewart Brand: <www.gbn.org/staff/sbb/brand.html>
- Copyright Clearance Center (CCC): <www.copyright.com>
- Copyright Licensing Agency (CLA): <www.cla.co.uk>
- Corporation for National Research Initiatives: <www.cnri.reston.va.us>
- Global Business Network: <www.gbn.org>
- International Data Corporation: <www.idc.com>
- Library of Congress: <www.loc.gov>
- TED: <www.ted.com>
- Richard Saul Wurman: <www.ted.com/rsw.html>

CHAPTER

2

INFORMATION RIGHTS

In America, information rights have evolved largely as a result of our experience with early attempts to control information. They are based on a combination of English common law, the Constitution and its Amendments, and a rich, diverse history of case law. Each American enjoys certain basic information rights, the most important of which is, arguably, the right to speak and write freely.

There are other rights that we enjoy, including the right to control the duplication and distribution of what we create, the right to access certain information collected or created by our government, and the right to privacy.

With these information rights come responsibilities. For the most part, our information responsibilities are also based on a combination of common law, the Constitution and its Amendments, and a history of case law.

INFORMATION CONTROL IN ENGLAND AND THE COLONIES

In 1275, the De Scandalis Magnatum was enacted to prescribe punishment for anyone who disseminated untrue information that could disrupt the atmosphere between the king and his people. In 1378, the law was extended to afford scandal protection for "peers, prelates, justices and other officials" of the monarchy.

When the first printing presses were established at the end of the fifteenth century, the De Scandalis Magnatum was reenacted in 1554 and 1559 to include "seditious words" as cause for punishment. This law was enforced by the Court of the Star Chamber to punish individuals engaged in political scandal.

In 1585, the Star Chamber required publishers to be licensed to publish books. An intentional monopoly was formed in what was known as the Stationers' Company. The Stationer's Company was endowed with the ability to seize the publications of all outsiders. Later, in 1637, an ordinance was passed to limit the number of printers, presses, and apprentices in the country.

The Court of the Star Chamber was abolished in 1641, but the licensing system remained in force. In 1662, the Licensing Act was instituted as a temporary statute, until it expired in 1679. In 1711, Queen Anne realized that licensing publishers was not a viable solution and enacted the Stamp Act. The Stamp Act imposed a duty on all newspapers and advertisements, effectively limiting publishing to the most wealthy segments of British society.

The first printing presses in America arrived at Harvard University in 1638 and were used to publish church information.

Each colony restricted the press, and the state of New York, for example, required publishers to be licensed until 1719.

The First Amendment, guaranteeing the right of free speech and assembly, was originally proposed as part of twelve amendments to the United States Constitution during the first session of Congress in 1789. On December 15, 1791, the Bill of Rights—minus two of the original amendments—became part of the Constitution.

CONSTITUTIONAL AMENDMENT PROTECTIONS

The United States Constitution extends four basic information protections to American citizens via several Amendments:

1. The First Amendment provides for freedom of speech and assembly:

"Congress shall make no law respecting an establishment of religion, or prohibiting the free exercise thereof; or abridging the freedom of speech or of the press; or of the right of the people peaceably to assemble and to petition the Government for a redress of grievances."

2. The Fourth Amendment protects against arbitrary government search and seizure:

"The right of the people to be secure in their persons, houses, papers, and effects, against unreasonable searches and seizures, shall not be violated, and no Warrants shall issue, but upon probable cause, supported by Oath or affirmation, and particularly describing the place to be searched, and the persons or things to be seized."

3. The Fifth Amendment guarantees due process and protects against self-incrimination and double jeopardy:

"No person shall be held to answer for a capital or otherwise infamous crime, unless on a presentment or indictment of a Grand Jury, except in cases arising in the land or naval forces, or in the militia, when in actual service in time of war or public danger; nor shall any person be subject for the same offense to be twice put in jeopardy of life or limb; nor shall be compelled in any criminal case to be a witness against himself, nor be deprived of life, liberty, or property, without due process of law; nor shall private property be taken for public use without just compensation."

4. The Ninth Amendment guarantees all rights to the individual not specifically delegated to the states and the federal government:

"The enumeration in the Constitution of certain rights shall not be construed to deny or disparage others retained by the people."

Of all the Constitutional Amendment protections, the Ninth Amendment is under the most fire and gets the least amount of attention in a highly consolidated, corporate controlled, mainstream press. The current trend in America is toward negating the Ninth Amendment rights vested in the individual and transferring those rights to government agencies and corporate entities whenever possible. It's not unreasonable to state that the trend in the United States is toward enacting laws that serve solely to benefit corporate interests.

For example, some city charters are being rewritten to convey all rights to the state that are not expressly retained by the city. Similarly, contracts between authors and publishers are being written to convey all rights to the publisher that are not expressly retained by the author. Since it is impossible to foresee any and all abuses a larger entity may impose upon a smaller entity, one wonders about the ultimate long-term effects on all smaller entities. It is important to remember that our forebears saw fit to *reserve unexpressed rights in favor of the individual and the smallest unit of government.*

COPYRIGHT AND INTELLECTUAL PROPERTY

American copyright is governed primarily by the Copyright Act of 1976 (Title 17 of the United States Code), implemented in January 1, 1978.

Congress made concerted efforts to create new copyright legislation in late May 1996. A House Judiciary subcommittee came very close to crafting the new law, but deferred further action. Negotiations between online services and copyright owners failed the day before final amendments were due.

The House Courts and Intellectual Property subcommittee, chaired by Representative Carlos Moorhead (R-California), refused to refer the bill to the House Judiciary committee until online services and copyright owners agreed on what, specifically, should constitute a copyright infringement by an online service provider. As of early July 1998, the proposed changes to the American copyright law remain in flux.

The proposed copyright bill would:

- Impose a fine of up to US$250,000 and a prison term of up to two years on any online or Internet service that willfully violates someone else's copyright.
- Limit damages to no more than US$1,000 for unwitting copyright infringement by any online or Internet service.

- Hold harmless any online or Internet service that has taken reasonable steps to educate employees to remove infringing material.
- Hold harmless an Internet or telephone company that acts solely as a conduit, merely transmitting unmodified information.

The House Judiciary Committee on April 1, 1998, endorsed a copyright bill authored by Howard Coble (R-North Carolina) that would criminalize technology used to reproduce intellectual property while simultaneously limiting the liability of Internet service providers who host or transmit infringing copies of copyrighted material. Under this proposed legislation, the process and technologies of "reverse engineering" would be criminalized. The process of reverse engineering is regularly used by software companies to analyze competing products and to ensure compatibility with complimentary products. Software companies argue that any law prohibiting reverse engineering would be a severe hardship.

Under Representative Coble's legislation, it would conceivably become illegal to use photocopiers, tape recorders, video recorders, or computers.

Representatives Rick Boucher (D-Virginia) and Zoe Lofgren (D-California) proposed amendments to the bill that would criminalize the intentional infringement of copyrighted works instead of the technology used to reproduce intellectual property. All of the Boucher and Lofgren proposed amendments were rejected by the House Judiciary Committee.

Coble was quoted in the *New York Times* as saying his proposed legislation is needed because "while most people would never shoplift, many have no second thoughts about stealing intellectual property." Coble's bill was subsequently combined with proposed legislation by Representative Robert Goodlatte (R-Virginia) that would hold Internet service providers harmless for unknowingly transmitting or storing pirated material. The combined bill would require Internet service providers to remove pirated material from their networks when copyright infringement is called to their attention.

The Coble-Goodlatte bill was designed to bring American copyright law into compliance with the World Intellectual Property Organization Copyright Treaties Implementation Act that was proposed in December 1996.

Opponents of the legislation argue that the Coble-Goodlatte bill would strengthen and extend the market position and monopolistic tendencies of leading software companies such as Microsoft Corporation. Microsoft, for its part, supports the bill as it's currently written, emphasizing that the proposed law equitably maintains the balance between fair use and the rights of copyright owners.

Virginia's Democratic Representative Rick Boucher crafted an alternative piece of legislation, the Digital Era Copyright Enhancement Act, that would punish copyright circumvention only when the intent was to infringe upon the rights of a copyright owner. Proponents of the Boucher bill argue it would strengthen fair use and enhance competition within the high technology industry.

WORLD INTELLECTUAL PROPERTY ORGANIZATION

The December 1996 World Intellectual Property Organization (WIPO) conference in Geneva attempted to wrest copyright from the sole hands of content creators and initiated a new debate between content creators, transmitters, and consumers.

An agenda forwarded by the Clinton administration on behalf of the Hollywood studios and other major American copyright industries was resoundingly defeated at the Geneva WIPO conference. The Clinton administration agenda was originally set forth in the "Intellectual Property and the National Information Infrastructure" white paper published in September 1995.

Legislation to implement the Clinton administration recommendations was introduced in Congress in late September 1995, and the first hearings on the proposed legislation (S 1284 and HR 2441) took place in December 1995. The legislation offered nothing to protect the creators of intellectual property while focusing its efforts in favor of corporate entities that may have licensed a creator's original content. Opposition to the proposed law was so great that neither bill made it out of subcommittee.

The initial Clinton position on copyright and intellectual property focused on seven central issues. These seven issues largely applied only *after* a publisher had secured a license to original content. This essentially enhanced the licensor's rights while eclipsing the creator's rights. Copyright law was originally intended to protect *creators* of intellectual property to an extent great enough to keep them interested in producing worthwhile content. The Clinton administration's seven-point plan is outlined below.

1. Granting publishers rights over even temporary reproduction of a work in a computer's memory, such as that which occurs while browsing the Web.
2. Amending existing law so that digital transmission of a copyrighted work would be regarded as a distribution to the public.
3. Eliminating the fair-use provision whenever a use might be licensed.
4. Treating electronic forwarding of a copyrighted work as a violation of both the reproduction and distribution sections of the copyright statute.
5. Attaching copyright management information to digital versions of a work, enabling publishers to

track every digital copy and locate every copy on a network.

6. Protecting every work technologically (presumably by encryption) and making any attempt to circumvent the protection illegal.
7. Placing the burden of enforcing copyright of works in digital form on online services and Internet service providers.

The Clinton copyright agenda was largely championed by Bruce Lehman, chair of the Clinton administration's Working Group on Intellectual Property Rights. Lehman's approach was to attempt to force Congress to adopt the Clinton copyright agenda by getting the measures adopted in the international WIPO forum. Lehman knew if the measures were integrated into the WIPO treaties, it would be virtually impossible for Congress to pass less restrictive intellectual property laws in the future. It was a seemingly safe bet, but the gambit failed miserably and completely in the international forum.

American citizens once again, naively assumed that a presidential administration would never try to subvert or circumvent the democratic process—this time by promoting an international treaty that stood in direct opposition to Congressional intent and tone. But it certainly appears that is exactly what was attempted by the Clinton administration through Lehman.

In addition to the Clinton administration's seven-point plan, Lehman also proposed the creation of a new form of intellectual property rights in the underlying factual content of databases. Lehman's proposal was based on the European Union's database protections that allow some ownership and attendant copyright rights to anyone who expends effort to collect facts.

During the closing days of the WIPO conference, Lehman, having seen his proposals to extend intellectual property rights in favor of corporate interests roundly defeated, adamantly claimed that without new information ownership rights, the largest American content creators would simply ignore the Internet.

The WIPO Copyright Treaty requires the United States to implement legislation to protect only the integrity of Rights Management Information (RMI). This prevents the removal or alteration of electronic RMI that may be attached to digital forms of protected works in the future. Distribution of digital copies with removed or altered RMI would be prohibited. The Clinton agenda called for a much broader RMI provision that would make any attempt to block monitoring software (even on the grounds of privacy invasion) a felony. Under the provision adopted by the WIPO, blocking monitoring software would not be illegal.

In late 1996, the WIPO Copyright Treaty was signed by almost one hundred countries, but even a year later none of the signing countries had ratified the copyright treaty. Intellectual property owners—mostly recording and publishing trade associations and lobbyists representing enormous corporate media conglomerates—continue to push for the changes with the hope that the new laws will protect their works from being distributed without permission, globally, on the Internet.

Library groups and academics, on the other hand, argue that the treaty is severely flawed and virtually eliminates the concept of fair use of copyrighted works.

Fair use is a provision of American copyright law that allows portions of copyrighted works to be used for certain, specific purposes. In very general terms, fair use is considered to be permissible so long as it does not exploit the commercial value of the original work. The most often cited examples of fair use are review, criticism, and parody.

In September 1997, the Digital Future Coalition, a collaboration of educational and consumer groups and trade associations for the electronics and telecommunications industries, testified before the House Judiciary Committee's Subcommittee on

Courts and Intellectual Property. The coalition voiced concerns that the WIPO treaty language would allow copyright owners to restrict the flow of public domain materials in addition to copyrighted works.

The treaty, as currently endorsed by the Clinton administration, would also overrule the Supreme Court's "Betamax" decision that specifically allows the electronic recording of materials by consumers for their personal use. Specifically, a part of the bill to ratify the WIPO treaty in the United States—HR 2281—contains a provision that would criminalize the manufacture or distribution of any technology that could be used to circumvent copyright protection. The WIPO conferees explicitly rejected any punishment for manufacture or distribution of such devices, but the Clinton administration reintroduced the penalties. Some critics argue that if passed, the legislation would outlaw consumer use of audio and video tape recorders as well as personal computers.

The copyright demarcation line was clearly drawn. On one side of the line were the mostly multinational film, recording, software, and publishing conglomerates. On the other side of the line were educators, librarians, and consumers in what has to be an uncomfortable liaison with the electronics and telecommunications manufacturers.

On December 16, 1997, President Clinton signed the No Electronic Theft Act into law. The copyright legislation, authored by Representative Robert Goodlatte (R-Virginia), punishes willful copyright infringement of at least US$1,000 of value even if no profit is made from the infringing activity. Previously, copyright infringement actions could only be brought if the violator profited from the infringement. The new law introduces a sliding scale of penalties based on the degree of severity of the copyright infringement:

- For infringements with a retail value of US$2,500 or more, a copyright violation carries a US$250,000 fine and a three year prison sentence.
- For less severe violations, with a retail value between US$1,000 and US$2,500, the penalty is a US$100,000 fine and a one year prison sentence.

The No Electronic Theft Act enables copyright owners to dictate how their materials can be used by others. Under prior law, the federal Copyright Act, not contract law, governed the use of copyrighted material. Some copyright owners argue that the new law moves the United States closer to recognizing the moral rights inherent in intellectual property. Others, including smaller copyright owners, readily point out that the No Electronic Theft Act—by removing the emphasis from standardized federal law and placing it in nonstandard contract law—is intended to benefit only mammoth corporate interests.

Many industrialized nations extend what are called moral rights to copyright and intellectual property protection. In France, for example, copyright falls under the aegis of the Ministry of Culture which sees its responsibility with regard to copyright as protecting the artist. In America, on the other hand, copyright falls under the jurisdiction of the Department of Commerce where, predictably, the protection of a publisher's business interests is considered more important. Where the Europeans traditionally extend the civilized right to control any changes with the creator, American law generally and indecorously extends all control rights in a creative work solely to the publisher.

Academics and technology experts warn that a balance must be struck between intellectual property rights and the public's right to access information. Many fear the development of a sort of information feudalism under the new law. As copyright ownership continues to aggregate, coalesce, and consolidate in the hands of a few immense media conglomerates, ordinary people will find themselves having to pay for it piece by piece.

Welcome to the information eclipse, when rights and protections of smaller entities are completely overshadowed by the interests of commercial gain for a minority elite.

In late April 1998, Internet service providers and content producers reached a tentative copyright agreement that will be considered by the Senate Judiciary Committee and hopefully enacted into law by Congress.

Under the terms of the negotiated agreement, Internet service providers and telephone companies will not be held liable for damages if they unknowingly transmit material that infringes a copyright. If service providers become aware of a copyright infringement within any systems under their control, however, they must stop it.

Reversing their previous position that Internet service providers should be treated the same as any other business under existing copyright law, copyright owners agreed to the compromise that broke a two-year stalemate.

In the last week of April 1998, the Senate Judiciary Committee adopted the Digital Millennium Copyright Act which, if signed into law, would actually make illegal any *equipment* used to infringe copyrights in addition to the act (or intent) of infringing a copyright. Imagine the bumper stickers: "Tape recorders don't infringe, people infringe," "Free the DAT Seven," and "You can take my VCR remote when you pry it from my cold, dead fingers." Critics of the proposed legislation argue that the basic issue of fair use is not adequately addressed. A similar version of the bill has already passed the House Judiciary Committee.

It's clear that copyright law has not kept pace with either advancing technology or a changing economy. Changes need to be made, and there must be a balance struck between intellectual property rights and the public's right to access information. Individuals and small organizations will continue to be at a clear disadvantage as long as the laws continue to be enacted to support commerce at the expense of all else.

There exists a powerful need to strengthen copyright law to protect the rights of creators of intellectual property. And let's be clear: individuals create all original intellectual property and it's with individual rights that we should be most concerned. Simultaneously, moral rights and fair use should be not only recognized, but strengthened, to assist individuals and small organizations.

LEGISLATIVE PROTECTIONS

In addition to the basic protections provided by the Constitution and its Amendments, a variety of legislative protections have evolved over the years to provide basic information rights to the American citizenry. The remainder of this chapter briefly outlines some of the more important of these legislative protections, as well as the rights and responsibilities they convey.

CURRENCY AND FOREIGN TRANSACTIONS REPORTING ACT ("BANK SECRECY ACT")

Currency and Foreign Transactions Reporting Act of 1970 ("Bank Secrecy Act") requires any bank or other depository organization to keep certain records and to report certain types of financial transactions to the federal government.

Records of all deposits or credit transactions of more than US$10,000 and records of transactions of more than US$10,000 that send money out of the country must be retained.

Any "unusual domestic currency transaction" of more than US$10,000 must be reported to the Internal Revenue Service.

The most controversial aspect of the Bank Secrecy Act requires that all checks of US$100 or more must be copied and retained for five years. Most banks simply retain records of all checks without regard to the transaction amount.

Privacy Act

The Privacy Act of 1974 set up certain safeguards against the misuse of federal records by government or third parties. However, the legislation contains only minimal protection from abuse of private sector records.

The Act prohibits federal agencies from disclosing individual personal information or records without the "prior consent of the individual to whom the record pertains." A very wide exception exists, however, allowing the disclosure of any information or record if the intended use is a "routine use for purposes compatible with the purpose for which [the information] was collected."

Federal agencies interpret this "compatible purpose" exception to allow the transfer of computer data between agencies for the purpose of computer matching. Computer matching is the process by which information from disparate computer databases can be combined to enable searching for common records. For example, the Department of Education matches computer records with the Internal Revenue Service to determine the current address of those in default on a student loan.

The Internal Revenue Service goes further by maintaining that it derives your consent for information disclosure with a statement contained within its *Instructions for Preparing Form 1040*:

> "We may give the information to the Department of Justice and the other Federal agencies, as provided by law. We may also give it to the states, the District of Columbia, and U.S. commonwealths, or possessions to carry out their tax laws. And we may give it to foreign

> governments because of tax treaties they have with the United States."

The Privacy Act also gives you the right to see and correct all records that are held about you by the federal government. The Act does not provide a method or system for informing or notifying you of this right, however.

As an example of the impact of this lack of notification, consider that the Social Security Administration maintains the benefit records of more than 150 million Americans. In 1986, only twenty-three people asked to see their Social Security records.

The Privacy Act prohibits federal agencies from selling or renting an individual's name and address unless specifically authorized by law to do so. It's important to note that the Privacy Act applies only to government agencies; it specifically does not apply to the private sector.

Tax Reform Act

Since 1910, tax returns submitted to the Internal Revenue Service (IRS) had been public records. In 1976, however, the Tax Reform Act was signed into law, placing restrictions on the use of IRS records. This action was taken in reaction to allegations that the Nixon administration had used tax returns to harass political opponents.

The revised Section 6103 of the IRS code establishes confidentiality of all American tax returns unless disclosure of the tax return is specifically authorized by law. The Tax Reform Act also prohibits federal government agencies from distributing or redisclosing tax information. Since 1976, exemptions to the rule have regularly and steadily been added. There are now at least twenty-nine different exceptions to the tax disclosure rule, allowing our personal information to be passed between various government agencies without our knowledge or consent.

Right to Financial Privacy Act

The Right to Financial Privacy Act of 1978 requires the Internal Revenue Service to provide a taxpayer with fourteen days' notice when it issues a summons to see his or her records at any financial institution.

Upon receipt of this notice, the taxpayer has the right to intervene and suspend compliance with the summons within the fourteen day period. If the taxpayer files the intervention with the bank and IRS, a federal district judge decides whether or not to enforce the summons.

The Financial Privacy Act of 1978 provides limited protection to prevent a record keeper from disclosing information about an individual to government agents. The Act also provides individuals with the right to contest the disclosure of the information.

Employee Polygraph Protection Act

In July 1988, President Reagan signed into law the Employee Polygraph Protection Act of 1988. The Act prohibits the use of polygraph ("lie detector") tests by private companies for pre-employment screening and for random testing of employees. Pharmaceutical companies and private security firms are exempt from the polygraph testing ban.

Polygraph tests in general can be seen as invasions of privacy because examiners ask sensitive personal questions, and because there is no such thing as a volunteer polygraph test. Refusal to take a lie detector test is generally perceived as an admission of guilt or at least of having something to hide.

Freedom of Information Act

The Freedom of Information Act (FOIA) requires disclosure of most information collected by the federal government, unless there is a "clearly unwarranted invasion of privacy." The FOIA allows anyone to access *all* federal government records held by the federal executive branch unless the records are *specifically* covered by one of the Act's exemptions.

Do you find the compatibility of the Privacy Act and the FOIA confusing? To keep it all straight, remember that the Privacy Act states that information available under the FOIA cannot be exempted under the Privacy Act. The President, Congress, and the federal courts are all exempted from the FOIA.

Electronic Fund Transfer Act

The Electronic Fund Transfer Act of 1980 requires any financial institution providing electronic transfer of funds to notify its customers about third-party access to customer accounts and records. The Act also imposes liabilities on financial institutions for transmission or documentation errors.

Computer Software Act

The Computer Software Act of 1980 adds the definition of a computer software program to the Copyright Act of 1976 and extends all copyright protections to computer software.

Fair Credit Reporting Act

The Fair Credit Reporting Act allows rejected credit applicants to request the reason for an adverse credit decision. You have the right to learn the nature and substance of the information contained in your credit file. If information in the file is inaccurate or false, you have the right to challenge it and learn the source of the information. Adverse information about you that is more than seven years old should be purged from the file.

The Fair Credit Reporting Act does not assure the correction of adverse information disclosed by a creditor to a credit-reporting bureau in error and most credit reports carry a disclaimer similar to the following example:

> "This information is furnished in response to an inquiry for the purpose of evaluating credit risk. It has been obtained from sources deemed reliable, the accuracy of which this organization does not guarantee. The inquirer has agreed to indemnify the reporting bureau for any damage arising from misuse of this information and this report is furnished in reliance upon that indemnity. It must be held in strict confidence, it must not be revealed to the subject reported on, except by a reporting agency in accordance with the Fair Credit Reporting Act."

Citizens cannot sue for invasion of privacy, negligence, or defamation of character under the Fair Credit Reporting Act, and the credit report we receive from most reporting agencies is not the same report provided to our potential creditors.

Commercial reporting services, such as Dun and Bradstreet, are not subject to the Fair Credit Reporting Act.

In the mid-1990s, New York Democrat Charles Schumer sponsored a bill to amend the Fair Credit Reporting Act. One of Schumer's proposed changes would have banned something known as "pre-screening." Pre-screening is the process used by banks and other creditors to secure a list of qualified consumers from a credit bureau based on a defined set of criteria. The credit bureau then matches the criteria against its database and supplies the creditor with a list of pre-screened potential customers.

Another area of contention is a proposed change concerning obsolete information. As the law is currently framed, most adverse information is removed from each credit file after seven years. Proposed changes would establish a graduated scale of obsolescence. Certain kinds of information would be removed from the report after three years, other kinds of information would be removed after five years, and so on. The proposed changes would prevent reporting agencies from furnishing Chapter 13 bankruptcy information after seven years.

Under the existing law, when a consumer is denied credit, the creditor sends out an "adverse action" notice. The consumer has the right to inquire further and obtain a free credit report from the credit reporting agency that supplied the creditor with the report. A proposed change in the law would require that the creditor automatically supply a copy of the credit report every time credit is denied. Another proposal would force banks and other lenders to notify consumers each time they provide information to credit reporting agencies.

Associated Credit Bureaus, Inc. research shows that only two percent of the credit files sold result in a request for disclosure of the file. That accounts for nine million disclosures each year and 90 percent of those are the result of "adverse action" notices.

The Fair Credit Reporting Act of 1971 has its roots in the mid-1960s when consumers became aware of the role that local credit bureaus had in making credit decisions. During that same period, a House of Representatives committee began considering the possibility of creating a federal computer database for credit records. The House committee discovered that a network of such databases already existed with the credit bureaus.

Senator William Proxmire (D-Wisconsin) enlisted the support of the credit-reporting industry and the banking community to draft the framework of the Fair Credit Reporting Act that guaranteed a number of important consumer protections:

- The right to be given the name and address of the credit bureau that generated a report which contributed to the decision to deny a consumer credit.
- The right to know who has received a credit report.
- The right to have inaccurate or unverifiable information deleted from a file.
- The right to have most adverse information deleted after seven years.

FAIR CREDIT BILLING ACT

The Fair Credit Billing Act (FCBA) supplements the Fair Credit Reporting Act. It covers the billing practices of creditors and provides remedies for billing disputes. In general, the FCBA applies only to open-ended credit accounts like credit cards and revolving charge accounts. Disputes governed by the FCBA include charges you didn't make or authorize, inaccurate charges, bill mailing problems, and charges for goods or services that weren't delivered as agreed upon.

You must notify the creditor, in writing, within sixty days of receiving the first bill that contains the item(s) you are disputing in order to be protected under the FCBA. The creditor must acknowledge your letter within thirty days of receiving it. The creditor must reasonably investigate the dispute and either correct the mistake or explain why the bill is believed to be correct.

EQUAL CREDIT OPPORTUNITY ACT

The Equal Credit Opportunity Act (ECOA) prohibits discrimination based on race, national origin, sex, marital status, receipt of welfare payments, or age (except in the case of an individual not being old enough to enter into a binding contract).

Under the ECOA, a creditor may not discourage you from applying for credit because of your age, sex, marital status, nationality, or because you receive public assistance. While a creditor may ask what your residence or immigration status is, you may not be asked to reveal your personal information such as sex, age, or national origin.

Similarly, a creditor may not ask your marital status if you are applying for an unsecured account, separately from your spouse. Married couples can elect to have credit information listed in each spouse's name separately.

When deciding to grant credit to an applicant, a creditor may not consider the racial makeup of the applicant's neighborhood or whether or not the applicant has a telephone in his or her own name (although it is permissible to consider whether or not there is a telephone in the applicant's home).

The ECOA confers the right to keep your own accounts after you change your name, change your marital status, or retire. The ECOA requires creditors to report credit histories on accounts shared by married couples in both names for accounts opened after June 1, 1977.

FAIR DEBT COLLECTION PRACTICES ACT

The Fair Debt Collection Practices Act prohibits debt collectors from using false, deceptive, or misleading representations in collecting a debt. The Act also prohibits debt collectors from harassing, oppressive, or abusive behavior including threats of violence or use of profanity.

The statute requires a debt collector to stop contacting consumers who write a letter telling them to stop. After receiving such a demand letter, the only time a debt collector may contact a consumer is to notify the consumer that the creditor intends to take some specific action.

Debt collectors are specifically prohibited, by the Fair Debt Collection Practices Act, from using obscene language, repeatedly using the telephone to annoy anyone, using threats of violence, advertising a debt, making false statements, misrepresenting the involvement of an attorney in the collection activity, or misrepresenting the legal status of any document they send a consumer.

ELECTRONIC COMMUNICATIONS PRIVACY ACT

In 1986, President Reagan signed the Electronic Communications Privacy Act (ECPA) into law. The ECPA is designed to expand the scope of telecommunications covered under the protection of the 1968 federal wiretapping laws.

The Electronic Communications Privacy Act protects electronic mail, cellular telephones, pagers, and various other forms of electronic data transmission. It also requires government agencies to obtain a court order before intercepting electronic communications.

If I took a letter from your postal mailbox, opened it, and read it, I'd be guilty of a federal offense. If I did the same thing by intercepting or retrieving your email, chances are I would not be committing a crime.

The ECPA, as currently written, has two main objectives:

1. Protecting all electronic communications systems, including email, from outside intrusion.
2. Protecting the privacy of certain messages transmitted over public-service email systems.

The ECPA makes it a federal crime to intercept certain electronic communications, but makes a distinction between public and private electronic communications systems. Most importantly, email messages transmitted within private systems that are used solely for interoffice communications are not subject to the privacy provisions of the ECPA. This means that a corporation can read internal or interoffice email messages without invading the privacy of employees.

Electronic mail messages that are transmitted within private email systems that allow outside access can be read by the owner of the system with impunity. Reading email messages exchanged over public systems, such as America Online or the Internet, by anyone other than the sender and recipient, is a felony under the ECPA.

Extending privacy to electronic communications would appear to be quite straightforward, on the surface. These issues become quite complicated, however, when one takes into account the Privacy Act of 1974 and almost 200 state laws that cover wiretapping, electronic eavesdropping, and access to personal information.

There are signs that even though the legal community isn't keeping up with the technology, the populace at large is starting to ask pointed questions and make serious demands concerning privacy issues with respect to electronic communications.

Corporations that promise to protect the privacy of office email are coming under fire when that privacy is compromised. It's currently a crime in only three states—California, Colorado, and Florida—for an individual or a company to eavesdrop on or record confidential communication without the knowledge and consent of both parties to the communication. Federal law requires only the knowledge and consent of one of the parties.

In the summer of 1990, the City Council of Colorado Springs, Colorado became outraged when council members discovered the mayor was secretly intercepting and reading their private email messages.

In August 1990, Alana Shoars, a network administrator in charge of the electronic mail system at Epson America, Inc., filed a lawsuit against the company. Shoars' lawsuit alleged that her supervisor had intercepted her MCI Mail messages on a regular basis as they were passing through the company's network gateway.

When Shoars complained about her supervisor's activities, she was fired. Shoars filed a lawsuit for wrongful termination as an individual and also filed a class action suit with 2,500 other current and former Epson employees asking for unspecified damages of up to US$3,000 per violation. That's US$3,000 for each message that was intercepted. The class action suit was filed as an invasion of privacy under Section 631 of the California Penal Code.

Also during 1990, a lawsuit seeking unspecified damages was filed in the Superior Court of California against Nissan Motor Corp. alleging invasion of privacy, violations of constitutional right of privacy, and wrongful termination of employment.

The lawsuit was brought by plaintiffs Bonita Bourke and Rhonda Hall, both of whom were employed as Information Systems Specialists within the Nissan Infinity Support Group at Nissan's Carson, California facility.

The lawsuit alleged that a Nissan supervisor illegally eavesdropped on the private email of both plaintiffs. Bourke and Hall alleged that the supervisor showed them a "large stack" of email messages and that they were each given written warnings about personal use of the email system. Both plaintiffs also allege they were threatened with discharge.

Nissan had reportedly presented the email system to its employees as an alternative to postal mail, telephone, and fax. Because all email users were required to use a password to access their messages, an expectation of privacy was reasonable and warranted.

Bourke and Hall alleged that the personal nature of the email messages in question quickly became common knowledge within their workgroup when the email messages were published by Nissan within its dealer services department.

The lawsuit alleged that Bourke and Hall filed employee complaints with Nissan's human resources department at the end of December 1990. According to Bourke and Hall's court filing, the result was that both individuals were terminated by Nissan in early January 1991, allegedly in retaliation for the human resources complaints.

A United States Secret Service Director, John Simpson, admitted in a letter to California State Representative Don Edwards that the United States government has been intercepting private email and surreptitiously monitoring computer bulletin boards in order to track the activities of suspected hackers.

Counterfeit Access Device and Computer Fraud and Abuse Act

The Computer Fraud and Abuse Act makes it a federal crime to access a computer system across state lines for fraudulent purposes. Under the Act, it's a felony offense to access a computer to gain classified information and carries a punishment of a US$10,000 fine and ten years imprisonment. The statute also makes it a misdemeanor, carrying a US$5,000 fine and one year imprisonment, to fraudulently access a computer of a financial institution or credit-reporting agency.

Federal Trade Commission Protections

The Federal Trade Commission (FTC) was formed to protect consumers against unfair and deceptive business practices and to promote commercial competition with antitrust measures. In mid-1996, the FTC and Christine Varney, Federal Trade Commissioner, made it clear that online companies risk FTC regulation if they don't start regulating themselves.

In October 1996, three members of the Senate Commerce Committee asked Varney and the FTC to look into privacy issues with regard to various online directory services like Lexis-Nexis, Inc.'s P-Trak that sell personal information to the highest bidder. At roughly the same time, Representative Edward Markey (D-Massachusetts) and Representative Bruce Vento (D-Minnesota), each proposed separate pieces of legislation to regulate the kinds of information that can be gathered from consumers online and the distribution of that individual personal information.

In April 1997, Senator Diane Feinstein (D-California) and Senator Charles Grassley (R-Iowa), introduced bills to prohibit the purchase, sale, or other exchange of social security numbers by third parties. The legislation, dubbed the Personal Information Privacy Act, would make illegal the purchase, sale, or exchange of certain personal information—including mothers' maiden names and unlisted telephone numbers—by credit bureaus.

In early 1997, Varney began pressing Web publishers, direct marketers, and research firms to develop a means of self-regulating their information tracking and harvesting activities. Varney has suggested three basic principles that should be followed by commercial Web sites:

1. Consumers should be informed how Web sites handle personal information.
2. Web sites should be honest in providing that information to consumers.

3. Consumers should be able to control how much personal information they release.

Several Web sites targeted at children were roundly criticized by consumer privacy advocates because they are essentially stealth online marketing surveys. These sites create detailed dossiers on children including their names, ages, birthdays, number of siblings, and family demographics. In one case, children were encouraged to report reams of information in exchange for "locker loot" points that could be redeemed for merchandise. One only has to be reminded of all the abducted children in the world to consider the potential for abuse with this kind of information.

Perhaps the best attempt at self-regulation as of mid-1998 is the TRUSTe system. Companies participating in the TRUSTe system promise to reveal exactly what personal information they gather before gathering it, in exchange for the TRUSTe seal of approval, called a trustmark. TRUSTe participants are randomly audited for compliance on a regular basis.

In late March 1998, the Internet Content Coalition—a group of mostly large, multinational media companies including Ziff Davis, Sony, Time-Warner, CNET, and CBS—announced it would actively support the TRUSTe system as the standard for disclosing to consumers what information is being collected about them on the Web, how it is being used, and with whom it is shared.

Web publishers can participate in the TRUSTe trustmark program by signing a standards and license agreement. However, in addition to paying an annual fee, Web publishers must submit to an *ongoing* audit process. The annual fee is based on revenues and ranges from US$249 (for organizations with revenues under US$5 million) to US$4,999 (for entities with revenues more than US$75 million).

To display the TRUSTe trustmark, a Web publisher must provide the following information to all users on its Web site:

- What information the site gathers or tracks about users
- What the site does with the information
- With whom the site shares the information
- The site's "opt-out" policy that allows visitors to remove themselves from mailing lists and other marketing activities
- The site's policy on correcting and updating personal information
- The site's policy on deleting users' names from its database

It remains to be seen how TRUSTe will handle the audits and who might have access to them. For more information, see Internet Privacy on page 181.

FURTHER...

This snapshot of information rights of the American citizenry should provide us all with at least a small sense of security in our dealings as consumers, citizens, and professionals. Unfortunately, many of these basic information rights for individuals are being weakened.

In the next chapter, various actions by the United States government to weaken and subvert its citizens' information rights is examined.

RESOURCES

- Digital Future Coalition: <www.ari.net/dfc/>
- TRUSTe: <www.truste.org>

- Federal Trade Commission: <www.ftc.gov>
- Internet Content Coalition: <www.netcontent.org>
- No Electronic Theft Act: <dev.abanet.org/intelprop/hr2265.html>
- United States Constitution: <www.house.gov/Constitution/Constitution.html>
- United States Copyright Law: <lcweb.loc.gov/copyright/title17/>
- United States Copyright Office: <lcweb.loc.gov/copyright/>
- World Intellectual Property Organization (WIPO): <www.wipo.org>

CHAPTER

3

FEDERAL AGENCY ACTIONS

In 1982, the United States government maintained 3,530 million—that's 3.5 billion, with a "b"—personal files—paper and electronic—on American citizens, an average of fifteen files for every person in the country. The plan is to eventually maintain every record in electronic form. A vast majority of this data—fully 75 percent of it—is held by five federal government agencies or departments:

- Health and Human Services
- Treasury
- Education
- Defense
- Commerce

By themselves, standing in isolation, each of these files is intrusive enough. But when the individual files are computerized and used collectively, the total information on each of us available to the federal government is extensive and getting even more complete.

NATIONAL CRIME INFORMATION CENTER

The Federal Bureau of Investigation (FBI) is planning to upgrade and expand its criminal justice database, the National Crime Information Center (NCIC) database. The FBI, together with a Congressional subcommittee headed by Don Edwards (D-California), maintain that the present NCIC database is vulnerable and has an unacceptably high error rate.

As we'll see in later chapters, computer database errors are widespread and problematic. That the United States' premier law enforcement agency even acknowledges that it has an error rate that it considers unacceptable is alarming.

In pursuit of upgrading and expanding the NCIC system, the FBI awarded a multimillion-dollar contract to McLean, Virginia-based Mitre Corp. The contractor was engaged to design a new system that would allow "in-depth statistical analysis, rule-based search algorithms, increased data integrity, and detection of system abuses," according to the FBI.

Congress, the Computer Professionals for Social Responsibility (CPSR), and the American Civil Liberties Union (ACLU) all voiced concern over the proposed system.

ACLU representatives claim that the FBI originally wanted to link the NCIC database with other national databases. This interconnection of information systems was cut from the new proposal for cost reasons, not because the FBI was concerned about civil liberties, said the ACLU.

In addition, the ACLU and CPSR are concerned about two file sections within the present NCIC database that contain no public information. The concern arises because there is no way to verify the accuracy of the suspicions that comprise the information stored there.

Federal Agency Snapshots

Events and actions like the ones outlined in the following four vignettes could be complicated by disgruntled employees or even by excellent agency employees suffering from a case of "bad judgement," though they may normally be law-abiding citizens. Whether or not there exists any infiltration of these agencies by criminal elements is beyond the scope of this work.

National Security Agency

In 1982, a Federal Appeals Court ruled that the National Security Agency (NSA) can legally eavesdrop on any conversation between a United States citizen and foreigners, even when there is no reason to suspect that the American citizen is an agent of a foreign government.

At the same time, the NSA argued that the government's own telephone conversations should be protected. In 1985, for instance, the NSA initiated a five-year program to encrypt government information sent across the country's telephone and data networks.

Internal Revenue Service

During the administration of President Jimmy Carter, plans were abandoned that called for an US$850 million, 8,300-terminal computer network the Internal Revenue Service had proposed called the Tax Administration System (TAS). The Carter administration cited personal privacy issues in scrapping the IRS plan. The plan would have given IRS employees virtually instant access to all tax records.

The IRS has continued to refine its Taxpayer Compliance Measurement Program (TCMP), however. The TCMP is a computer process by which the Internal Revenue Service is able to predict the behavior of taxpayers using a computer model based on a random selection of taxpayers.

SECURITIES EXCHANGE COMMISSION

Under the 1934 Securities Exchange Act, the Securities Exchange Commission (SEC) is allowed to inspect stockbroker records. This Act has been applied to such an extent that now an SEC official can visit your stockbroker's office and examine your account without a warrant or summons of any kind.

CENTRAL INTELLIGENCE AGENCY

The Central Intelligence Agency (CIA) has been found guilty of opening United States citizens' mail to and from the former Soviet Union between 1953 and 1973. The U.S. Post Office says that it no longer allows the CIA to intercept mail, although the FBI may still get warrants to do so. Approximately 200 such court orders are issued each year, allowing the FBI to intercept private mail.

In 1976, the United States Supreme Court ruled that the government's practice of opening international postal mail does not violate the Fourth Amendment so long as "reasonable cause" exists that the mail contains dutiable goods or contraband.

COMPUTERS AND PRIVACY REPORT

In the late summer of 1990, the General Accounting Office (GAO) released a report entitled *Computers and Privacy: How the Government Obtains, Verifies, Uses, and Protects Personal Data* detailing the pathetic record of compliance with existing privacy regulations by the various agencies of the United States government. The report examined the 910 largest computerized systems of personal data among the more than 2,000 systems maintained by 178 agencies of the government.

The GAO report states that agencies did not issue the required Federal Register notices for fully 35 percent of the systems. This is significant because more than half of the 910 systems included in the report can be accessed by government agencies other than the *originating* agency. In some cases the systems can even be accessed by *private companies*—including health care agencies, financial institutions, and insurance companies. And, as stated earlier, private sector organizations are not subject to the Privacy Act.

According to the report, government agencies responsible for seventy-eight of the systems included in the study did not know to what purpose the personal information contained in the systems was being put by other governmental agencies or organizations accessing the information.

Many of the government agencies covered in the GAO study are involved in using their records for various programs, including law enforcement, with the following breakdown:

- Twenty-six agencies were involved in computer matching.
- Twenty-eight agencies were involved in front-end verification.
- Thirty-seven agencies were involved in computer profiling.

Most disturbing of all is the fact that 707 of the 910 systems covered in the GAO *Computers and Privacy* report are completely internetworked.

The government agencies complain that it is too difficult and burdensome for them to keep up with, let alone comply with, all the various information and privacy regulations:

- Privacy Act
- Computer Matching and Privacy Protection Act
- Right to Financial Privacy Act
- Electronic Communications Privacy Act
- Computer Security Act
- Federal Managers' Financial Integrity Act
- Freedom of Information Act

Just how poorly are the government agencies doing?

The 1990 GAO report specifically highlighted a total of 292 violations of the Privacy Act alone in 1989. According to the report, one third of the largest personal records systems administered by the various agencies of the federal government failed to notify the public about the records they collect and maintain. The Privacy Act requires government agencies to publish a description of the kinds of records they maintain, the types of sources for that information, and the purposes they have for the information. No such legislation regulates personal information use in the private sector.

Computer Matching Restrictions

Computer matching is the comparison of different computerized lists or files of individuals intended to discover duplication, fraud, or other abuse of any government program. Comparisons can be made using almost any personal identifier such as address, name, or social security number, enabling various uses for information in addition to those originally intended.

In 1977, the Secretary of Health, Education, and Welfare (HEW) announced Project Match. Project Match was aimed at identifying government employees who were illegally receiving Aid to Families with Dependent Children (AFDC) benefits. The software program compared the computer files of welfare roles and federal payroll records in the Washington, DC area. The pilot project eventually grew into a national match of five million employee records with the welfare records of twenty-six states.

In 1982, the Internal Revenue Service records of taxpayer addresses were compared with Selective Service System lists of individuals born in 1963 to identify and locate individuals who had violated the draft registration requirement.

Computer matching is a *prima facie* violation of the Fourth Amendment. The courts have consistently disallowed "fishing expeditions" in homes or businesses and similar protections should be afforded against electronic information safaris. Computer matching of unrelated data is intentionally designed as a general search and is not based on any pre-existing evidence.

In April 1989, the Office of Management and Budget (OMB) released a set of draft guidelines that would restrict federal agency use of computer matching to verification of eligibility for federal benefits programs, to monitor compliance with requirements for one of the benefits programs, or to recoup payments and delinquent debts.

Under the draft guidelines, the federal agencies would also be required to notify individuals in advance that their records might be searched and matched. The guidelines would mandate agencies to report to individuals any adverse data found and allow them to refute the information.

Agencies were required to comply with the draft guidelines for the Computer Matching and Privacy Protection Act by July 19, 1989. The revised law extended the 1974 Privacy Act to government agency computer matching programs. The Act's revisions did not, however, extend into the domain of highly consolidated, multinational corporate interests.

INSLAW AND OUTLAWS

In its second issue, *Wired* magazine published one of the best written and most important pieces of high-technology investigative journalism to date. The article, "Inslaw Octopus" by Richard L. Fricker, painstakingly outlined the curious case of how the United States Department of Justice conspired with private individuals to commit fraud, obstruct justice, tamper with a witness, retaliate against a witness, and receive stolen goods, among other crimes.

Bill and Nancy Hamilton started a company named Inslaw specifically to enhance the Prosecutors Management Information System (PROMIS), a piece of software designed to manage legal cases. Enhancement of the PROMIS software was funded by the Justice Department when it recognized that its case management system was in urgent need of automation.

The underlying PROMIS software was originally created in the 1970s under a Law Enforcement Assistance Administration (LEAA) grant. Like any other piece of information generated by the government, the original version of PROMIS was in the public domain.

Recognizing that the market in the United States alone for legal automation software was more than US$3 billion, Inslaw made significant improvements to the public domain version of the PROMIS software and went private in the early 1980s.

The Inslaw-enhanced version of PROMIS had the capability to combine disparate databases and could track people by their involvement with the legal system. Many claim that the United States Department of Justice has stolen and modified the Inslaw-enhanced version of the PROMIS software to aid in the tracking of intelligence operations, agents, and targets instead of legal cases.

Databases maintained by the Department of Justice, the United States Attorney, the Internal Revenue Service, and other government agencies were all separate, stand-alone systems and could not be combined. Until PROMIS. The PROMIS software could combine information from all of the agencies' databases without the need for reprogramming the underlying software.

At the end of President Jimmy Carter's administration, LEAA was phased out, and Bill Hamilton converted Inslaw to a private, for-profit business. Inslaw claimed ownership of the enhanced PROMIS software that was funded with Inslaw's money.

Hamilton's lawyers sent the Department of Justice a letter asserting ownership of the enhanced version of the PROMIS software and asked the Department to waive any proprietary rights. In an August 11, 1982 letter, the Justice Department agreed, in general, with Hamilton's claim of ownership of the enhanced software.

In March 1982, Inslaw won a US$9.6 million grant from the Department of Justice to install the public domain version of PROMIS—not Inslaw's proprietary enhanced version—in 20 U.S. Attorney's offices as a pilot program.

During the Inslaw pilot installation of the PROMIS system, the Department of Justice claimed that Inslaw was on the verge of bankruptcy. Even though Inslaw was engaged to provide only the public domain version of PROMIS, the Department of Justice demanded that Inslaw turn over the enhanced version of the PROMIS software in case the company couldn't complete the contract. Inslaw agreed to release the enhanced PROMIS, on the condition that the Department of Justice recognize Inslaw's proprietary rights to the enhanced version of the software and that the Department not distribute enhanced PROMIS outside of the U.S. Attorney's offices.

Once the Department of Justice had control of enhanced PROMIS, it refused to acknowledge that Inslaw had created the enhancements. When Inslaw protested, the Justice Department withheld all payments. Two years later, Inslaw was forced into bankruptcy.

In early June 1986, Inslaw filed a US$30 million lawsuit against the Department of Justice in bankruptcy court. Inslaw's attorney filed the suit in bankruptcy court on the theory that the Department of Justice—the creditor—had control of PROMIS, Inslaw's primary asset. It is against the law for a creditor to exercise control over the property of a debtor.

In 1987, Washington, DC bankruptcy judge George Bason ruled that the Department of Justice had stolen PROMIS and awarded Inslaw US$6.8 million in damages. Judge Bason also ruled that Justice Department officials had made a concerted effort to drive Inslaw into bankruptcy and had placed the enhanced PROMIS up for public auction.

The Department of Justice appealed Judge Bason's ruling to the federal district court, which affirmed the Bason judgment. The Justice Department then appealed to the Washington, DC Circuit Court of Appeals, which reversed Judge Bason's decision, finding the bankruptcy court had no jurisdiction to hear the damages claim. In October 1991, a review petition to the Supreme Court was denied.

On November 20, 1990, the House Judiciary Committee asked Central Intelligence Agency director William Webster to determine whether the CIA was in possession of the enhanced PROMIS software. CIA Director Webster claimed to be unable to find any evidence that the CIA had ever obtained the enhanced

PROMIS software, but a retired CIA official reportedly insisted that the Department of Justice gave PROMIS to the CIA. Canadian documents place enhanced PROMIS in the possession of various Canadian government agencies. Fricker's article in *Wired* reported that the enhanced PROMIS software found its way to the governments of more than 80 countries, allegedly through the United States Department of Justice.

On August 11, 1992, the House Judiciary Committee, after a three-year investigation, voted 21–13 to ask then-Attorney General William Barr to "immediately settle Inslaw's claims." Barr refused to appoint an independent prosecutor to the Inslaw case, instead appointing Nicholas Bua, a retired federal judge. Bua reported directly to Barr, resulting in the strange situation of the Department of Justice being entirely responsible for investigating itself.

Oliver North reportedly used the software to track dissidents within the United States as part of a domestic emergency preparedness program commissioned under President Ronald Reagan's Federal Emergency Management Agency (FEMA).

When House Judiciary Committee Chairman Representative Jack Brooks (D-Texas) asked Oliver North about using the PROMIS software during the Iran-Contra hearings, the hearing was immediately suspended pending an executive (secret) conference. When the hearings reconvened, the issue of North's use of the PROMIS software was dropped.

Freelance reporter Danny Casolaro was found dead on August 10, 1991 in a Martinsburg, West Virginia hotel room. Both of his wrists were deeply slashed. Casolaro had been actively investigating the Inslaw case and maintained that Inslaw was only a part of a larger story of how intelligence agencies, the Department of Justice, and organized crime had subverted the federal government for profit.

Casolaro had gone to Martinsburg to meet with an informant. Martinsburg police allowed Casolaro's body to be embalmed before family members were notified and allegedly warned hotel employees not to talk to reporters. The hotel room was immediately cleaned by an outside service and Casolaro's notes, which witnesses report they saw him carry into the hotel, were never found.

FURTHER...

As this chapter has shown, no government can ever be completely competent or completely benevolent. The best any of us can do is work to change what's wrong and ensure that what's right doesn't get lost in the process.

America is seen as a shining star for freedom of the press and held up as an example for the rest of the world. The next chapter explores the depths of this myth. Indeed, governmental intrusion on the First Amendment is relatively rare and almost always quickly and appropriately addressed. The same cannot be said for corporate intrusions on our information rights, however. This sphere of intrusion will likely continue to get a lot worse before it gets better.

American media is undergoing unprecedented consolidation pressures, and the range and number of voices are clearly being diminished. The threats to our information rights are coming from a variety of corners, not just government.

RESOURCES

- American Civil Liberties Union: <www.aclu.org>
- Computer Professionals for Social Responsibility: <www.cpsr.org>
- Central Intelligence Agency: <www.odci.gov/cia/>

- Federal Bureau of Investigation: <www.fbi.gov>
- General Accounting Office: <www.gao.gov>
- "Inslaw Octopus" (Richard L. Fricker): <www.wired.com/wired/1.1/features/inslaw.html>
- Internal Revenue Service: <www.irs.ustreas.gov>
- National Crime Information Center: <www.fbi.gov/2000/ncicinv.htm>
- National Security Agency: <www.nsa.gov>
- Office of Management and Budget: <www.white-house.gov/WH/EOP/OMB/html/ombhome.html>
- Securities Exchange Commission: <www.sec.gov>
- Supreme Court Decisions (FindLaw): <www.findlaw.com/casecode/supreme.html>

Chapter 4

Myth of a Free Press

America's founders took the idea of a free press very seriously. (For more information on why the founders felt so strongly about a free press, see Information Control in England and the Colonies on page 20.) The framers of the Constitution were so serious about the idea of a free press being crucial to a democracy, that they guaranteed it, almost unconditionally, in the First Amendment:

> "Congress shall make no law respecting an establishment of religion, or prohibiting the free exercise thereof; or abridging the freedom of speech or of the press; or of the right of the people peaceably to assemble and to petition the Government for a redress of grievances."

Two hundred years later, it's arguably true that the guarantees precluding *government* intrusion upon a free press have been, for the most part, admirably upheld. But the tend toward consolidation within the international media industries throughout the 1980s and 1990s has led to a state where diminution of unique voices is clearly undeniable. When the diversity of voices is reduced—for whatever reasons—the threat to a free press is both clear and present. Unfortunately *corporate* intrusion upon a free press now presents at least as great a threat, and no Constitutional guarantees exist to prevent it.

For example, consider the established, mainstream media coverage of the sexual harassment allegations against President Clinton throughout his administration. For the sake of this exercise, put aside the question of whether or not the story was newsworthy. Just think back to the actual coverage you saw, heard, and read.

Well after the dismissal of Paula Jones' sexual harassment lawsuit against the President, the facts regarding the bankrolling of her legal representation were only beginning to trickle out in the mainstream media. The online publication *Salon* broke the story of a conservative political organization with ties to the Rev. Jerry Falwell that paid more than US$200,000 to people who made damaging allegations about President Clinton's behavior. For weeks the story was completely ignored by mainstream media outlets.

Salon, in the same series of articles by investigative reporter Murray Waas and others, also broke the story that David Hale, the central witness against President Clinton in Kenneth Starr's Whitewater investigation, received payments from an anti-Clinton campaign funded by billionaire Richard Mellon Scaife.

Neither of these stories were picked up by the mainstream media organizations until weeks after they ran in Salon, and then coverage was limited in scope. One has to ask what purposes—

or perhaps more accurately, whose purposes—were being served by ignoring what was surely one of the most important political stories of the 1990s.

In early April 1998, two former Fox Television journalists—Steve Wilson and Jane Akre—filed a lawsuit against a Florida affiliate of the Fox television network for killing their investigative piece on the possible health risks of a synthetic growth hormone for dairy cattle. According to the lawsuit, the Fox affiliate, WTVT, was ready to broadcast the four-part series in February 1997, but changed its mind when Roger Ailes, Fox News Corporation's president, received a threatening letter from Monsanto, the manufacturer of the synthetic growth hormone. Wilson and Akre alleged that WTVT concerns about an expensive legal battle caused the affiliate to expand the editing process for nine months until the journalists could be fired.

WTVT responded to the lawsuit with a news release denying the charges and blaming the drawn-out editing process on Akre's and Wilson's unwillingness to check facts and present a balanced report.

Wherever the truth lies, Monsanto's five-page letter of February 21, 1997 to Fox executive Ailes contains a particularly disturbing passage calling into question the integrity and professional behavior of Akre and Wilson. "In the aftermath of the Food Lion verdict," the letter read, "such behavior would alone be cause for concern."

The reference to the Food Lion verdict is especially threatening. A month earlier, in January 1997, a jury had ordered ABC to pay Food Lion US$5.5 million in damages for reporting that the grocery store chain repackaged spoiled meat for resale. The truth of the ABC story's allegations was never disputed. Food Lion sued ABC for trespass and fraud when the television network's producers posed as Food Lion employees and used a hidden camera to record employee actions.

What troubles media critics (and probably many "beat" reporters as well) is that mainstream media outlets have collectively decided to consciously avoid stories that would upset the deep pockets of Corporate America. For instance, a 1997 article in the *American Journalism Review* surveyed a collection of television consultants, journalists, and executives: "What passes for investigative reporting on local TV news these days is often a mishmash of self-serving, superficial reports on consumer rip-offs and government waste," the publication reported. In short, mainstream media outlets are concerned about expensive litigation and boring viewers, not educating or enlightening the populace.

PUBLISHING VS. DISTRIBUTING

When you create original content and put it on the Internet, you become a publisher. If, on the other hand, you store content that was created by others on your Internet server, you become a distributor.

Publishers are required to take responsibility for the material they publish. Distributors are not required to know the contents of what they distribute, and a distributor is responsible only for content that it knows is illegal.

The defining American court case with regard to this issue is Cubby v. CompuServe. In the case, a New York federal judge held that CompuServe was not liable for a false statement that one of its users made about Cubby on the CompuServe Information Service.

More recently, organizations (and individuals) have found ways to get around the distinction between a publisher and a distributor when it comes to responsibility for content.

The Church of Scientology, for example, has been known to bring a lawsuit whenever it finds that church documents are being distributed on the Internet without permission. When it finds an individual distributing church documents without permission, the Church of Scientology notifies the Internet service provider from whom the individual purchases his or her connectivity and informs the provider that the individual is infringing the church's copyright.

If the Internet service provider fails to address the alleged infringement situation to the church's satisfaction, the Church of Scientology then sues both the individual and the Internet service provider, claiming that the Internet service provider contributed to the copyright infringement because it knew it was distributing copyrighted material without permission.

Abundant examples of organizations, individuals, and even entire countries attempting to restrict the free flow of information are just as common.

In late May 1996, Vietnam's telecommunications authority implemented strict rules to control the use of the Internet and to empower the Ministry of the Interior to monitor all traffic entering and leaving the country. Any information seen to be "damaging" to the country's interests would be banned.

In a proposed ruling from the Vietnamese Department General of Posts and Telecommunications, only authorized telecommunications companies would be allowed to provide Internet services. This ruling would outlaw the country's Institute of Information Technology that currently provides four-times-a-day email service to almost two thousand subscribers. The proposed rule goes so far as to say that full access to the Internet need not be seen as a priority.

In an example closer to the American home, cable television's History Channel announced in June 1996 that it would be producing a new series entitled "The Spirit of Enterprise." The series promised an "inside look" at America's corporate elite, including AT&T, DuPont, Anheuser-Busch, Boeing, American Express, and General Motors. The problem arises when one discovers that the content will be decidedly one-sided since each company is co-producing the hour-long profile of itself in addition to buying advertising time during the series. Each company is also being given complete editorial control over all content in its segment.

This escapade redefines the notion of checkbook journalism. The History Channel began cablecasting in January 1995 and at the time of the announcement (mid 1996) enjoyed a subscriber base of 19.2 million. Its owners include the corporate parents of ABC and NBC (Disney and General Electric, respectively).

FIRST AMENDMENT CHALLENGES

There are numerous examples of governmental censorship and instances of prior restraint. Here's one of the worst instances from the past few decades.

In 1983, the Reagan White House issued a directive—NSDD 84—requiring more than 120,000 government employees with access to classified materials to sign a lifetime agreement. The agreement specified that they would submit any material they wished to publish to the appropriate agency for prior clearance before the material was published.

In 1984, the Department of Housing and Urban Development (HUD) drafted a research contract with a Harvard scholar that would have required him to submit results of HUD-sponsored research for review six months before publication. The scholar would also have had to submit results on related work not funded by HUD, and would have given the agency the right to demand that the scholar make "corrections" in data, methodology, and analyses. After months of negotiation, Harvard decided to refuse the contract.

Through prepublication reviews such as the example cited above, the federal government's funding of many activities puts it in a unique position to influence the content of research or restrict its publication.

A 1980 Supreme Court decision opened the door for the government to exercise prepublication reviews. In Snepp v. United States, the Supreme Court found in favor of the government's argument that a former CIA agent's book violated his agreement to give the CIA a chance to determine if the material "would compromise classified information or sources," *prior to publication*.

This case led to NSDD 84, requiring 120,000 employees and contractors of the federal government to agree to lifetime prepublication reviews.

The NSDD 84 directive also gave the government the power to require employees to take polygraph tests while investigating unauthorized disclosures of classified information.

Under Congressional pressure, Reagan's administration suspended the prepublication review directive in September 1984. A 1981 mandate was left in place, however, requiring government employees with high-security clearances to sign a lifetime agreement (known as Form 4193) allowing prepublication review by the government of all documents, including *fiction*.

The General Accounting Office reported in 1986, however, that the suspension of the prepublication review directive had little effect. The GAO report cited 21,718 instances of governmental prepublication review of books, articles, and speeches in 1984 alone. By 1985, the number of prepublication reviews rose slightly to 22,280. To provide context and a frame of reference, the total number of unauthorized disclosures of classified information during the 1984–1985 two year period was fifteen.

By the end of 1985, according to the GAO report, a minimum of 240,776 individuals had signed Form 4193.

Press Freedom and Responsibility

One of the more compelling examples of the responsibilities of an allegedly free press comes from an incident that took place the year I moved to Minnesota.

In October 1982, Dan Cohen looked for a journalist to help him drop a political bomb in that year's Minnesota gubernatorial election. Cohen, an Independent-Republican activist and member of the Wheelock Whitney gubernatorial campaign, found interested reporters from both Twin Cities dailies: Bill Salisbury of the *Saint Paul Pioneer Press* and Lori Sturdevant of the *Minneapolis Star Tribune*.

The information Cohen gave to the reporters—both of whom agreed not to reveal Cohen as the source of the information—was proof that Marlene Johnson, the Democratic-Farmer-Labor Party candidate for lieutenant governor, had been convicted of shoplifting some fifteen years earlier. Johnson had failed to pay for less than US$10 worth of sewing materials. Johnson was disoriented by the recent death of her father, and the conviction was subsequently set aside in 1970. Cohen's political bomb and the attendant news stories did not change the outcome of the election: Johnson and Governor Rudy Perpich were elected on November 2, 1982.

Interestingly, Cohen's investigation also revealed that Johnson had been charged with unlawful assembly in 1969, when Johnson had participated in a protest against the city of Saint Paul's failure to hire minority employees. That case was dismissed in 1970.

Editors of both newspapers overruled their reporters' promises of confidentiality and ran the stories identifying Dan Cohen as the source. Both newspapers decided it was important to inform the public that the information came from a Wheelock Whitney supporter. Reports indicate that both newspapers had initially considered attributing the information to an unidentified Whitney supporter, but the Perpich-Johnson campaign had already accused the Whitney campaign of using smear tactics, something Whitney was vehemently denying.

Cohen subsequently brought suit against the *Pioneer Press* and *Star Tribune* for breach of contract.

Cohen won his case against the two newspapers in 1988. His lawyer was Elliot Rothenberg, the Independent-Republican candidate for attorney general in the 1982 election, whose campaign went down in flames with Wheelock Whitney's. The 1988 jury awarded Cohen US$200,000 in compensatory damages and US$500,000 in punitive damages. The Minnesota Court of Appeals upheld the compensatory damages award in 1989, but threw out the punitive damages award. In 1990, the Minnesota Supreme Court ruled that the promise made by the two journalists was not a legally binding contract and held that Cohen was not entitled to any damages.

In March 1991, the case was heard by the United States Supreme Court. Cohen and his attorney argued that the First Amendment does not protect the newspapers from liability when they dishonor promises of confidentiality. Cohen also contended that newspapers should not be exempt from laws that cover the general population.

Cohen maintained that while the First Amendment protects the press from government compulsion to name a source, it does not protect newspapers from the results of violating promises made voluntarily. By making the voluntary promise of confidentiality, the newspapers gave up any First Amendment protections, he argued.

The attorney for the newspapers, John French, argued that a journalist's promise of confidentiality in the field, before he or she knows what sort of information will be revealed, must be protected under the First Amendment and that the core issue was one of scope.

French cited other news organizations that have revealed or identified sources when the identity of the source was deemed to be of central editorial importance. French also cited the best-known example of a *Newsweek* report that identified Oliver North as the source of previously reported secret information about the *Achille Lauro* hijacking. *Newsweek* identified North as the source, after the good Colonel publicly accused members of Congress of leaking the information.

Publishers and broadcasters in twenty-eight states, including Minnesota, have traditionally relied on "shield laws" that prevent anyone from forcing them to reveal or identify a source. In the states that don't have shield laws, journalists, publishers, and broadcasters have always relied on the privilege granted them by the First Amendment in refusing to reveal or identify their sources.

Some argue that the media organizations want to eat their cake and have it too. They want the right to reveal an anonymous source if and when it suits their purposes, but the media also want to prevent the government (or anyone else for that matter) from forcing them to reveal their sources when it doesn't fit media objectives.

In 1991, the Supreme Court found in favor of Cohen, ruling that a breach of contract outweighs the protections offered by the First Amendment—an author can be sued for violating a good-faith agreement to keep a source's identity confidential.

In the 5–4 decision, two conservative justices (Souter and O'Connor) joined two liberal justices (Marshall and Blackmun) in forming the dissenting opinion. The majority ruled that "promissory estoppel," a legal doctrine covering a person's reliance on a promise to his or her detriment, factored heavily in Cohen's favor, even though the court found that no formal breach of contract occurred.

This decision threatens to change forever the way broadcasters, publishers, and journalists deal with their sources.

Minnesota Free Flow of Information Act

In the 1998 Legislative Session, Minnesota passed the Free Flow of Information Act, commonly referred to as the "Reporters' Shield Law." Previously, Minnesota state courts had held that journalists were granted protection only for confidential sources and, more specifically, that unpublished notes or unbroadcast images were not protected. The Minnesota Free Flow of Information Act reinstated complete and unqualified protection for unpublished notes and unbroadcast images in all civil cases. A qualified privilege for the same material was also granted in all criminal cases.

Under the new law, in criminal cases, prosecutors or defense attorneys must prove that information held by a journalist cannot be obtained in any other way. The information being sought must also be critical to the case. If a journalist is an eyewitness to a felony, no shield privilege is granted.

The Reporters' Shield Law protects journalists, publishers, and broadcasters, but does nothing to protect the public interest against consolidation of ownership and attendant conflicts of interest in the mainstream media.

The amended text of the Minnesota Free Flow of Information Act follows.

> **595.021. News media; protection of sources; citation**. Sections 595.021 to 595.025 may be cited as the Minnesota free flow of information act.
>
> **595.022. Public policy**. In order to protect the public interest and the free flow of information, the news media should have the benefit of a substantial privilege not to reveal sources of information or to disclose unpublished information. To this end, the freedom of press requires protection of the confidential relationship between the news gatherer and the source of in-

formation. The purpose of sections 595.021 to 595.025 is to insure and perpetuate, consistent with the public interest, the confidential relationship between the news media and its sources.

595.023. Disclosure prohibited. No person who is or has been directly engaged in the gathering, procuring, compiling, editing, or publishing of information for the purpose of transmission, dissemination or publication to the public shall be required by any court, grand jury, agency, department or branch of the state, or any of its political subdivisions or other public body, or by either house of the legislature or any committee, officer, member, or employee thereof, to disclose in any proceeding the person or means from or through which information was obtained, or to disclose any unpublished information procured by the person in the course of work or any of the person's notes, memoranda, recording tapes, film or other reportorial data which would tend to identify the person or means through which the information was obtained.

595.024 Exception and procedure.

Subdivision 1. Disclosure; application. A person seeking disclosure may apply to the district court of the county where the person employed by or associated with a news media resides, has a principal place of business or where the proceeding in which the information sought is pending.

Subd. 2. Disclosure allowed; conditions. The application shall be granted only if the court determines after hearing the parties that the person making application, by clear and convincing evidence, has met all three of the following conditions:

(1) that there is probable cause to believe that the source has information clearly relevant to a specific violation of the law other than a misdemeanor,

(2) that the information cannot be obtained by any alternative means or remedy less destructive of first amendment rights, and

(3) that there is a compelling and overriding interest requiring the disclosure of the information where the disclosure is necessary to prevent injustice.

Subd. 3. Determination; appeal. The district court shall consider the nature of the proceedings, the merits of the claims and defenses, the adequacies of alternative remedies, the relevancy of the information sought, and the possibility of establishing by other means that which the source is expected or may tend to prove. The court shall make its appropriate order after making findings of fact. The order may be appealed directly to the court of appeals according to the rules of appellate procedure. The order is stayed and nondisclosure shall remain in full force and effect during the pendency of the appeal. Where the court finds that the information sought has been published or broadcast, there shall be no automatic stay unless an appeal is filed within two days after the order is issued. Either party may request expedited consideration.

595.025 Defamation.

Subdivision 1. Disclosure prohibition; applicability. The prohibition of disclosure provided in section 595.023 shall not apply in any defamation action where the person seeking disclosure can demonstrate that the identity of the source will lead to relevant evidence on the issue of actual malice.

> Subd. 2. Disclosure conditions. Notwithstanding the provisions of subdivision 1, the identity of the source of information shall not be ordered disclosed unless the following conditions are met:
>
> (a) that there is probable cause to believe that the source has information clearly relevant to the issue of defamation;
>
> (b) that the information cannot be obtained by any alternative means or remedy less destructive of first amendment rights.
>
> Subd. 3. Determination; appeal. The court shall make its order on the issue of disclosure after making findings of fact, which order may be appealed to the court of appeals according to the rules of appellate procedure. During the appeal the order is stayed and nondisclosure shall remain in full force and effect.

Minnesota Governor Arne Carlson allowed the Minnesota Free Flow of Information Act to become law without his signature but wrote of his concerns in an April 6, 1998 letter to Secretary of State Joan Growe.

"We do not provide such confidentiality in a wide array of professional relationships," Governor Carlson wrote. "I would argue that if the media has the right to scrutinize our operations in government, we should also have the right to scrutinize theirs." Governor Carlson went on to adroitly criticize the driving forces of the market on media actions:

> "Over the nearly 25 years since the Minnesota Free Flow of Information Act was passed into law, we have watched the media become increasingly driven by the forces of market competition, ratings and circulation. Now, more than ever, money is an irrefutable factor in the business of news. As CBS pioneer Fred Friendly

asked, 'how in television can we do our best when television makes so much more money doing its worst?'"

Communications Decency Act

The Communications Decency Act, signed into law by President Clinton in February 1996, made it a felony to knowingly send or show "indecent" material to a minor over the Internet. Violators were subject to up to two years in prison and a US$250,000 fine.

The Communications Decency Act defined "indecency" as "any comment, request, suggestion, proposal, image, or other communications that, in context, depicts or describes, in terms patently offensive, sexual, or excretory activities or organs."

"Obscenity" can be proved to be illegal by applying the Miller test: "Material that appeals to the prurient interest of the average person, describing sexual conduct in a way that is 'patently offensive' to contemporary community standards; and when taken as a whole lacks serious literary, artistic, political, or scientific value is said to be 'obscene' (and therefore illegal)."

Opponents of the Communications Decency Act argued that there is no way to determine the age of users of email lists, newsgroups, and Web sites. Methods of age verification—like the use of credit cards—are available only to larger enterprises, effectively muzzling individuals, nonprofit groups, and smaller businesses.

The Communications Decency Act, introduced by Senator James Exon (D-Nebraska), intended to criminalize online publication of any material deemed "obscene, lewd, lascivious, filthy, or indecent." The Exon legislation was buried within the complexities of the telecommunications reform package. Even conservatives like House Speaker Representative Newt Gingrich (R-Georgia) denounced the bill as "clearly a violation of free speech and it's a violation of the rights of adults to communicate with each other."

On February 16, 1996, U.S. District Court Judge Ronald L. Buckwalter of Philadelphia issued an order temporarily blocking enforcement of the Communications Decency Act, ruling that the Act's "indecent materials" provision was unconstitutionally vague and would "leave reasonable people perplexed in evaluating what is or what is not prohibited in this statute."

A three-judge federal panel in Philadelphia blocked the law on July 12, 1996, ruling that it was unconstitutional in that it imposed prior restraint on free speech in a "unique and wholly new medium of communication." Judge Stewart Dalzell, eloquently captured the panel's unanimous position when he stated in his ruling:

> "... the Internet has achieved, and continues to achieve, the most participatory marketplace of mass speech that this country—and indeed the world—has yet seen. The plaintiffs in these actions correctly describe the 'democratizing' effects of Internet communication: Individual citizens of limited means can speak to a worldwide audience on issues of concern to them.... The government ... implicitly asks this court to limit both the amount of speech on the Internet and the availability of that speech. This argument is profoundly repugnant to the First Amendment principles."

A separate three-judge federal panel in Manhattan concurred with the Philadelphia panel later that same month, on July 29, 1996. Joe Shea, editor of the *American Reporter*, an online news publication, sued on the grounds that the Communications Decency Act limited the right to publish material on the Internet that would be protected under the First Amendment if it appeared in a print publication.

On June 30, 1996 and again on August 15, 1996, the Justice Department, citing a desire to "assist parents in protecting children from sexually explicit material on the Internet," appealed both rulings to the Supreme Court. The Supreme Court struck down the Communications Decency Act in June 1997. For more information about the Act with regard to censorship issues, see Communications Decency Act Sequels on page 217.

Further...

The Constitution guarantees a press free from government intrusion, but is silent about corporate intrusion.

Another shining star of the American system is our supposed free market economy. Markets should be the sole determination of which products and companies succeed, so the free marketers chant. The next chapter investigates the substance behind that myth.

Resources

- American Reporter: <www.american-reporter.com>
- BGH Bulletin: <www.foxbghsuit.com>
- Church of Scientology: <www.scientology.org>
- Communications Decency Act: <www.fcc.gov/telecom.html>
- Department of Housing and Urban Development: <www.hud.gov>
- Department of Justice: <www.usdoj.gov>
- Fox Television: <www.fox.com/tv.html>
- General Accounting Office: <www.gao.gov>
- History Channel: <www.historychannel.com>

- Minneapolis StarTribune: <www.startribune.com>
- Saint Paul Pioneer Press: <www.pioneerplanet.com>
- Salon: <www.salon1999.com>

CHAPTER

5

MYTH OF A FREE MARKET

It's fashionable these days to preach the gospel of techno-libertarianism; a weird concoction of traditional libertarianism combined with a healthy dose of don't-worry-be-happy-technology-will-find-the-answer Pollyannaism. Basically it boils down to: reduce the size of government and get whatever government is left out of the way of the free market. The market will regulate itself naturally, and everything will be fine.

If you're a member of the privileged classes—that's anyone who can grab a loaf of bread off the grocery shelf without looking at the price tag—the idea of smaller government probably sounds like a wonderful idea. So does the idea of a free market. The problem is, the existing markets are anything but free. And contrary to popular belief, government is only half to blame for the state of our markets.

Microsoft Industry Control

Until mid-1998, Bill Gates and the company he co-founded, Microsoft Corporation, had both managed to maintain inordinately low political profiles, flying below the radar of political analysts and observers. That highly cultivated profile, however, was never anything more than a thin patina.

In 1997, for example, Bill Gates and Microsoft managed to get the House Ways and Means Committee to attach the Software Export Equity Act (SEEA) to the 1997 tax bill. SEEA gives an estimated US$1.7 billion tax break over the next decade to software exporters. Never-you-mind that SEEA benefits fewer than one hundred companies and that Microsoft is by far the biggest beneficiary of this Big Government largesse.

Microsoft didn't even have an internal lobbying department or office until 1995. Before that, when Microsoft needed representation before the government, Bill Gates turned to his father's Washington, DC-based law firm, Preston, Gates, Ellis & Rouvelas Meeds. In 1996, Microsoft spent a total of US$1.1 million on lobbying efforts and by 1997, Microsoft employed no less than ten outside lobbying firms.

Microsoft is an active member in the Business Software Alliance (BSA), a trade association that helps enforce international copyright law on behalf of the American software industry. According to various industry reports, there have been several alleged instances when the BSA would drop its copyright infringement actions in exchange for "special agreements" whereby alleged copyright infringers would then replace all of their software with Microsoft products.

In the past, information was inseparable from its delivery mechanism "wrapper." A great book, for example, was only so much ink stains smeared on dead trees. A classic music recording was nothing more than a lump of molded vinyl with grooves. With the advent of electronic commerce and the information economy, everything changed. Information of any kind can now be retrieved instantly, without need for local storage or a traditional delivery mechanism.

Microsoft clearly wants to control the point at which information ceases to exist in physical space, except at the point of consumption. In order to do this—to merge our collective information space into its software—Microsoft will have to own the rights to most information on the planet. By all indications, the company collectively—and Bill Gates individually—are well on the way to doing just that.

Microsoft Information Licenses

Microsoft's Sidewalk Web site carries the predictable Terms of Use agreement that has become ubiquitous in the software industry's "shrink-wrap" licenses. On the Web, these agreements are referred to as "click-wrap" licenses. Microsoft's begins:

> "This Web site is offered to the user conditioned on the user's acceptance without modification of the terms, conditions, and notices contained herein. By accessing and using this Web site, the user is deemed to have agreed to all such terms, conditions, and notices."

Pretty standard fare until you realize that by merely accessing the Microsoft site, you are agreeing to Microsoft's terms and conditions for use without possibly knowing what those uses will be.

And at least one of those conditions—Use of Information—is ominous indeed:

> "By being a user of this Web site, the user agrees that Microsoft may share with other parties both aggregate information, individual information, and locator infor-

> mation gathered by Microsoft in the course of the user's continuing individual use of this Web site."

Microsoft goes on to define "locator information" as consisting of a "user's name, email address, physical address, and/or other data about the user that enables the recipient to personally identify the user."

Even worse, these notices appear on virtually every Microsoft Web site: Sidewalk, Expedia, Investor, Carpoint, and Slate.

By using any of these Microsoft Web sites you are giving Microsoft permission to collect personal information about who you are and what material you look at on its sites. Microsoft can easily learn your travel habits, taste in politics and culture, and sexual proclivities. Worst of all, Microsoft can do whatever it likes with that information, because you have given it your permission by merely using the Microsoft Web site(s).

As Microsoft's Internet Explorer browser becomes the *de facto* standard, Microsoft gains yet another way of gathering personal information about you without your knowledge. Internet Explorer is inherently capable of tracking your Web browsing activities—your "clickstream"—and passing that information to Microsoft whenever you visit one of the company's Web sites.

MICROSOFT AND ITS COMPETITION

It's very fashionable within the computer industry to profess to hate—*really despise*—Bill Gates and Microsoft. Whether or not there's a cogent case to be made for the government stepping in and splintering the software leviathan is beside the point. Any convincing argument to contain the giant tends to get overwhelmed by a thick fog of hyperbole and corporate envy.

In January 1998, the U.S. Justice Department opened hearings to decide, presumably once and for all, whether Microsoft is just exceptionally successful or engaged in anti-competitive tactics to establish a monopoly over the software industry. Microsoft's rise to the top of the software pile is as simple as it was uncertain. The company was able to establish its operating systems as industry standards by extracting a royalty on every PC sold. No small feat. Microsoft then was able to leverage its operating system dominance to create and subsequently assure market share for the company's office productivity software programs.

Microsoft detractors, like a chorus, point out in unison and on cue that Microsoft receives royalties on *all* PC systems, regardless of whether or not a Microsoft operating system is installed on that computer system. They also allege that Microsoft's programmers are granted access to secret information that makes its business software work better than competing products. Except—the most outspoken critics argue—Microsoft products are inferior to similar products from other operating system and application software vendors. When this contradiction is pointed out, the unblinking critics cite the philosopher's proposition that the sign of sure genius is the ability to hold two opposing thoughts in one's mind simultaneously.

Microsoft critics are also quick to point out that the company is a master at marketing vaporware (software that doesn't yet exist). When Microsoft realizes that competitors have an edge, so the theory goes, the software giant issues a press release to instill fear, uncertainty, and doubt in consumers and competitors alike. Fear that if a competitor's product is chosen, the consumer will miss out on great—but nonexistent—features to come from the promised Microsoft product. Microsoft bets that the consumer will adopt a wait and see attitude. Sometimes Microsoft ships a product and sometimes it doesn't, but its gambles almost always pay off. Either way, the competition is quashed or at least dealt a severe blow.

Even when Microsoft releases a catch-up product—and the vast majority of all of its products are catch-up products—it usually takes the company several years to refine the product to a competitive level.

In a truly free market, competitors would be able to withstand the Microsoft onslaught. Critics argue that when Microsoft encounters a competitor that it can't handily beat in the market, it simply buys it. "Exit strategy through acquisition" is a catchphrase heard time and again. Microsoft calls the tactic "embrace and extend." Consider these four enormous forays Microsoft has conducted outside the computer software industry since the mid-1980s:

- Photography archive: Bettman
- Cable television: MSNBC and Comcast
- Satellite communication: Teledesic
- Leonardo DaVinci's notebook

Bill Gates claims there's no way to really monopolize the computer industry because it moves too fast, with breakthrough products created on an almost daily basis. His argument is as abominable as it is disingenuous, of course, but it tends to deflect attention away from his remarkable personal wealth. At the beginning of 1998, Bill Gates' personal fortune was estimated to total US$40 billion, at which time mathematically-inclined observers noted that Gates makes about US$500,000 per hour or close to US$150 per second. At that rate, the more cynical observers noted, if Bill Gates were to drop a US$500 bill, it wouldn't be worth the four seconds of his time it would take him to pick it up. (As of this writing, Bill Gates' personal wealth is estimated to be more than US$50 billion.)

MICROSOFT V. DEPARTMENT OF JUSTICE

Beginning in the third quarter of 1997, the United States government turned its intense gaze upon Microsoft and its cofounder in earnest. On October 20, 1997, the U.S. Justice Department asked a court to fine the software behemoth US$1 million per day for violating a 1995 court order against anti-competitive behavior.

The core of the government's case against Microsoft revolved around the software vendor's requirement of personal computer manufacturers to bundle its Internet Explorer Web browser along with its Windows 95 operating system. One could argue an analogy of NIKE Corporation requiring the corner shoe store to carry NIKE socks, shoelaces, hats, t-shirts, and underwear if it wanted to carry NIKE shoes.

Microsoft's main competition in the Web browser market is Netscape, which still commanded 60 percent of the market at the end of 1997. Netscape representatives indicated that it supported the Justice Department request.

For its part, Microsoft's response was that the Justice Department was misinterpreting the court order and that the company would defend its right to add technological innovations to its products. According to Microsoft representatives, the 1995 consent decree allows the software company to integrate new features into its operating system products and that is how the software industry has always operated. Microsoft argues that its requirement of manufacturers to include Internet Explorer on systems they sell is merely Microsoft's attempt to achieve that integration of new features and the government should just mind its own business.

The 1995 court order was a result of an extensive Justice Department investigation under then-Assistant Attorney General Anne Bingaman.

In December 1997, U.S. District Court Judge Thomas Penfield Jackson rejected the Justice Department's request for a contempt-of-court citation and US$1 million-a-day fine. But he simultaneously ordered Microsoft to stop requiring PC manufacturers to include Internet Explorer with the Windows 95 operating system. Judge Jackson also appointed Harvard law professor Lawrence Lessig as a special master to gather additional information, examine the issues, and present his findings in the Justice Department's antitrust case against Microsoft.

Legal observers were in general agreement that while finding that Microsoft had not violated his 1995 order, Judge Jackson firmly and clearly warned Microsoft to watch its corporate step with regard to anti-competitive behavior. Microsoft, in a somewhat peculiar interpretation, said that it felt Judge Jackson's preliminary ruling gave the software giant a window of opportunity to demonstrate that the bundling of Internet Explorer is good for consumers.

The high-technology community's perception of Judge Jackson's preliminary ruling was all over the map. Word from the anti-Microsoft camp was jubilant, while Microsoft defenders took mostly a wait-and-see posture. The most level-headed members of the community saw the ruling as foreboding for the industry as a whole: Either all of Microsoft's operating systems will include Web browser functionality—effectively putting competing browsers out of business—or the government will find itself in the business of regulating what features software companies can include in their products.

Within days of the ruling, Microsoft appealed the decision. The company argued that Judge Jackson improperly expanded the scope of the case when he issued the preliminary injunction against the browser bundling, even though he had previously rejected the Justice Department's contempt-of-court request. "The matter before the court was whether Microsoft could be held in contempt for violating a consent decree entered in 1995," said William Neukom, Microsoft's senior vice president for law and corporate affairs, in a news release. "The court denied the Justice Department's petition for contempt; the case should have ended there," Neukom concluded.

Microsoft went on to disingenuously claim that what Judge Jackson and the government were insisting upon—removing

Internet Explorer from the Windows operating system—was *impossible* and would create an operating system that was "degraded... deficient... [and] dysfunctional."

Judge Jackson, at a December 19, 1997 hearing, noted for the record that his court clerk walked him through the process of removing Internet Explorer 3.02 from his computer in about ninety seconds.

The software company said it would comply with Judge Jackson's order by offering computer manufacturers three options: a "nonfunctional" browser-stripped version; the original Windows 95 release; and the current Windows 95 release which includes the Internet Explorer browser software.

In mid-January 1998, Microsoft lawyer Richard Urowsky told Judge Jackson that the software giant should not be cited for contempt-of-court because it had carefully followed the government's requests in its briefs to the court. Judge Jackson made it clear that Microsoft should have followed his order, not the government's requests.

Microsoft reiterated its position that if all of the Internet Explorer files were removed from Windows 95, the operating system would fail to work. If it were required to comply with the letter of Judge Jackson's order, Microsoft argued, it would be forced to offer a non-functioning operating system.

Justice Department attorney Phillip Malone argued that Judge Jackson's order was broad enough to allow Microsoft ample latitude for compliance and that Microsoft was taking an "extreme and illogical course." Malone noted that almost all Windows applications would break the operating system if they were removed in the way Microsoft removed Internet Explorer.

A Denver-based computer consultant, Glenn Weadock, demonstrated several methods of removing the Internet Explorer software by using directions included in Microsoft documentation (using Microsoft Windows 95's Add/Remove Programs control panel). Microsoft vice president for consumer platforms, David Cole, testified that using the Windows operating system's Add/Remove Programs control panel removes only twenty-six Internet Explorer files, *retaining most of the browser software's functionality.* Cole testified that Microsoft's marketing literature describes the process of removing Internet Explorer as "uncomplicated" and having "no adverse effects" on the operating system.

When asked, "What is Internet Explorer 3.02?" by Justice attorney Malone, Cole responded, "that is a feature of the operating system that allows you to browse the Web, among other things." Microsoft's position was clearly that Internet Explorer wasn't a program or software application at all, but rather an integrated function of the operating system.

Never known for being left out of the action, the United States Senate entered the fray in early February 1998 when Senate Judiciary Committee Chairman Orrin Hatch (R-Utah) warned Microsoft it could be risking regulation by an "Internet Commerce Commission" if it monopolizes the Internet.

"It seems far better to have antitrust enforcement today than heavy-handed regulation of the Internet tomorrow," Hatch said, as he announced his plans for the Senate Judiciary Committee to conduct antitrust hearings centered on Microsoft. Novell, one of Microsoft's fiercest operating system competitors, is based in Senator Hatch's home state of Utah.

Senator Hatch's comments provoked a quick defensive response from Senator Slade Gorton (R-Washington), who said that he found it hard to believe that his "colleague from Utah will be able to make good on the written promise he recently made to me that the 'Judiciary Committee has no intention of interfering' with the Microsoft litigation." Microsoft is based in Senator Gorton's home state of Washington.

Senator Hatch's Judiciary Committee hearings were conducted in early March 1998. One of the most interesting developments of the hearings was Microsoft's agreement to allow its PC manufacturer customers to talk to the Senate Judiciary Committee. Microsoft has nondisclosure agreements with its PC manufacturer customers that preclude the discussion of topics that Microsoft considers to be confidential with any third party.

A similar agreement was reached between Microsoft and the Justice Department when the government agency expressed concern that its investigation would be impeded by nondisclosure agreements between Microsoft and its customers.

In mid-April 1998, Microsoft told reporters that it would be including Internet Explorer in its Windows 98 operating system. Microsoft representatives were quoted in various publications as saying the company hadn't been asked to remove Internet Explorer from Windows 98, only from Windows 95.

As of early July1998, Microsoft won the right to distribute Internet Explorer with Windows 95, but the software company's problems with the Justice Department continue, with no solution in sight.

Project to Promote Competition and Innovation in the Digital Age

What happens to losing presidential candidates and rejected Supreme Court nominees? They form lobbying groups. In some cases they form a lobbying group that's bizarre enough to make a reasonable person almost feel sorry for Microsoft's public grilling at the hands of the Justice Department. Almost, but not quite.

In mid-April 1998, former Senator and presidential candidate Bob Dole (R-Kansas) and former appeals judge Robert Bork (who was also the Nixon administration's Solicitor General) announced they had formed a group to lobby against Microsoft's allegedly anti-competitive business practices.

The Dole-Bork lobbying group, called the Project to Promote Competition and Innovation in the Digital Age (or "ProComp") includes the usual suspects from the computer industry: Netscape, Sun, and Oracle among others.

What's especially bizarre about the Dole-Bork group is that both founders are unabashed conservatives who built reputations on opposing any and all government regulation of the market. How that history is reconciled with calling for government regulation of Microsoft is curious. Do Dole and Bork know something the "rest of us" do not? Do they sense something might be out of control in the economic atmosphere? What has precipitated this about-face with regard to government regulation? Could they, too, think that the public interest is being eclipsed?

Microsoft has studiously and quietly begun to garner the support of a wide range of conservative politicians to help in its lobbying efforts. Former members of Congress Jack Kemp and Vin Weber as well as Haily Barbour—the former chairperson of the Republican party—have all jumped on the Microsoft bandwagon.

Microsoft Business Practices

Legal questions aside, when one asks if Microsoft is a monopoly, the only appropriate response is another question: In which markets? Through whatever means, Microsoft is deeply involved in every aspect of the computer software market. As of late 1997, the company controls the operating system of more than 94 percent of all personal computers sold everywhere in the world. In 1995, Microsoft's word processing application, Microsoft Word, commanded just over 33 percent of the market; by 1997 Microsoft Word's market share had grown to more than 80 percent. International Data Corporation analysts report that more than 65 percent of all new intranets run on Windows NT, and the market penetration of Microsoft's Windows

NT Workstation software is growing at the annual rate of 177 percent.

For years Microsoft's competitors have floated various proposals to dismantle the software giant, mostly in the name of fair competition and a level playing field. In late 1997 and early 1998 the tone of these proposals changed in an important way. Previously, the proposals were floated anonymously or at least very quietly, usually behind the scenes. By the late 1990s, however, practically every high technology executive seemed to be publicly calling for Microsoft's corporate head on a virtual pike and taking their proposals to any federal regulator willing to listen.

In early April 1998, the *New York Times* reported that the Justice Department was not considering breaking up Microsoft, but was said to be considering a range of other possibilities. According to the *New York Times* article, computer industry trade associations reportedly made ten proposals, including:

- Force Microsoft to divest its operating system business from its applications businesses.
- Force Microsoft to honestly disclose and document the parts of its operating systems to which its programmers have access.
- Prohibit Microsoft from tying new software products to its operating systems.

Microsoft dismissed the proposals as a "wish list with no basis in the facts of this industry or the laws of this country," and indicated that there was no reason to believe that any scenario would delay the release of the Windows 98 operating system by the company's targeted June 25, 1998 release date.

On April 11, 1998, the *Los Angeles Times* reported that it had uncovered an elaborate Microsoft plan to put its corporate spin on the Justice Department's investigations of the software company's business practices. The plan, according to confidential Microsoft documents obtained by the *Los Angeles Times* reporters, called for the planting of news articles and opinion pieces commissioned by Microsoft's public relations firms in local newspapers across the country. The articles and editorials would reportedly be presented as "spontaneous testimonials" indicative of a groundswell of grassroots support for Microsoft.

The Microsoft plan was highly targeted, aimed at news outlets in the twelve states that are considering antitrust actions against the software company.

At first, Microsoft spokesperson Greg Shaw, denied he was aware of the plan. When informed by the *Los Angles Times* journalists that his name appeared throughout the confidential documents, Shaw acknowledged the plan but dismissed it as a dead proposal. The status of the plan was contradicted by *Los Angeles Times* sources who said it was presented as an active objective to Microsoft's regional public relations firms. The plan called for the planted stories to be followed with studies and surveys designed to illustrate Microsoft's impact on each state's regional economy.

Within days of the *Los Angeles Times* story, Microsoft began its uncommon public relations onslaught in earnest. Newspaper ads posed as unsigned editorials that painstakingly explained why government regulation of Microsoft would be bad for the company, but even worse for America. The keystone of Microsoft's campaign appears to be the concept of innovation. "At Microsoft, the freedom to innovate for our customers is more than a goal, it is a principle worth standing up for," read the warm and fuzzy marketing copy cloaked as editorial.

Ironically, Microsoft is widely disparaged within the computer industry as not innovative at all. Rather, the software behemoth is almost universally seen as an excellent marketing organization that acquires innovation instead of developing it. Many

Microsoft detractors readily point out that the company is best seen as a consolidator of technology products.

Microsoft's ad campaign states that innovation "results from a spirited competitive environment…." But just how competitive is Microsoft's environment? Most small, innovative software companies are shuddering in fear; or spending imaginary profits at the whiff of a mention of Microsoft interest in either the company or the market segment within which they operate.

Most disturbing of all, the practice of planting news articles and opinion pieces presented as a groundswell of grassroots support isn't even a Microsoft innovation or invention. It's not even new. It's been happening for so long that political flacks even have a code name for it: "Astroturf lobbying."

In early May 1998, Microsoft followed up with a letter signed by its manufacturing partners, predicting all sorts of famine and pestilence if the software giant were prevented from releasing its Windows 98 operating system on schedule.

Microsoft and its Independent Contractors

Reports and court records indicate that Microsoft holds some classes of its workers in the same high regard as its competitors and the Justice Department.

Microsoft is well known in the high technology industry for making a lot of its employees very wealthy virtually overnight. The company generously rewards its employees' hard work with relatively opulent benefits.

Central to Microsoft's employee benefits package is its employee stock purchase plan. The employee stock purchase plan was established in 1986 and allows employees to buy Microsoft stock at 85 percent of its market value at certain times of the year, through a payroll deduction program.

For years, most of these benefits—including the employee stock purchase plan—were denied to anyone who, heaven forbid, chose to work at Microsoft and retain some semblance of independence.

For many Microsoft contractors this didn't pose a problem; they were comfortable working independently, with the company as a client, gladly trading stock options and other employee benefits for a measure of independence. There was, many found, an intangible—but very real—benefit in being able to select the projects one wanted to work on or even being able to take some extra time off between contracts.

For other independent contractors—particularly those who wanted the security of full-time employment with Microsoft—the limited benefits policy proved to be unfair and exploitative. After all, they argued, they were doing the same work as their employee counterparts but were being denied the offer of a full-time job and the same level of benefits, especially access to that lucrative employee stock purchase plan.

A court agreed with the disgruntled independent contractors, holding that Microsoft's independent contractors were entitled to participate in the company's employee stock purchase plan. Microsoft appealed the ruling to the Supreme Court, which rejected the appeal in late January 1998.

A variety of trade associations—including the U.S. Chamber of Commerce, the American Electronics Association, the Software Publishers Association, and the Information Technology Association of America—supported Microsoft's appeal. The lobbyists criticized the appeals court ruling as undermining alternative work arrangements and imposing a "draconian penalty on employers for worker misclassification."

FURTHER...

Capitalism holds high the promise of free markets, but in America most markets are not free at all, as evidenced by taking a look at just a sliver of activity by a single corporate behemoth. It is when this sliver is repeated over and over again throughout the economy by consolidated corporate entities that eclipses begin their path.

One thing that will prove helpful, as our culture lumbers toward the next millennium, is unfettered access to information we need to make informed decisions about our personal and professional lives. As citizens we must remain vigilant with regard to our information access rights. The twin eclipse of government and corporate interests threatens to obstruct our view, as explored in the next chapter.

RESOURCES

- Business Software Alliance: <www.bsa.org>
- Department of Justice: <www.usdoj.gov>
- Microsoft Corp.: <www.microsoft.com>
- Microsoft Sidewalk: <sidewalk.com>

Chapter 6

Information Access

John Perry Barlow—former Wyoming rancher and lyricist for the Grateful Dead—has identified a phenomenon he calls the "learning curve of Sisyphus:" what happens when technology develops faster than anybody's ability to learn it. This phenomenon can be broken down into two basic, closely interrelated components:

- Knowledge workers' skills become obsolete faster than they can be completely learned.
- Everyone feels they have no control over their lives and identities.

Who controls access to information, and how can we be assured that we have access to the information we need?

PRODIGY

The Prodigy electronic information service proved that limiting access to information will result in failure, every time, no matter how much money you throw at it. Prodigy, a service provided jointly by Sears and IBM, failed miserably for the sole reason that it attempted to limit access to information.

Prodigy maintained a staff of editors who decided what sort of information could be posted to the public messaging sections. When users complained about censorship, and began to complain to Prodigy advertisers, their user accounts were deleted. One cancer researcher reportedly lost access to crucial patient correspondence.

Prodigy misjudged the medium. It saw its audience as the advertisers; the users were merely an annoyance that had to be tolerated, so long as they could be "delivered" to the advertisers.

The Prodigy user community got smart and quickly learned how to create large email distribution lists in order to bypass the service's censors. Prodigy fought back by instituting a policy whereby users were charged US$0.25 for every email message beyond an allotted thirty messages per month. This flew in the face of Prodigy's original offering—which was aggressively advertised—of a flat rate of US$9.95 per month for all services, including unlimited email.

Prodigy maintained that because it owned the service, it was a *publisher*, and entitled to enjoy the freedom to censor anything that it saw fit in its private fiefdom. The Prodigy user community felt that the service had more in common with a *common carrier*, like the telephone company, and that Prodigy couldn't censor what information they posted to the service.

This is going to be a very important issue over the next few years. Are these networks and service providers publishers, or are they common carriers? If they're common carriers, then censorship is out of the question. If, on the other hand, they're publishers like Prodigy claimed, then they're going to have to pony up payment for the information they distribute and accept responsibility for what passes through their servers. Most Internet service providers consider themselves more closely (but not completely) related to common carriers. (For more information, see Internet Plumbing Problems on page 126.)

THOMAS

Thomas, the Web site of Congress (named for Thomas Jefferson), was a little too egalitarian for Republican tastes when it first debuted. Shortly after launch of the Thomas Web site in mid-1996, the rules governing Internet use for House committees were rewritten. Under the original rules, each committee was allocated an equal amount of server space and nothing prevented any party from setting up their own sites.

Representative Bill Thomas (R-California), chairman of the House Oversight Committee, had a problem with Democrats potentially having the freedom to put up information that would bypass Republican-controlled sites. Representative Thomas was instrumental in getting the rules changed for placing information on the Thomas Web site. Under the new rules, all subcommittees can have separate pages, but those pages must be "linked to, and accessible only from the committee's page." In effect, the committee chair must approve all content on the Web sites. It probably seemed like a good idea at the time.

SELF-CENSORSHIP IN THE PRESS

In late 1990, HR 4079, sponsored by Representative Newt Gingrich (R-Georgia) and the Senate version (S. 2245) sponsored by Senator Phil Gramm (R-Texas), called for what amounted to concentration camps to be built and for the government to round up *suspected* drug users and force them to work without compensation for the state.

In order to do this, the Constitution would have to be suspended for a period of five years, with the Fourth Amendment, the Eighth Amendment, and *habeas corpus* either suspended, redefined, or disallowed completely. The proposed legislation called for a declaration of a national state of emergency for a period of five years; in essence, martial law would be instituted.

Old Japanese internment camps used during World War II and active and inactive military bases would be used as concentration camps along with the establishment of a new privately owned prison system.

All camp internees would be forced to work and if they were caught with drugs, an additional year would be added to their sentences for each instance, with no right of appeal.

News releases for this bill were sent to all national and local media outlets, but there was virtually no mention of the legislation in the mainstream media. It's impossible to ascertain if this was an instance of nearly universal self-censorship or a case of the media having motive for not covering such a newsworthy event.

ACCESS TO GOVERNMENT RECORDS

Computers, modems, and high-speed Internet connections have been touted as implements for enhancing the democratic process by allowing access to previously inaccessible information. The power of these tools is now being cited by the United States government as reason to bar access to government records.

In the early 1970s, CBS News correspondent Robert Schakne conducted an investigation of a corrupt politician—Daniel

Flood (D-Pennsylvania)—who later pled guilty to soliciting illegal campaign contributions. Schakne requested criminal records from the FBI, under the Freedom of Information Act (FOIA), on Medico Industries, a defense contractor alleged to have received political favors from Flood.

The FBI refused Schakne's FOIA request, citing an exemption that allows government agencies to withhold "records [that] could reasonably be expected to constitute an unwarranted invasion of personal privacy."

Schakne appealed the case to the United States Supreme Court, which upheld the FOIA exemption, stating that while most FBI records were public, private citizens "benefited from the practical obscurity" held in government files. Justice John Paul Stevens, writing for the majority in the 1989 Justice Department v. Reporters Committee decision:

> "There is a vast difference between the public records that might be found after a diligent search of courthouse files, county archives, and local police stations throughout the country and a computerized summary located in a single clearinghouse of information."

Not all information access issues are as sensational or high-profile as Robert Schakne's FOIA folly. Many are much more mundane but can potentially have a much wider impact upon the populace.

Robert Westbrook's California-based Crimeline sells criminal background information to virtually anyone—public agency or private individual—who can meet his asking price. Westbrook sued Los Angeles County, California in 1992, when court officials refused to sell him computer tapes of the court's daily log.

In 1994, Judge Arleigh M. Woods ruled that the privacy provisions in California's Constitution and the state's penal code reserve the use of court databases to law enforcement agencies:

> "It is the aggregate of the information which makes it valuable... it is the same quality which makes its dissemination constitutionally dangerous."

In the late 1980s, federal courts required that the White House save and make public all executive office email. The Executive branch of the federal government argued that personal email was similar to personal telephone calls, not public documents. The courts disagreed, on two separate occasions.

As recently as March 1998, a federal judge was still threatening to hold John Carlin, Archivist of the United States, in contempt of court for resisting the release of the government's electronic records. A former National Archives regulation—General Records Schedule 20—allowed the destruction of email and other computerized records, once they had been copied to paper. Carlin, however, continued to advise federal agencies that the regulation was still in effect, according to Public Citizen, the consumer advocacy group. United States District Judge Paul Friedman ruled in favor of Public Citizen, and voided General Records Schedule 20.

Public Citizen and other critics had effectively argued that the General Records Schedule 20 regulation was analogous to an electronic shredder. The biggest problem, according to critics, was that email at low-level offices of government agencies were declared to be the equivalent of high-level government offices including the State Department and the White House.

Various federal agencies, including the Justice Department and National Archives, appealed Judge Friedman's ruling. Representatives of the Justice Department disingenuously argued that "many government computer applications will grind to a halt or crash entirely" if an "oppressive, 'no delete'" order were upheld. At the same time, the agency argued that mandatory backups "would cause huge difficulties, especially if the data ever needs to be retrieved."

Does the government have a duty to protect the data it collects? Privacy advocates argue that when federal law was enacted to help states set up criminal databases, the databases were intended to make law enforcement more effective—not turn sensitive criminal data into easy pickings for marketers. Government records can be dangerously inaccurate, incomplete, and misleading. For example, only about one-half of the FBI's 17.5 million criminal background reports list the final outcome of warrants and arrests, and the FBI readily admits that its systems contain errors.

Journalists, on the other hand, note that reporters with computers have effectively used government computer records for the public good, uncovering everything from election fraud to convicted sex offenders driving school buses. Information abuse can easily be prevented by aggressively prosecuting illegal use of private data, not by restricting public access to that data, according to members of the fourth estate.

The essence of the entire argument is a debate about who owns the information. Is the information government collects on its citizens the property of the citizen or of the government? Surprisingly, in almost all cases, personal information gathered by government agencies or private parties belongs to whomever collected it, not the subject of the information.

RESTRICTIONS WITHIN GOVERNMENT

In 1985, the Department of Defense required the Society of Photo-Optical Instrumentation Engineers (SPIE) to restrict attendance at a conference where unclassified papers would be presented to United States and Canadian citizens and permanent U.S. residents. Scientists that were allowed to attend the conference had to sign an "Export Controlled DoD Technical Data Agreement," promising that they would obtain an export license before sharing the information from the conference with foreign citizens.

Information is an important national resource that the government understandably wants to manage. But the government's efforts in managing information need to be fundamentally different from its management of other public resources: the government's management of this valuable resource must be guided by the basic assumption that open communication and free flow of information have great social utility. This is the foundation of our national heritage and a keystone of our Constitution. This assumption might be overridden only in specific instances where the government can show a substantial public necessity, such as a concrete and immediately verifiable risk to national security.

Advocates of governmental restriction of access to information often cite national security as a justification. In recent administrations this has come to be a pseudo-justification applied to a wildly disparate and ever-broadened base of information that has never before been restricted. This action is in opposition to the beliefs of administrations prior to President Truman.

Vannevar Bush, President Roosevelt's science advisor, held the view that "a sounder foundation for our national security rests in a broad dissemination of scientific knowledge upon which further advances can more readily be made than in a policy of restrictions which would impede our further advances in the hope that our potential enemies will not catch up with us."

A second reason commonly given for restricting the flow of information is that the government necessarily needs to check its deficit spending and its excessive regulation activities. The policies that result from this position—such as the FCC decision not to publish the complete text of its proposed rules—limit public access to crucial information about the governmental decision making process.

In April of 1987, the National Academy of Sciences published a report finding that controls on the export of manufactured goods and information cost the United States economy

188,000 jobs and US$9 billion each year. Moreover, a full 40 percent of all doctoral engineers entering the American work force every year are foreign citizens. One can cogently argue, from the government's own study, that its position of impeding the free flow of information is detrimental to our economy.

The American tradition of openness with regard to public information access is based in the Constitutional requirement that obliges the federal government to regularly publish information on its spending and taxing activities, and on the corresponding impact this has on the citizenry. Yet, there have been concurrent, opposing trends since World War II to simultaneously open and to restrict the flow of information.

In 1940, President Roosevelt instituted a series of procedures for classifying information based on a 1938 law restricting public access to military installations, equipment, and related information. World War II also saw the beginning of a large intelligence bureaucracy. After the war, Congress gave certain agencies—such as the Atomic Energy Commission and the Central Intelligence Agency—broad authority to restrict information availability for the sake of national security.

The counter-trend toward a less restrictive information environment, advocated by President Roosevelt's science advisor, Vannevar Bush, finally culminated in the enactment of the Freedom of Information Act in 1966. In 1974, Congress strengthened the FOIA and then, in 1976 passed the Government in the Sunshine Act. The Government in the Sunshine Act requires federal agencies to open more of their meetings to the public.

The administrations of Presidents Ford and Carter moved to curb the tendency toward governmental secrecy and President Nixon and President Carter both moved to narrow the information classification system.

President Carter went so far as to issue an executive order in 1978 specifying that even if information fell into one of seven restricted categories, it was not to be classified unless its disclosure would cause "identifiable damage" to national security. President Carter's executive order also called for documents to be *automatically declassified* after six years and prohibited them from being reclassified. Perhaps most significantly, President Carter ordered that an agency could not restrict access to information as a response to a request for it under the Freedom of Information Act.

In the 1980s, the administration of President Reagan used a broad definition of national security, imposing restrictions on multitudinous categories of previously accessible government information. In 1983, Richard V. Allen, President Reagan's national security advisor, said that "national security must include virtually every facet of international activity, including (but not limited to) foreign affairs, defense, intelligence, research and development policy, outer space, international economic and trade policy, and reaching deeply into the domains of the Departments of Commerce and Agriculture."

During this same period, the Reagan administration put forth the notion of an "information mosaic." The concept of an information mosaic represented that an unknown enemy could use sophisticated search techniques to assemble disparate bits of seemingly harmless information into insights that would threaten national security. Once the inherent power of techniques such as computer matching are fully grasped, it's not much of an intellectual leap to recognize a wide variety of unintended applications for the techniques.

In 1982, President Reagan issued an executive order authorizing federal officials to classify more information than ever before. Displacing President Carter's idea of "identifiable damage," federal officials today need only suggest that "disclosure reasonably could be expected to cause damage to the national security."

President Reagan's order also allowed information to be classified—or even reclassified—at any point in time and maintained as classified indefinitely. This superseded President Carter's six year automatic declassification policy. Perhaps most shocking of all, was the clause of the Reagan order that allowed federal officials to classify any information they deemed necessary, *even if that information had already been placed in the public domain*.

The effect of President Reagan's policy is chilling in the extreme. Consider the language of a Department of Energy research contract, for example:

> "If the grantee believes any information developed or acquired may be classifiable, the grantee shall... protect such information as if it were classified."

When presenting their collective position with regard to surveillance and search of suspects, government intelligence and law enforcement agencies have relied upon the peculiar language of "lawful access" when articulating views and making demands. When lobbying for mandatory key escrow, for example, (see Government Cryptography Control on page 246) federal agencies have consistently stated that "lawful access" would be required to recover private cryptography keys. One could reasonably assume that "lawful access" means—or at least implies—a valid search warrant issued by a judge.

That reasonable assumption may be wrong.

President Reagan's 1981 executive order 12333 casts new light on just what "lawful access" means and clearly subverts the intent of the Fourth Amendment. Executive order 12333 states, in part:

> "**2.5 Attorney General Approval**. The Attorney General hereby is delegated the power to approve the use for intelligence purposes, within the United States or against a United States person abroad, of any tech-

> nique for which a warrant would be required if undertaken for law enforcement purposes, provided that such techniques shall not be undertaken unless the Attorney General has determined in each case that there is probable cause to believe that the technique is directed against a foreign power or an agent of a foreign power. Electronic surveillance, as defined in the Foreign Intelligence Surveillance Act of 1978, shall be conducted in accordance with that Act, as well as this Order."

According to some privacy advocates, this executive order would permit the Attorney General to simply declare that an investigative target is an agent of a foreign power, thereby making no search warrant necessary to surveil or search the target.

In October 1986, John Poindexter issued a National Security Council directive designed to restrict *unclassified* information that involved not only national security but also "other government interests, [including] government or government-derived economic, human, financial, industrial, agricultural, technological, and law enforcement information."

In 1987, the Reagan White House withdrew the Poindexter directive under pressure from Congress, but the basic policy—NSDD 145—was left untouched. NSDD 145 calls for a "comprehensive and coordinated approach" to restricting foreign access to all telecommunications and automated information systems.

In December 1987, Congress passed the Computer Security Act, which basically transfers responsibility for developing a government-wide computer-security system from the National Security Agency to the National Bureau of Standards.

Freedom of Information Act and Electronic Information

In early 1989, the Administrative Conference of the United States recommended that electronically acquired and stored information should be covered under the Freedom of Information Act. According to a conference statement, "the FOIA was written with paper records in mind. However, in this age of widespread computer usage, the conference recommendation urges agencies to interpret the FOIA to include electronic information."

Some members of Congress, including Representative Glenn English (D-Oklahoma), have proposed amending both the Freedom of Information Act and the Privacy Act to include electronic information. As of this writing, none of these proposals have passed beyond the subcommittee level.

A Freedom of Information Act Folly

Eric Corley (a.k.a. Emmanuel Goldstein), editor and publisher of *2600 Magazine: The Hacker Quarterly*, claims that a November 6, 1992 meeting sponsored by the magazine at a shopping mall in suburban Washington, DC, was disrupted by a raid of private security officers and local police officers under the direction of the federal government. Material distributed at the meeting—including Computer Professionals for Social Responsibility (CPSR) membership applications—was reportedly confiscated.

Craig Neidorf, present at the meeting, claimed guards confiscated photographic film from a person trying to take pictures of the private security officers. Neidorf also claimed that when a meeting attendee attempted to copy down the names of the security officers, they confiscated his pencil and paper.

Al Johnson, chief of security for the Pentagon City Mall, told the electronic journal *Newsbytes* on November 9, 1992, "No one said that we were acting on behalf of the Secret Service. We were merely enforcing our regulations. While the group was not disruptive, it had pulled tables together and was having a meeting in our food court area. The food court is for people eating and is not for meetings. We therefore asked the people to leave."

That same day, November 9, 1992, Johnson was quoted in a *Communications Daily* article by Brock Meeks as saying, "As far as I'm concerned, we're out of this. The Secret Service, the FBI, they're the ones that ramrodded this whole thing."

Presumably because its membership applications were confiscated, the Computer Professionals for Social Responsibility organization filed a Freedom of Information Act request with the United States Secret Service.

On April 21, 1993, CPSR received a response from the Secret Service with regard to the trade association's FOIA request. It appears that the Secret Service wanted the names of the attendees of the Pentagon City Mall meeting and had the mall security people obtain them. The Secret Service maintained that the information it possesses with regard to the shopping mall incident was obtained "in the course of a criminal investigation that is being conducted pursuant to the Secret Service's authority to investigate access device and computer fraud."

The Secret Service FOIA response indicates that the government agency possesses two documents, consisting "solely of information identifying individuals" that was obtained from a "confidential source."

The Secret Service went on to claim that "premature release of the identities of the individual(s) at issue could easily result in interference to the Secret Service's investigation by alerting these individual(s) that they are under investigation and thus allowing the individual(s) to alter their behavior and/or evidence."

CPSR, the Electronic Frontier Foundation, and the American Civil Liberties Union challenged the actions of the Pentagon City Mall security officers, the local police, and the Secret Service on the grounds that the meeting raid was a warrantless search and seizure conducted at the behest of the Secret Service.

Minnesota Data Practices Act

There appears to be little, if any consistency, among what government information is available from state to state. Some states have a Freedom of Information Act (or equivalent) and some do not. Minnesota, for example, does not. Instead, Minnesota has a Data Practices Act (Chapter 13, Government Data Practices). While it's beyond the scope of this book to provide in-depth coverage of the legislation of every state, this section offers a citizen's overview of the current law in my home state of Minnesota. (For more information about Minnesota's Data Practices Act with regard to personal privacy and government information, see Minnesota Data Practices Act on page 163.)

In the early 1970s, government officials in Minnesota, as in most states, began to voice concern about the impact of information on the lives of its citizenry. The state's intention was to regulate information when it had a negative impact on people's lives, especially when the information in question was collected by the government. Journalists resisted the new restrictions on information that had previously been freely available, and in 1979, the Data Practices Act was amended to provide public access to government information.

The Minnesota statute is unique, partly because Minnesota—unlike some other states—does not have a state-level equivalent to the federal Freedom of Information Act. In Minnesota, all government information is presumed to be public unless specifically classified by a statute (or temporary ruling) as not public. Minnesota's definition of "information" is wide ranging and includes computerized data, video and audio tapes, and "non-traditionally collected" information. The definition also includes the more pedestrian mountains of forms and reports that most of us recognize as government information.

Ironically, the judiciary—including "any office, officer, department, division, board, commission, committee, or agency of the courts"—is exempt from the Data Practices Act. Access to court information is understandably governed by information access rules adopted by the state supreme court. However, information from the lawyer's professional responsibility board, the board of judicial standards, the lawyer's trust account board, the state law library, the state court administrator's office, the district court administrator's office, and the office of the court administrator is simply not addressed under the legislation. Therefore, in Minnesota, almost all information about the professional responsibilities and behaviors of lawyers and judges is protected.

Our judiciary was Constitutionally designed to be independent, and with good reason. Sooner or later, units of government will test their powers against each other. But an independent judiciary does not mean an exempt judiciary. Access to information that would serve to hold judges accountable for behavior and protocol is not the same thing as attempting to hold judges accountable for rulings that may simply be unpopular.

When the citizenry or the media, like mad bees, swarm an unpopular judicial ruling, it often serves only to eclipse the more fundamental issues of the case law and its fair application. Such distractions could ultimately open the door for members of the judiciary to hide behind privacy when threatened.

In Minnesota, government data is classified into three main categories:

- **Data on individuals** is said to be *public* if it is accessible by the public for any reason. Data is said to be *private* if it is accessible by the subject, but not by the public. Data is said to be *confidential* if it is accessible by neither the subject nor the public.

- **Data on decedents** is said to be *public* if it is accessible by the public for any reason. Data is said to be *private data on decedents* if it is accessible by the decedent's representative, but not by the public. Data is said to be *confidential data on decedents* if the information is accessible by neither the decedent's representative nor the public.

- **Data not on individuals** is said to be *public* if it is accessible by the public for any reason. Data is said to be *non-public* if it is accessible by the subject (if any), but not by the public. Data is said to be *protected non-public* if the information is accessible by neither the subject (if any) nor the public.

In any case, private and confidential data on decedents becomes public ten years after the death of the subject and 30 years after the creation of the data. In Minnesota, only living human beings can be individuals for the purposes of the Data Practices Act; *corporations and other created business entities are specifically excluded*.

The Data Practices Act allows anyone to inspect government information at no charge. If you want copies of the data, you'll have to pay the costs associated with making the copies. A request for inspection access allows one to look at how the data is actually laid out, which can help immeasurably in refining an information request for specific government data. In Minnesota, limits on the cost of access to government information are clearly defined:

> "If a person requests copies… the responsible authority may require the… person to pay the actual costs of searching for and retrieving government data, including the costs of employee time, and for making, certifying, compiling… the copies of the data…."

A Minnesota government agency cannot charge for its costs to redact the data to meet the inspection request while removing protected information. The statute is specific:

> "… the responsible authority… may not charge for separating public from not public data."

For example, if you request inspection of the salaries of all the employees in the state attorney general's office, the agency will likely have to create a report that includes employee social security numbers. Social security numbers are protected personal information under the Data Practices Act, and have to be removed from the report. The attorney general's office, however, cannot charge you for its costs to redact the protected information.

Unlike most information access legislation, Minnesota's Data Practices Act is as inclusive as possible. The wording of the law, "All government data shall be public unless…." allows only limited government information to be excluded. The act specifies that the information must be kept in an accessible form:

> "The responsible authority shall keep records containing government data in such an arrangement and condition as to make them easily accessible for convenient use."

Don Gemberling, director of the Public Information Policy Analysis Division of the Minnesota state Department of Administration, has spent twenty-five years of his life crafting the Minnesota Data Practices Act and helping people understand it. Gemberling plots government information access along the continuum illustrated below.

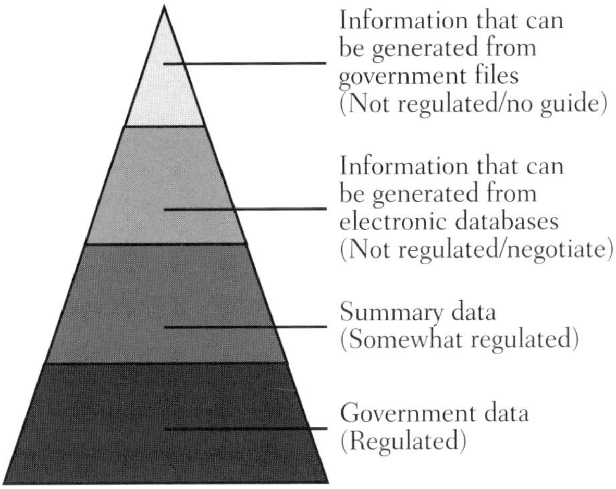

Figure 6-1: Minnesota Data Practices Act information access continuum.

The key to any successful government information request in Minnesota is, after first making an *inspection* request, to make the actual *information* request in such a way that the information sought clearly falls within the base section of the pyramidal continuum, "Government data." Information that falls within this area—and that is not about people—is generally not protected. The other three sections of the continuum are each progressively more problematic—the levels of regulation are either much more loose or nonexistent. That doesn't necessarily mean that the information is private or protected, it just means that the agency responsible for it is more likely to set its own rules for access.

It has become fashionable for government agencies to declare that the databases they have compiled—such as a drivers license database—have commercial value. No one disputes that these databases, compiled with citizens' tax dollars, have commercial value. In these cases, however, the Minnesota law specifically limits the fees assessed to the information's actual development costs:

> "When a request under this subdivision involves any person's receipt of copies of public government data that has commercial value and is a substantial and discrete portion of or an entire formula, pattern, compilation, program, device, method, technique, process, database, or system developed with a significant expenditure of public funds by the agency, the responsible authority may charge a reasonable fee for the information in addition to the costs of making, certifying, and compiling the copies. Any fee charged must be clearly demonstrated by the agency to relate to the actual development costs of the information. The responsible authority, upon the request of any person, shall provide sufficient documentation to explain and justify the fee being charged."

In the case of state-collected information that is deemed to have commercial value, intellectual property provisions have been made in the Data Practices Act:

> "Nothing in this chapter or any other statute shall be construed to prevent a state agency, statewide system, or political subdivision from acquiring a copyright or patent for a computer software program or components of a program created by that government agency. In the event that a government agency does acquire a patent or copyright to a computer software program, the data shall be treated as trade secret information…."

The statute clearly places the burden of justifying any denial of an information access request squarely on the agency from whom the information was requested:

> "If the responsible authority… determines that the requested data [are not public], the responsible authori-

> ty… shall inform the requesting person of the determination either orally at the time of the request, or in writing as soon after that time as possible, and shall cite the specific statutory section… on which the determination is based."

If an information access request is denied, the agency from whom the information was requested must provide written justification:

> "Upon the request of any person denied access to data, the responsible authority… shall certify in writing that the request has been denied and cite the specific statutory section upon which the denial was based."

Gemberling acknowledges that the statute was refined with public information access rights in mind. According to many journalists, this written justification requirement has done more than anything to loosen the information grip of recalcitrant government agencies

Information about government employees is a mixed bag of public and not public data. The statute specifically limits personnel public information to:

- name
- gross salary
- contract fees
- gross pension
- paid fringe benefits
- expense reimbursement
- job title and description
- education and training background
- previous work experience

- date of first and last employment
- complaints or charges against employee
- final disposition of any disciplinary action
- terms of dispute settlement
- payroll time sheets that do not reveal any protected data (such as medical leave)

State government employees have some latitude, allowing them—at times—to play fast and loose with the release of information about disciplinary action. If a government employee that is not covered by a collective bargaining agreement resigns before being disciplined, the disciplinary information is private. If that same employee doesn't resign or resigns after being disciplined, however, the disciplinary information is public.

The rules are different for government employees that are covered by a collective bargaining agreement. In these cases, disciplinary information is public if the employee doesn't file a grievance for the disciplinary action or if the disciplinary action is upheld in arbitration. Otherwise the disciplinary information is protected.

It has become something of a spectator sport for government agencies in Minnesota to push the compliance envelope with regard to the Data Practices Act. If a state agency hires a private attorney to investigate a problematic agency employee, for example, the agency can cleanly sidestep any information access legislation issues. The action taken by the agency as a result of the investigation is public information, but the actual information uncovered by the investigation itself is not "government information" and therefore not covered by the Data Practices Act. Subsequently, the uncovered information is protected. The information is also likely to be separately protected as attorney-client privilege and attorney work product.

The practice is especially tiresome because there are currently no enforcement provisions in the Minnesota Data Practices Act except to bring a lawsuit. According to Gemberling, fully 65 percent of the time an opinion from his office helps resolve the issue even though Department of Administration opinions are not binding.

Platform for Internet Content Selection

The Communications Decency Act (CDA) attempted to restrict access to a specific category of speech. Follow-up legislation will likely mandate the availability of technologies that allow access to selected types of speech to be restricted. Technology will allow any individual or organization to accomplish what the CDA couldn't do with legislation.

The World Wide Web Consortium (W3C), in response to the mainstream-media-borne cyberporn hysteria, developed a technology called the Platform for Internet Content Selection (PICS) to meet the need of restricted access, especially in the case of children, to selected types of content on the Web.

PICS is an extension to the Hypertext Markup Language (HTML) standard, allowing anyone to filter material on the Web. PICS accomplishes this task, not through filtering technologies, but rather, through a labeling standard for rating content and optionally blocking access to that content.

Any individual or organization will be able to develop their own content rating schemes based on PICS in order to enforce their own worldview. Imagine the possibilities of an enforced worldview of, say, Jerry Falwell (or Larry Flynt, for that matter) and you'll quickly get the idea.

What's so disturbing about PICS is that the labeling standard can be transparently implemented at any point of the Internet distribution chain: individual user, proxy server, Internet service provider, state, or even nation. With PICS, access to certain content can be restricted *without the users' consent or even knowledge*. This means that not only will parents be able to restrict access to certain types of information within their homes, but that businesses will be able to restrict employee access to certain bodies of information. And even entire countries will be able to restrict access to information they deem disruptive or inappropriate.

The ability for parents to control information access within their homes is wholly appropriate, but perhaps better accomplished in other ways. The concept of a business, organization, or state controlling access to information, however, is without exception inappropriate.

(For more information about PICS in relation to corporate censorship, see Platform for Internet Content Selection on page 208.)

ONLINE JOURNALISM

In early 1972, Tom Wolfe—one of America's true literary lions—introduced the concept of The New Journalism to the world by authoring a thirteen-page piece for *New York* magazine, entitled, "The Birth of 'The New Journalism'; Eyewitness Report by Tom Wolfe." According to Wolfe, the novel was dead, replaced by creative nonfiction and its attendant narrative tools—and the participant observer had arrived.

In 1995 Joshua Quitner rang the death knell for Wolfe's print-bound New Journalism and rang in what he called Way New Journalism. The watermark of Way New Journalism is the process whereby anyone, for the price of a Web server and an Internet connection, can compete with traditional, mainstream publications. For the first time writers will be able to bypass Big Media's distribution cartel, taking their readers with them.

Tom Wolfe changed forever the way journalists worked their skill. Suddenly it was okay to have fun with facts and write with a distinctive voice. Where Wolfe's New Journalism combined the forms of the novel and standard reportage, Quitner's Way New Journalism added video, sound, and hypertext links to the mix. But most observers agree that the practitioners of Way New Journalism are still experimenting with their tools, honing their craft as the medium itself struggles to walk.

ONLINE JOURNALISM REVIEW

In February 1998, the faculty and students of the University of Southern California's Annenberg School for Communication launched the *Online Journalism Review*, an online publication with a mission to criticize news coverage on the Internet.

The *Online Journalism Review* promises to validate deserving Net-based publications as reliable sources of information. This is the first publication—electronic or print—that promises to take Net-based news organizations like C|Net's news.com, Microsoft's *Slate*, and *Salon* as serious as their print and broadcast counterparts.

Featuring a combination of breaking news, commentary, features, and resource databases, the publication explores the traditional standards of journalism—ethical, legal, and commercial—as applied to the emerging new media that comprise the Web. Because the *Online Journalism Review* is funded by academia and isn't required to turn a profit, one would reasonably assume that commercial interests and business pressures will not hold sway at the publication. "We want to identify who is best serving the public on the Web and who, hiding in the cloak of journalism, belongs in different garb," writes executive editor Larry Pryor, in the publication's mission statement. "We want to support the truth tellers, label the entertainers and expose those who would let excess commercial interests sway their judgment."

Pryor identifies several Internet-specific problems that must be addressed before Web-based journalism will be perceived as legitimate. Reportage on these areas will form the core coverage of publication. Among the problems:

- Bias
- Incompetence
- Fraud and commercial exploitation
- Gossip and rumor-mongering
- Copyright infringement
- The "scoop" mentality (errors caused by deadline pressures)
- Technical elitism
- Deliberate distortion through image and text manipulation
- Plagiarism
- Commercial interest over editorial content
- Privacy invasion

The *Online Journalism Review* also contributes to the curriculum at the Annenberg School by participating in a new program to train high-school students in ethical journalistic practices.

Technorealism

In the first quarter of 1998, a small group of Internet cognoscenti took a look at the state of technology in general and the Net in particular. They didn't much like what they saw. They saw two opposite views, each championed by extremists. In one view, the Internet was seen as an unsettled utopian frontier, holding the future of humanity. In the opposing view, the Net was seen as a teeming cesspool of pornography, perversion, and predators.

This group of Internet experts, calling themselves technorealists, published a manifesto—yes, a *manifesto*—in response to these two opposing views, calling for what they called technorealism. Technorealism attempts to dismiss the "louder voices at the extremes" and calls for a balance between "technoutopianism and neo-Luddism."

The technorealist position is expressed concisely through eight general—but evolving—principles that will appear to be almost painfully obvious to anyone who's been paying attention to the growth of the Internet and technology's impact on society:

1. Technologies are not neutral.
2. The Internet is revolutionary, but not Utopian.
3. Government has an important role to play on the electronic frontier.
4. Information is not knowledge.
5. Wiring the schools will not save them.
6. Information wants to be protected.
7. The public owns the airwaves; the public should benefit from their use.
8. Understanding technology should be an essential component of global citizenship.

Nothing radical, outrageous, or even new there, right? For anyone who's been awake during the 1990s, these are mildewed bromides, right?

Well, maybe in real life, but not on the Internet.

On the Internet, these eight simple platitudes were met with either wild enthusiasm or flaming outrage. Only on the Internet is it possible for something so seemingly uncontroversial to generate so much controversy. But it's certainly great fun to watch the hyperbole hurled from one side to the other and back again, like a virtual tennis match in cyberspace with fireballs.

The pro-technorealist camp gathered in a virtual drum circle to celebrate the wonders of level-headedness, proclaiming neither their love nor hate for technology. The technorealist detractors, on the other hand, were quick to point out that narcissism mixed with technology is a recipe for trouble if not disaster.

Technonarcissism, for better or worse, has become something of a cottage industry within the larger high technology industry. From pompous declarations of virtual independence to calls for two laptops in every soup pot to proclamations of an ever-growing, continually-booming economy, the stakes for legitimacy—or at least credulity—are stretched to the breaking point.

Internet Plumbing Problems

As the Internet becomes more and more fundamental to information gathering, education, and commerce, the physical-world access problems become very real. These problems will grow as the Net's population continues to grow. Take, for instance, the business that exists *only* in cyberspace. Cut off that business's Net connection and you've dealt the business a critical, potentially fatal, blow.

Some state legislatures are beginning to realize the potential severity of this problem and have begun to craft laws to address the situation. In Illinois, for example, State Representative Jack McGuire (D-Joliet) introduced a bill in February 1998 that would allow consumers who suffer network outages of more than four hours to demand (and get) refunds from Internet service providers.

Internet service providers actively resist legislation that would provide such levels of consumer protection for service outages.

Almost all outages, the providers claim, are beyond their control. The Internet service providers argue that any law requiring service guarantees would hold them liable for outages on networks that they do not control from end to end. For the most part this is true. Most of the Internet's plumbing is owned by a very small group of very large companies.

Mike O'Connor, co-founder of gofast.net, Inc., a Saint Paul, Minnesota Internet service provider is known for his clear thinking and wit:

> "I love the plumbing analogy, because the parallels are pretty strong. Would you sue your plumber if the water in your building stopped flowing? Most likely the water stopped because of a problem at the utility company."
>
> "Are Internet service providers more like plumbers—integrating products and services from a variety of third-party suppliers—or are they more like utility companies that deliver a service to your door? In the long run, either definition will work. If Internet service providers are plumbers, they will get less regulation (and less protection). If they're viewed more like utility companies, they'll get more regulation, but they'll also get a guaranteed margin of profit through the tariff process. We can't expect to have it both ways."
>
> "Another thought is to break the Internet up into layers. A physical plumbing layer of wires and fiber at the bottom; integration services in the middle; and applications on the top. Each of these layers will probably need different regulation, with the physical layer being treated more like a utility, the application layer treated like the software it is, and the integration services provided by companies like gofast.net somewhere in the middle."
>
> "Meanwhile, no amount of legislation is going to make some of the current technology limits go away. Maybe

> some day we'll be able to provide quality of service guarantees, but not right now. So, in a way, this [quality of service guarantees] is like trying to pass a law to override the theory of relativity. No amount of shouting is going to make the power grid, or the natural gas delivery system, or the Internet 100 percent reliable."

FURTHER...

Responsible citizenship requires access to information collected and created by the government. In order to be well informed, we must have access to the information we need, when we need it. As shown in this chapter, any number of organizations—in both public and private sectors—have elected themselves as the sole arbiters of what we need to know.

If the demand for access to information can be viewed as an eclipsing body, the body that information access manages to eclipse is personal privacy.

RESOURCES

- 2600 Magazine: The Hacker Quarterly: <www.2600.com>
- American Civil Liberties Union: <www.aclu.org>
- John Perry Barlow: <www.eff.org/~barlow/>
- C|Net news.com: <www.news.com>
- Computer Professionals for Social Responsibility: <www.cpsr.org>
- Electronic Frontier Foundation: <www.eff.org>
- Freedom of Information Act: <www.aclu.org/library/foia.html>

- Freedom of Information Act: <www.seas.gwu.edu/nsarchive/nsa/foia.html>
- gofast.net, Inc.: <www.gofast.net>
- House Oversight Committee: <www.house.gov/cho/>
- Minnesota Data Practices Act: <www.revisor.leg.state.mn.us/stats/13/>
- Newsbytes: <www.newsbytes.com>
- Online Journalism Review <www.ojr.org>
- Prodigy: <www.prodigy.com>
- Public Citizen: <www.citizen.org>
- Salon: <www.salon1999.com>
- Slate: <www.slate.com>
- Technorealism: <www.technorealism.org>
- Technorealist Conspiracy: <www.technorealist.org>
- Thomas: <thomas.loc.gov>
- World Wide Web Consortium: <www.w3.org>

CHAPTER

7

PERSONAL PRIVACY

Contrary to the sensationalistic headlines that occur on a regular basis and then fade into distant memory, privacy is not a temporary issue that will fade over time. If anything, privacy concerns will intensify in the coming years.

Virtually every poll ever taken on the importance of privacy has shown that it is regarded as a major concern by individuals. Equifax, the large credit reporting agency, conducted an extensive opinion survey in 1990 and found that nearly four out of five people surveyed expressed concern that their privacy is "threatened." In 1978, just less than one-third of those surveyed (31 percent) said they were "very concerned" about their privacy being threatened. Almost one-half of those surveyed in 1990 (46 percent) felt "very concerned."

In an address at the first conference on Computers, Freedom, and Privacy in 1991, constitutional scholar Laurence Tribe called for a 27th Amendment to the Constitution,

> "... in order to preserve privacy and other individual rights threatened by the spread of computer technology... to cope with the many questions raised by the advent of 'cyberspace,' a place without physical walls, or even physical dimensions, where an increasing amount of the world's communications and business—ranging from ordinary letters to huge global transfers of money—is taking place, via computer and telephone lines."

According to Tribe, there is a serious possibility that the Constitution's fundamental protections for individuals will be "metamorphosed into oblivion" unless policymakers come to terms with the ramifications of technological change. Tribe's remedy is simple: Constitutional protections for free speech and against unreasonable search and seizure would be fully applicable in all situations, regardless of the technological method or medium used.

HOW IMPORTANT IS PRIVACY?

Personal privacy has long been important to Americans because most of our forebears came to this country to escape a government that was both intrusive and oppressive. Privacy has always been perceived as an important defense against a powerful government.

It sometimes comes as a surprise to citizens that privacy is not explicitly mentioned in the United States Constitution, yet most experts agree that privacy is implicitly protected in various amendments. Furthermore, many individual state constitutions recognize privacy rights for individuals. Many privacy rights experts insist that we need to start speaking in terms of limiting *surveillance* instead of protecting individual *privacy* in order to put the issue in proper perspective.

Do we have a reasonable expectation of privacy in public spaces? If so, certainly not for long. A former aerospace engineer, David Aviv, has patented a surveillance system that he intends to market as a crime deterrent. Aviv's system, called Public Eye, uses pattern recognition to distinguish between an innocuous event (like withdrawing cash from an automatic teller machine) and a violent one (like a mugging).

In Aviv's system, a series of cameras in a variety of public spaces send real-time images to a computer that compares the image to a database of threatening gestures. If the computer determines the act to be malevolent, an alarm notifies the police or a guard. One has to wonder if the system is specially tuned to properly interpret physical gestures of the handicapped.

Aviv has also used a specialized form of computerized pattern recognition called "word gisting" to distinguish between innocuous and malevolent speech. It's reasonable to wonder how the system deals with all the linguistics of non-English speaking people.

The varied ways in which technology can germinate privacy abuses is well substantiated. The other side of the argument, however, is usually given short shrift. Advancement in technology can strengthen an individual's privacy every bit as much as it can increase the likelihood that an individual may be subjected to surveillance.

A multitude of transactions that used to be carried out in person, face-to-face, are now handled remotely: home shopping, computer conferencing, telecommuting, and online banking, to name just a few. Concerned individuals who enjoy a vast diversity of interests can communicate very rapidly over networks to unite in support of a common cause. Because this can occur without personal identification information being tied to the activity, activists and whistle-blowers can voice concerns without fear of undue retaliation.

Of course, detaching personal identification information from statements can also make false representations more frequent and potentially more problematic.

The solution for protecting personal privacy as well as ensuring accountability is quite simple: ubiquitous strong public key cryptography and digital signatures. If messages can be exchanged in a manner that guarantees privacy and authenticity, false representations will quickly disappear. (For more information, see Cryptography on page 237.)

GRISWOLD V. CONNECTICUT

Although the United States Constitution does not specifically mention an individual's right to privacy, most legal scholars agree that case law has consistently established that a basic right to privacy must exist in modern society. Privacy rights were established only by the courts and a representative government, not by the founding fathers and the underlying documents used to establish our republic.

In the early 1960s, a New Haven, Connecticut doctor—the executive director of the New Haven Planned Parenthood office—was arrested, tried, and fined US$100 for providing birth control counseling to married couples. On June 7, 1965, in its landmark Griswold v. Connecticut decision, the United States Supreme Court overturned the Connecticut statute that made it a crime to use—or counsel the use of—contraceptives.

The Supreme Court issued six different opinions. The majority of the Court deemed it unimaginable that the government could regulate the size of a family without violating the Constitution. The decision clearly affirms the right for couples to make decisions about contraception privately. The majority opinion, written by Justice William O. Douglas, argued that while the country's founding documents were silent on the matter of an individual's right to privacy, they emanated specific legal "penumbras" that established "zones of privacy."

"We deal with a right to privacy older than the Bill of Rights," wrote Justice Douglas in his opinion. He went on to note that many rights not specifically mentioned in the Constitution are derived from certain Constitutional provisions. Specifically, freedom of association isn't specifically mentioned in the Constitution, but has been protected as an extension of the Constitutional guarantees of free speech and assembly.

Justice Hugo Black dissented from the majority opinion. "I like my privacy as well as the next one, but I am nevertheless compelled to admit that the government has a right to invade it unless prohibited by some specific constitutional provision," wrote Justice Black in his opinion. Justice Potter Stewart was the other dissenting voice: "I can find no such general right of privacy in the Bill of Rights, in any other part of the Constitution, or in any case ever before decided by this Court."

The other six Supreme Court justices agreed with Justice Douglas's majority, but differed on underlying or originating guarantees for the right to privacy.

When the League of Women Voters studied the "choice" issue a few decades ago, enforcement emerged as one of the main concerns in its position supporting privacy and individual choice. The League makes a good point. If we start with the assumption that society has an anti-abortion statute in place, where and how does enforcement begin? Do we start with cameras in our hospital operating rooms (they already exist in some). In our physician's offices? In our bedrooms?

Fortunately, the members of the League of Women Voters managed to see beyond the emotional hot-buttons of the day and look at the broader perspective.

Credit Privacy

Three enormous companies provide the bulk of credit reporting services in the United States: Experian, Inc. (formerly TRW Credit Data Corp.), Trans Union Corp., and Equifax Credit Information Services. These three companies together provide information to some seven hundred online automated credit bureaus across the country. Each of the three systems maintains an estimated 150 million credit files for use by banks and credit bureaus around the country. Today Americans are using more than US$700 billion in consumer credit and more than 450 million credit reports are issued each year.

Each credit file contains information about an individual and his or her spouse, including:

- Typical identifying information including name, address, telephone number, and social security number;
- Financial status and employment information including income;
- Complete credit history including types of credit granted, credit grantors, and payment records;
- Existing lines of credit, payment habits, and outstanding debt;
- Public-record information including newspaper clippings, arrest and conviction records, bankruptcies, tax liens, and lawsuits;
- List of credit bureau subscribers that have requested credit reports on the individual.

Equifax has been the staunchest opponent to any legislation that would regulate the credit reporting industry. The credit reporting agencies have all begun cross-indexing their credit reports against United States Census data, addresses, and marketing surveys to develop sophisticated "profiles" of individual consumers. These profiles are sold to direct marketers and are broken down into various lifestyle categories. The Equifax consumer database, for example, reportedly uses fifty lifestyle categories such as "Upper Crust" (families with high incomes and education) and "Stars and Stripes" (young military families). These profiles include names, addresses, and spending habit details.

The credit privacy alarm was sounded in March 1970 by Alan Westin, a Columbia University professor, in a *New York Times* article. In 1970, the company now known as Equifax was then called Retail Credit, and Westin argued that the company's credit files "may include facts, statistics, inaccuracies and rumors… about virtually every phase of a person's life; his martial troubles, jobs, school history, childhood, sex life, and political activities." In 1970, credit was routinely denied to anyone who was considered "morally deficient," and consumers had no right to inspect the information collected on them. And Equifax (née Retail Credit) was planning to computerize its files. "Almost inevitably, transferring information from a manual file into a computer triggers a threat to civil liberties, to privacy, to a man's very humanity because access is so simple," contended Westin in the *New York Times* article.

The Fair Credit Reporting Act became law in October 1970, granting consumers the right to know what information credit agencies were reporting about them. Retail Credit changed its name to Equifax five years later. (For more information, see Fair Credit Reporting Act on page 36.) Alan Westin was eventually hired as a privacy consultant by Equifax.

Equifax doesn't just want to be in the credit reporting business. Equifax is expanding into areas that impact virtually every aspect of life in America. In the mid-1990s, the company began its push into the following areas:

- Insurance application investigation and verification
- Medical testing
- Physician profiling
- Medical claims review
- Medical insurance claims clearing
- Networked medical records (joint venture with AT&T)
- Automobile accident loss investigation
- Motor vehicle records
- Credit- and debit-card processing
- Check authorization

Atlanta-based Equifax commissioned a study, conducted by Louis Harris & Associates in 1990, that discovered almost 80 percent of all Americans would agree with the statement, "If we rewrote the Declaration of Independence today, we would probably add privacy to the list of 'life, liberty, and the pursuit of happiness' as a fundamental right." The study found that almost 90 percent of American citizens voiced concern about privacy threats.

In April 1991, Consumers Union published a report citing a finding that nearly one-half of the credit records it studied from TRW, Equifax, and Trans Union contained inaccuracies. The report also cited the fact that about 20 percent of those inaccurate reports were serious enough to cause denial of credit.

More recently, in March 1998, the United States Public Interest Research Group (PIRG) released a study that found that almost one-third of all consumer credit bureau reports contain errors serious enough to result in denial of credit or even a job. In addition, some of the study participants were unable to obtain copies of their credit reports, even after repeated calls.

In June 1991, the Federal Trade Commission (FTC) reported that it had received 9,000 written complaints about consumer credit reports in 1990, a 50 percent increase from 1989. The most serious complaints centered around inaccurate information, and inaccurate or outdated information that was supposed to have been deleted from a credit report but wasn't.

In July 1991, TRW asked a federal judge to set aside a US$290,000 jury award made in April of that year. The jury award—comprised of US$15,000 in compensatory damages and US$275,000 in punitive damages—was made in the case of a Wyoming man who was turned down for a car loan because of numerous errors in his credit report. The man had informed TRW that the information was inaccurate and belonged to his father who had the same first name but a different middle initial.

That same month, New York state Attorney General Robert Abrams filed suit against TRW charging the credit reporting agency giant with misleading consumers, disregarding consumers' privacy, and failing to maintain reasonable procedures to assure accuracy in its reports.

Abrams noted that TRW received approximately 500,000 complaints each year from consumers who allege inaccuracies in the firm's credit reports. (TRW maintains credit information on roughly 170 million American consumers.) Abrams also charged that TRW secretly rates and evaluates consumers for "creditworthiness" and offers credit grantors access to its point-scoring systems that rate an individual's creditworthiness. The suit alleged that TRW maintains a separate credit report within its files, about which consumers are not informed. The second credit report provides credit grantors a concise, easily readable summary and, in about 30 percent of cases, credit-scoring information.

Abrams was quoted in a *New York Times* article as saying, "TRW has a legal obligation to disclose to consumers its true role in the credit-granting process. Consumers are entitled to see the same information that credit grantors reviewed when making a critical decision as to whether to grant or deny credit. TRW is illegally denying them this right."

The states of Texas, Alabama, California, Idaho, and Michigan jointly filed a similar suit against TRW.

TRW denied any wrong-doing and filed a counter-suit against the states of New York and Texas, requesting a judgment allowing it to continue supplying information to its customers.

By late summer 1991, Congress was debating five different pieces of legislation that would revise the twenty-year-old Fair Credit Reporting Act. Proposed legislation ranged from penalizing credit reporting bureaus and credit grantors for not correcting mistakes to allowing consumers access to one free credit report per year.

In September 1997, the Fair Credit Reporting Act was changed to improve both accuracy and accessibility to credit reports, yet the 1998 PIRG study indicates that there are more credit report errors, and that individual credit reports are more difficult to obtain—all this after the *strengthening* of the Fair Credit Reporting Act. The new requirements of the Fair Credit Reporting Act include the following:

- Lenders must give accurate information to the credit bureaus;
- Credit reporting agencies must correct any mistakes within thirty days;
- The three major credit reporting agencies—Experian, Inc. (formerly TRW Credit Data Corp.), Trans Union Corp., and Equifax Credit Information Services—must provide non-automated toll-free telephone lines during business hours;
- Credit reports must be easy to read.

Fully 29 percent of the credit reports studied by PIRG contained serious errors, including false reports of delinquent payments and accounts that did not belong to the consumer. Of even greater concern, 70 percent of the credit reports contained errors of some kind.

Until credit reporting agencies are held accountable for the accuracy of the information they collect and disseminate, this situation is likely to further deteriorate. Privacy experts point to three simple things that credit reporting agencies can do to ensure accuracy in their files:

- Provide a free credit report to every individual, asking for error corrections.
- Institute a system of random checks for accuracy and information verification.
- Alert consumers whenever anyone accesses their credit report.

While the chances of credit reporting agencies taking the initiative to act on the above are slim, consumers, nevertheless, must make demands for accuracy or fair credit reporting will become a thing of the past.

Transaction and Behavior Information Privacy

The flip side of "access to information" is the "right to privacy." As networked hypermedia systems—like the World Wide Web—continue to come online, privacy issues will become of greater concern and are more complex. In networked environments like the Web, each user leaves telltale "crumb trails," leading into and out of the documents he or she accesses. Records are kept of all documents accessed and items purchased. New linkages can be easily forged that connect these and other seemingly disparate bodies of information. *Who* will have access to this crumb trail of information and purchasing habits? What limits will be placed on its use? Who will control the actual linkages that makes the privacy issue so closely revolve around the access issue?

This transactional and behavioral information has great value. Why else would store merchants ask for your zip code before they ask how your day is going? Merchants and marketers have always been aware of the value of personal information. As individual consumers, we're only now beginning to realize that the information surrounding what we buy, where we buy it, and how we pay for it has inherent, and possibly marketable, value.

Customers will soon begin to assert ownership rights of their personal information—both transactional and behavioral—and demand value in exchange for it. As a result, negotiating with customers for their information is likely to become both costly and complicated. Currently some companies are offering "club" memberships with small discounts to encourage customers to part with information that allows these companies to get the proverbial "foot in the door" of consumer's lives. Some of us are beginning to realize that our personal information, which we have so freely divulged in the past, has value and that we get very little in exchange for that value. When asked, most of us insist we are concerned about personal privacy issues yet opt in for every senseless "cents-off" offer we receive.

Consumers will eventually bargain directly with vendors that want their personal information and will also likely be represented—in aggregate—by third-party *infomediaries* acting on their behalf. Infomediaries will market individual customer information, while simultaneously protecting consumer privacy.

The current privacy backlash may have less to do with privacy concerns and keeping personal information confidential than with consumers' pragmatic assessment that the returns on divulging personal information are unsatisfactory.

Microsoft caused an enormous uproar in 1995 when it acknowledged—under pressure from its customers—that its Windows 95 Registration Wizard was collecting (and reporting to Microsoft) information about installed software on its customers computers, without those customers' knowledge or permission.

America Online, Inc. (AOL) began to combine information it harvests from its customers with information from Donnelly Marketing Inc., a market research firm. AOL reportedly intends to sell the combined information to third parties through List Services Corp., a mailing list broker. The combined information includes customer names, addresses, telephone numbers, estimated household incomes, length of time at current residence, age and number of children, and past purchasing patterns. AOL representatives have claimed in the trade and general press that a mechanism exists for someone to remove his or her name from the list, but privacy advocates counter that AOL's removal mechanism is incomplete and difficult to locate.

Netscape faced a similar problem in early 1996 with its "cookie" technology. Cookies enable Web browser software to create a record of the Web sites an individual visits, and the specific pages clicked through (accessed) at each site—called the "clickstream." Clickstream tracking uses specialized and powerful software to analyze the Web server's log files. Similarly, a Web server's referer log file can be used to obtain the address of the last Web server visited by any user.

The cookie software was designed to store this information on the user's local computer, but it also allowed Web sites to develop user profiles based on the behavior of individual visitors. Cookies made this profiling possible by uploading the user's record of previous visits to the host server at the beginning of each visit. Netscape subsequently announced that future releases of its browser software would allow the user to turn off the cookie function.

Privacy concerns surrounding the World Wide Web mostly surround this cookie technology. A Web cookie is simply a string of text and numbers that serve to identify a particular browser to a Web site. Cookies, when used in a benign fashion, can actually help users. The *New York Times*, for instance, employs cookie technology, at the user's option, to store username and password information between sessions. Individuals retain complete control over their cookies on the site, and can elect whether or not to have the site store their user information on the local computer.

This specific example illustrates why the Web cookie technology has caused such an uproar in certain quarters: cookies are stored on the user's hard drive without the user's consent or even knowledge. When an unknown third party stores information that serves to monitor browsing activities on your hard drive, it's reasonable to feel that you are being surveilled.

Netscape assumed that as electronic commerce became commonplace, its cookie technology would be used by merchants to capture transaction information, including dollar amounts spent and items purchased. Users would have detailed personal behavior and transaction profiles on their computers, detailing all their activity on the Web including sites visited, pages viewed, and the amount of time spent at each site. Because these profiles would span multiple sites, the information would provide a rich and exceptionally accurate representation of an individual's interests. How many people never change their Home page from the Netscape factory default settings? It would be exceptionally simple and dangerously transparent for Netscape to transfer this information from the user's computer each time the user visited the Netscape site.

Indeed, cookies are useful for keeping track of "shopping cart" contents on commerce-enabled Web sites like Amazon.com (for books) and CDNow (for music). In most cases, these shopping cookies are deleted once the user leaves the Web site that generated them. Persistent cookies, however, are more problematic because they are stored for an indefinite period (or, more likely, linked to a database record) and are not deleted when no longer needed.

While some individuals consider privacy an absolute right—and most people voice privacy concerns in an abstract sense—many consumers currently are willing to release personal information so long as they are informed of the situation, retain final control over the information, and especially if they can profit from the disclosure. Airline frequent flyer programs, hotel frequent visitor programs, rental car programs, etc. all amass tremendous amounts of personal information. We willingly provide this information, with informed consent, because we receive something in return—for now. Haven't you noticed that putting those frequent flyer miles to use is becoming progressively more difficult?

Hertz Corp.'s #1 Gold Club, for example, has a record of several credit card numbers (with expiration dates), frequent flyer numbers of several airlines, business and home addresses, phone and fax numbers, email addresses, driver's license numbers, insurance carriers and policy numbers, personal auto preferences, and frequency and location of travel for each of its members. I will gladly release that collection of information to Hertz—provided that Hertz agrees not to redistribute the information without my permission—in exchange for not ever having to stand in a car rental line ever again. It's clearly a win-win exchange—so far.

Consider that the Quicken personal finance software is used by roughly eleven million households throughout the world. Quicken users can do their banking and pay bills electronically, online. In 1996, Intuit, Quicken's developer, introduced a Quicken affinity credit card that allows customers to download the details of their credit card transactions directly into Quicken. Intuit learns a lot about its customers, and customers gain convenience and more accurate record-keeping capabilities.

If consumers voluntarily elect (with informed consent) to make their personal information available in return for something of tangible value, they can hardly be concerned about their privacy—except for the possibility that information released to one vendor might be sold to other vendors (with no value to the consumer). The obvious solution is a contract between consumer and vendor prohibiting the redistribution of personal information—or use of the information for any purpose other than that for which it was originally collected—without the consumer's informed written consent.

In the first half of 1997, no fewer than a half-dozen bills were introduced in Congress, designed solely to restrict distribution of personal information online. At the same time, a Georgia Institute of Technology survey found that between 70–80 percent of respondents believe that gathering online information about individuals for sale to third parties is illegal (it's not).

Representative Bruce Vento (D-Minnesota) was the first out of the gate with a responsible Consumer Internet Privacy Protection Act. The act would prohibit Internet service providers and publishers from disclosing personal and behavioral information about what users do while online without written permission.

In April 1997, Senator Charles Grassley (R-Iowa) and Senator Dianne Feinstein (D-California) introduced a bill that would prohibit credit reporting bureaus from distributing confidential personal information, including mother's maiden names and unlisted telephone numbers. The proposed legislation would also prohibit the use of social security numbers for any purpose other than tax reporting requirements, benefits distribution, or other official uses.

Senator John Kyl (R-Arizona) introduced a measure that would increase penalties for fraud involving the use of someone else's credit card number or social security number (commonly referred to as identity theft).

Representative Paul Kanjorski (D-Pennsylvania) introduced a bill that would prevent the government from disclosing social security numbers online.

The Web offers consumers and producers unprecedented market access opportunities. The key seems obvious: establish commerce guidelines that protect and ensure consumer privacy. TRUSTe, a Web site privacy auditing service, aims to create an ecommerce business constitution that respects and promises to protect the individual's right to privacy.

According to a Boston Consulting Group study conducted for the TRUSTe initiative that surveyed 9,300 people, 26 percent said they felt comfortable disclosing personal health and financial information to companies they knew. Six percent of the respondents said they felt comfortable revealing that information to companies they didn't know. And 21 percent said they'd disclose personal health and financial information to companies they didn't know but who revealed their plans for the data.

Consumers voiced two general concerns with regard to Web-based ecommerce:

1. Can I tell when a merchant is taking my personal information?
2. If I give my personal information to a merchant, will the merchant sell (or trade) that information to other merchants?

In the spring of 1997, America Online announced that it would begin selling the clickstream information it had amassed on its more than seven million subscribers. AOL subscribers voiced their outrage and AOL's stock fell. The stock resumed its growth path only when the company reversed itself and stated it would not sell subscriber information.

Individual information has always been available, in the form of public records at the local and state levels. Public records are bought and sold legally by marketers. What has changed is that those public records are now available in digital form and the cost of mining those records has dropped drastically. Simultaneously, the *value* of the mined data has risen even more drastically. The speed with which the databases can be mined and the level at which disparate databases have been interconnected has also dramatically increased.

Some critics point out that privacy concerns take a distant second to exchanging personal information for a chance to win something. Business school pundits maintain that the quickest and easiest way to obtain *accurate* personal information (for future selling) is to require individuals to register for a contest. Not only will we gladly part with our personal information, we will provide exceptionally accurate information when a prize is at stake.

During the summer of 1997, for example, Volvo of North America ran a promotion on America Online, offering free test drives and free gifts. The trade press reported that the Volvo site received fifty-three million hits in three weeks.

Sometimes, we have no control over how information that we unknowingly leave behind us is used. Most of us will remember that the public hearing for Supreme Court justice candidate, Robert Bork, was almost single-handedly responsible for videotape rental behavior information becoming protected personal information—it cannot be released without our consent. Many of us would assume that similar protections are available for most of our other benign transactions—like records of the titles of the books we purchase.

Unfortunately, the law that protects our video viewing habits does not extend to our book purchasing patterns. In March 1998, special prosecutor Kenneth Starr issued a subpoena to Washington, DC-based independent bookseller Kramerbooks requesting information about the books purchased by Monica Lewinsky, the former White House intern, alleged to have had an affair with President Clinton. Kramerbooks eventually refused to cooperate with the investigation when several civil liberties organizations voiced concern and provided legal support. Kramerbooks initially agreed to provide the requested information when the prosecutor agreed to narrow the scope of the information request.

When the Barnes & Noble chain was served with a similar subpoena, its deep corporate pockets allowed it to file suit to block Starr's action. "The subpoena raises the issue of whether the government has the right to pry into the reading preferences of every individual purchasing a book, magazine or pamphlet. Barnes & Noble believes that the First Amendment is sacrosanct and that it protects our customers' right to privacy, and their right to obtain and receive information without public disclosure," the bookseller said in a news release.

Judge Norma Holloway Johnson, chief judge of the federal district court for Washington, DC, ruled that Starr must prove he has a "compelling need" to see records of a bookstore patron's purchases and must establish a direct connection between those purchase records and his investigation. In her memorandum to the prosecutor, Judge Johnson wrote, "the bookstores and Ms. Lewinsky have persuasively alleged a chilling effect on their First Amendment rights." If Starr fails to prove the "compelling need," the subpoena will be quashed.

Library Awareness Program

When 1984 passed with relatively minor whimpers of Big Brotherishness from the fringes of the society-at-large, it seemed that issues of governmental invasion of privacy and covert surveillance on the American citizenry were a thing of the past, or merely fiction after all. Those paranoiac years of the 1960s and early 1970s seemed filed away in a dusty corner of our collective gray matter.

The Federal Bureau of Investigation, however—in the mid-1980s to the mid-1990s—attempted to recruit librarians to keep an eye on "suspicious activity" on the part of library patrons, especially those who use the photocopy machines and speak with foreign accents. The FBI, under its Library Awareness Program, insisted that crucial national secrets were leaking out of the country and into the hands of The Enemy.

The American Library Association has consistently resisted the program from the time of the FBI's first visit to New York City's Columbia University in 1987. Librarians just refused to cooperate. Fortunately for the rest of us, libraries and librarians may prove to be among the most crucial agents of a healthy and free society.

LOTUS MARKETPLACE: HOUSEHOLDS

In 1990, because of consumer outrage, Lotus Development Corp. abruptly cancelled the pending release of its second product entry into the Macintosh market. The product, Lotus MarketPlace: Households, was a CD-ROM that contained extensive demographic data on 120 million U.S. consumers. The information was already available to marketing professionals in other forms, but consumers were outraged that all of that information would be concentrated on a single disc.

Lotus provided a way for consumers to remove their names from the database, although one wonders about the effectiveness of such an approach, given the relatively few people that even knew of the disc's existence. Nonetheless, more than thirty thousand people requested to have their names and other personal information removed from the database, citing privacy issues. Lotus cancelled the product.

FINANCIAL PRIVACY

Our financial transactions reveal a great deal of information about our lifestyles, personal interests, and political beliefs. It is common for banks and other financial institutions to exchange information with various private-sector organizations as well as law enforcement agencies. First Amendment rights may be at issue when financial records reveal information about our associations with others. Unfortunately, we're generally not able to defend ourselves against unwarranted access because most of the time we're never aware that a third party is seeking access to our records.

In January 1997, Decision Strategies announced an agreement with Inter Access Risk Management to provide its SyFact data analysis services to various financial institutions as a fraud deterrent. Decision Strategies' SyFact takes disparate data stored by financial institutions and links it with account histories. Financial institutions reportedly lose huge amounts of money to fraud each year. According to the California Bankers Association, California banks lost US$65 million in 1995 to check fraud alone. The American Bankers Association reported that 1994 national check fraud losses amounted to US$815 million. Banks already gather data on their clients and account activities, but that information isn't centralized. The SyFact system integrates all the disparate information into a single repository.

SyFact is configured to detect account activity that is frequently associated with fraud and money laundering. If a set of preconditions is met—frequent transfers to an offshore account, for instance—an electronic alert, including interactive graphical representations of account relationships, is sent across the network to a security officer. The security officer can follow the relationships between accounts and activities by clicking on any element in the graphical representation. This is the financial services equivalent of electronic dumpster diving. SyFact builds its internal profiles from publicly available information including mortgage applications, bank accounts, loan applications, transfer forms, and wire transfer records.

MEDICAL RECORDS

Reports indicate that more than 20 percent of all medical costs in the United States go to maintain the current paper-based record-keeping system. The average hospital moves five million pieces of paper every year. Paper records can be viewed by only one person at a time, and during an average hospital stay a patient's file is seen by an average of eighty people. Every doctor you visit has a record that is unconnected from your other medical records.

Or at least it used to be that way.

A centralized medical records database would address the access limitations inherent in paper records, but privacy and confidentiality concerns pose huge problems.

Remember one of the basic new principles of information: Information expands as it is used. Instead of all that paper being passed around, imagine the efficiencies of the digitized version of the same information available on a distributed network. Instead of each professional maintaining separate and distinct records, all of your records would be centralized and instantly accessible.

Such centralized database facilities are already under development, and in some cases currently being tested. As the health care industry continues to rapidly consolidate into a handful of providers, the potential for abuse becomes obvious.

More likely than not, you've never heard of the Medical Information Bureau. If you are one of the millions of American citizens on whom the organization has information, though, you've probably felt the impact of the Medical Information Bureau in various parts of your life. The Medical Information Bureau is an insurance company clearinghouse of medical information related to individuals.

Here's how it works. When you apply for insurance, you will likely be required to sign a release form allowing your potential insurance carrier to exchange information with other insurance companies. This exchange of information takes place through the Medical Information Bureau.

The organization was originally designed to prevent fraudulent insurance applications but quickly grew to include disparate bits of information that would be of interest to the insurance industry.

Consider this fictional scenario, for example. You visit your doctor for a routine checkup and sheepishly mention—in the course of the inevitable small talk conversation with your physician during the course of the examination—that you're having a bit of a hard time with a hangover from the office holiday party last night. The doctor idly makes note of this seemingly irrelevant information. You don't drink much at all and last night's festivities have left you feeling under the weather.

Your doctor routinely submits your patient records to your insurance company and the Medical Information Bureau. And the most recent entry includes your comment. This bit of information remains in your medical files but you don't know anything about it until you apply for life insurance.

You are shocked to learn that you've been denied life insurance coverage based on your history of alcohol abuse.

Your life insurance company is a Medical Information Bureau subscriber.

What seemed like an innocuously irrelevant comment in passing, during what you thought was a private conversation, has suddenly had a tremendous impact on your life.

What you thought was harmless, the Medical Information Bureau found significant.

No federal laws protect the privacy of medical records except those related to drug abuse and psychiatric care. Few states have medical privacy laws. Like most of the other information we provide about ourselves, our medical records don't belong to us; they belong to whomever assembled them.

And there is virtually no limitation on what can be done with them. Your medical records can be sold to your insurance company or employer, for example. In fact, if you work for a medium-sized or large corporation, chances are you signed away your rights to protect your medical records from being shared with both your insurance company and employer the first time you received medical care under your health plan.

In September 1997, the Clinton administration proposed legislation that would allow law enforcement agencies to gain almost unlimited access to individual medical records, without the knowledge or consent of the subject of the records. Law enforcement authorities insist they need access to all medical records in order to more effectively investigate fraud in the health-care industry, even though they are not medical experts and unqualified to interpret medical records. At the same time, the proposed legislation would restrict access to medical records by employers, researchers, and marketers (who are also neither medical experts nor qualified to interpret the records).

Imagine suffering an apparent stroke and the attending physician being able to access your medical history instantly. It could save your life. Now imagine your mortgage application being denied because the lending institution accesses your medical records and discovers your history of strokes.

An appropriate solution is to strip all personal identifying information from shared medical records using a system of strong cryptography while granting ownership rights of all records to the subject. We would each have the right to decide who has access to our records and what they could do with them.

Datawarehousing and Datamining

People, organizations, and government agencies with whom you transact personal or professional business have the right to collect personal information about you. Contrary to common sense, though, the personal information that is collected *about* you doesn't *belong* to you. In most cases, the collected information belongs to the individual, organization, or agency that collected it. The important question becomes: To what purposes may the collected information be put? Sadly, it's mostly available—for any use—to anyone willing to pay for it. This results in a relatively new industry called datawarehousing.

You've probably never heard of Acxiom Corporation. I certainly had never heard of the company until I began researching this book. Acxiom Corporation, based in Conway, Arkansas, is one of the country's largest datawarehousing businesses.

Acxiom Corporation gathers, sorts, and warehouses information like credit card transactions, telephone numbers, real estate records, automobile registrations, Post Office change of address forms, fishing licenses, magazine subscription information, and just about every other scrap of information you can imagine on more than 195 million American citizens. Think of the paper trail of information you leave in the wake of your daily life. Then imagine that companies like Acxiom actively collect and refine it. Finally, imagine how accurate and complete a profile—almost certainly more accurate than we'd readily admit—can be formed, or "datamined" from these unrelated infobits.

Consider just the information available on your driver's license. Age, height, weight, unlisted address, and medical conditions. In some states, your driver's license number and your social security number are the same.

Marketers insist that the ability to compile highly refined electronic dossiers on individual consumers is completely harmless and actually even beneficial because it allows direct marketing to be finely targeted. Consumers benefit, marketers insist, from quicker credit approval processes and better telemarketing to more accurate and personalized insurance service.

Unlike credit reporting bureaus, datawarehousing and datamining firms are under no legal obligation to reveal the personal information their databases hold about us. According to a March 1998 *Washington Post* article, there are more than one thousand datawarehousers in America, a tenfold increase since 1991. The datawarehouse industry is led by three major organizations: Acxiom Corporation, R.L. Polk & Company, and Metromail Corporation.

According to the *Washington Post* article, faster computers have helped the growth of the datawarehousing and datamining industry:

> "A database query that took six minutes on a giant mainframe computer in 1994 now takes nineteen seconds. Officials just announced they will soon be able to deliver massive amounts of data to customers over the Internet in a few hours—something that now takes up to a week."

Information Brokering

The practice of information brokering has been around for years, certainly longer than datawarehousing and datamining. Throughout the 1990s, information brokers witnessed explosive growth rates in their industry, largely mirroring the growth rate of the Internet.

If you are involved in a disaster—natural or man-made—what degree of personal privacy can you reasonably expect? Apparently not much.

In October 1992, an explosion at the Texaco oil refinery in Wilmington, California burned for three days and displaced hundreds in the poor Hispanic community that surrounded the refinery. In the aftermath, more than 4,500 property-damage claims and 14,000 personal injury claims were filed against Texaco.

Texaco quickly hired a private detective to investigate the claimants and their lawyers. The detective's investigation lasted almost five years and resulted in the accumulation of reams of sensitive personal information. In a September 1997 account in the *New York Times*, claimants allege that Texaco's investigator used information, such as two delinquent traffic tickets, to threaten claimants with arrest unless potentially damaging information about the claimant lawyers was immediately provided.

According to the *New York Times* article, a surprisingly diverse variety of information was gathered by the Texaco investigator, including Social Security numbers, dates of birth, names and telephone numbers of neighbors, welfare histories, work histories, telephone records, and medical histories among others.

The residents of Wilmington and one of their lawyers filed lawsuits alleging privacy violations by the private investigator, Texaco, and Texaco's law firm.

On the Web, information brokers offer a veritable smorgasbord of personal information services, offering volume discounts and even one-hour service. The amount and types of personal information available is eye-opening. The following table illustrates only a representative sample of the kinds of data (and pricing) available from a randomly selected information broker.

Service/Information	Price
Nonpublished number/address	US$260.00
Telephone records (50 calls)	US$150.00
Cellular telephone records (50 calls)	US$260.00
P.O. Box into physical address	US$160.00
Bank account location (3 accounts)	US$300.00
Safe deposit box locate	US$375.00
Mortgage history	US$250.00
Asset search (per county)	US$45.00
Complete background special	US$135.00

Figure 7-1: Sample of services available from Web-based information brokers.

Some privacy invasion by private investigators is well known and has been well reported in the mainstream media. One of the best known is the surveillance undertaken by Wackenhut Corp. against Charles Hamel in the early 1990s. Hamel was an outspoken oil-industry critic who provided crucial evidence of corrosion in the Trans-Alaska Pipeline to Congress and several media outlets. In order to identify Hamel's sources, Alyeska Pipeline, the operator of the Trans-Alaska Pipeline, engaged Wackenhut investigators to obtain Hamel's telephone records.

The sale of personal information by state agencies has blossomed into a growth industry across the United States. The *New York Times*, for instance, reported that Illinois harvests US$10 million per year from the sale of its public records, and

Rhode Island sees almost as much (US$9.7 million) from the sale of its motor-vehicle records alone.

These records—motor-vehicle registrations, real estate transactions, divorces, marriages, births, deaths, bankruptcies, etc.—used to be stored as paper files in musty courthouse basements. It took substantial perseverance and considerable work to put together a personal dossier on an individual.

With the advent of the information economy, of course, all that changed. Private companies have sprouted like mushrooms, making it their business to collect public information from disparate sources, combine it, package it, and sell it. For a few dollars, anyone can find out virtually anything about anyone else in a relative blink of an eye. What used to take considerable effort now takes only a few keystrokes.

The *New York Times* profiled a company with more than twenty thousand customers ranging from private investigators to insurance agents and journalists. For about US$1.50, the company will provide its subscribers with the ability to enter a name and obtain the associated Social Security number, date of birth, and telephone number of the assignee in less than three minutes.

"For a few minutes and a few dollars more," the *New York Times* reports, "the computer screen fills with other personal details: past and current addresses, names and telephone numbers of neighbors, names and Social Security numbers of relatives, in-laws and business associates, civil judgments and property-tax filings."

NATIONAL IDENTITY CARDS

In April 1994, at the CardTech/SecureTech Conference in Crystal City, Virginia, federal agencies—including the United States Postal Service and the Internal Revenue Service—proposed various approaches to providing a national identity card.

Presumably, every American citizen would be required to present the identity card in order to interact with any federal government agency.

The Postal Service proposed a "general-purpose U.S. services smart card" that individuals and corporations would use for identity authentication when sending and receiving email, transferring funds, and interacting with government agencies. The Postal Service card would be automatically connected with the Department of Health and Human Services, the United States Treasury, the Internal Revenue Service, the banking system, and a central database of digital signatures for use in authenticating email and electronic transactions. The Postal Service revealed that it could produce more than 100 million of the cards within months of approval.

The identity card would allow transactions to occur that depend upon authentication and would allow veterans, retirees, college students, and welfare recipients to check their federal benefits. The card would also allow instant access to medical records and health insurance information.

At the same time, President Clinton was considering signing two executive orders that would have allowed the interconnection of individual bank accounts and federal records to a government-issued identification card like the one proposed by the Postal Service.

This sort of action would result in a totalitarian government with a panopticon view of the entire citizenry and would provide the government with a better surveillance mechanism than anyone could possibly imagine.

In early 1997, the United Parcel Service (UPS) launched a new advertising campaign touting its ability to put digitized representations of handwritten signatures online. Customers could login to a service and use the shipping number to view the signature of the person who signed for the package. It would be a relatively trivial task for a low-level hacker to use the UPS software to capture any number of signatures within minutes. The system was quietly, but quickly, phased out.

Workplace Privacy

Quota-based offices are often referred to as "electronic sweatshops." 9-to-5, an organization for working women, studied almost 700 employees from 49 companies in 12 different industries. The study found that 81 percent of the individuals surveyed said monitoring makes their job more stressful. More than two-thirds of the respondents said their employer used monitoring results as a basis for disciplining employees and 23 percent said that individual statistics were posted publicly.

According to a 1997 survey by the Minneapolis *StarTribune*, eight out of ten workers in America believe their employers have invaded their privacy rights.

Minnesota, unlike other states including New York and Wisconsin, has no statutory right to privacy, and instead recognizes only a limited constitutional right to privacy. Some states recognize a common-law tort of "invasion of privacy" as defined by Dean William Prosser, a legal scholar, as four separate but related torts:

1. *Intrusion*. "Intruding (physically or otherwise) upon the solitude of another in a highly offensive manner."
2. *Private facts*. "Publicizing highly offensive private information about someone which is not of legitimate concern to the public."
3. *False light*. "Publicizing a highly offensive and false impression of another."
4. *Appropriation*. "Using another's name or likeness for some advantage without the other's consent."

The state of Minnesota recognizes no such common law. Not since early 1991 has there even been an effort to create a right to privacy within the state of Minnesota. Employees have still challenged invasion of privacy by employers under civil claims including defamation, false imprisonment, intentional infliction of emotional distress, and wrongful discharge.

An employee of a business in the state of Minnesota has the right to view his or her personnel file once every six months. An employer has seven days to comply with the request if the records are in the state, and fourteen days to comply if the records are out of state. Former employees have the right to view their personnel files once, provided the request is made within one year of leaving employment.

An employer in Minnesota is not required to put all employee information in the personnel file. Documents not required to be placed in the personnel file—and therefore not required to be accessible to the subject—include reference letters, information related to an incomplete investigation of employee conduct, notes by other employees, education records, and employment tests.

Minnesota law states that it is a misdemeanor for an employer to require a polygraph test or voice-stress analysis.

State law allows Minnesota employers to run credit checks on potential employees.

Minnesota law prohibits the interception of wire, electronic, or oral communications except when a law-enforcement agent is involved or one of the parties to the communication has consented to the interception. An employer can monitor any or all employee telephone calls in the "ordinary course of business" on a business extension line.

There is no statute in the state of Minnesota that prohibits an employer from searching employee lockers and workspaces and an employer can make a case for searching employee vehicles that are parked on company property. Furthermore, there is no Minnesota law prohibiting an employer from conducting body searches of employees.

In Minnesota, employers may hire undercover investigators to monitor workplace activities, including employee performance. Minnesota does not have a specific prohibition against surveillance of employees.

Minnesotans are, by nature, a trustful lot and like most of us feel we have nothing to hide. But even those who casually toss off privacy issues as irrelevant to their own lives recoil at the level of intrusiveness in such policies.

Minnesota Data Practices Act

There appears to be little consistency among government information privacy protections from state to state. Some states specifically mention individual privacy rights in their constitutions and some do not. Minnesota, for example, does not. Instead, Minnesota has a Data Practices Act (Chapter 13, Government Data Practices), portions of which cover individual privacy rights with regard to government information. (For more information about Minnesota's Data Practices Act with regard to access to government data, see Minnesota Data Practices Act on page 113.)

The state of Minnesota, in general does not recognize an individual's right to privacy. There are, however, certain rights recognized by the state with regard to government information.

Whenever a government agency asks you to provide personal information about yourself, you have the right to be informed:

- Why the agency wants to collect the information;
- How the agency collecting the data will use the information;

- Whether you are legally required to provide the information being requested;
- What the consequences are if you refuse to provide the information being requested;
- The identities of other persons, entities, and agencies that are authorized by law to receive the data being requested.

When you have been informed of the above—through an oral or written procedure generally referred to as a "Tennessen Warning"—the agency requesting the data may only use or disseminate the information in the manner described to you in the notice (except for specific circumstances).

In Minnesota, government data is classified into three main categories:

- *Data on individuals* is said to be *public* if it is accessible by the public for any reason. Data is said to be *private* if it is accessible by the subject, but not by the public. Data is said to be *confidential* if it is accessible by neither the subject nor the public.
- *Data on decedents* is said to be *public* if it is accessible by the public for any reason. Data is said to be *private data on decedents* if it is accessible by the decedent's representative, but not by the general public. Data is said to be *confidential data on decedents* if it is accessible by neither the decedent's representative nor the public.
- *Data not on individuals* is said to be *public* if it is accessible by the public for any reason. Data is said to be *non-public* if it is accessible by the subject (if any), but not by the public. Data is said to be *protected non-public* if it is accessible by neither the subject (if any) nor the public.

Under the Minnesota Data Practices Act, you have the right to inquire—and be told—if a specific government agency is maintaining data about you regardless of how the information is classified (public, private, or confidential). You have the right to view—free of charge—all public or private (but not confidential) information maintained about you by any government agency, regardless of the form in which it is stored. If you don't understand the information, the agency is required to explain it to you.

If you ask for copies of public and private information about you, the copies must be provided at the reasonable cost of copying the data. When you ask about or for public and private information about you, the agency must respond to your request within five days. If the agency tells you it will take longer to fulfill your request, they must respond within ten days.

Under the Minnesota statute, you can challenge public or private information about you by writing to the responsible authority (usually the head of the government agency that collected or maintains the information) and:

- Identifying the information you are challenging, and;
- Explaining how the information should be made accurate or complete.

If the responsible authority disagrees with your data challenge, you can appeal the disagreement to the Minnesota Commissioner of Administration. Until the data challenge is resolved, you have the right to include your statement of challenge with your data. The agency must include your statement of challenge with its data until the data challenge is resolved.

Wiretapping

In prior eras, citizens were assured of private conversations by simply moving out of earshot of any eavesdroppers. The telephone made it much easier, of course, to communicate across great distances, but the possibility of one's conversation being overheard or intercepted rose proportionately. Perhaps worst of all, conversations could be listened to or intercepted without the knowledge of either party.

Telephone operators of the 1960s and 1970s will recall how easily the equipment they used to verify busy signals could be abused. Phone callers who encountered busy signals for long periods of time would frequently request local operators to check a phone line to determine whether it was actually in use or in need of repair. Frequent monitoring, along with threats of dismissal, were necessary to prevent operators from hanging out on such equipment, which was merely another port among many on their switchboards.

In 1967, the Supreme Court ruled that the police could not wiretap telephone conversations without court authorization. It is generally assumed that wiretaps are a kind of search.

In 1992, however, the courts ruled that cordless telephone conversations were not protected and that the police could wiretap a cordless telephone without a search warrant. The feeling was that it was widely understood by the public that cordless telephones were much less secure than wired telephones and that cordless phone users did not have a reasonable expectation of privacy. In 1994, the Communications Assistance for Law Enforcement Act (CALEA) became law and cordless telephone conversations were again protected the same as conversations on wired telephones.

(For more information on CALEA, see Communications Assistance for Law Enforcement Act on page 172.)

In 1928, during Prohibition, Roy Olmstead and his partners ran a successful—but quite illegal—liquor distribution business. Federal agents installed wiretaps in the basement of Olmstead's office and on the telephone lines near the homes of Olmstead's employees. Olmstead was convicted, largely on the basis of information obtained through the wiretaps. No search warrants were obtained for the wiretaps because the federal agents did not enter the homes or Olmstead's interior office to install the wiretaps.

Olmstead appealed the decision, arguing that the wiretaps had violated his Fourth and Fifth Amendment rights. The Supreme Court, in a 5-to-4 ruling against Olmstead, found that the process of obtaining the evidence had not involved any trespass nor any search. The five justices comprising the majority opined that the Fourth Amendment protected only tangible property, not intangibles like conversation.

Justice Louis Brandeis's dissenting opinion—that the protections provided by the Bill of Rights should naturally extend to an electronic world—is the most widely quoted, however:

> "When the Fourth and Fifth Amendments were adopted, 'the form that evil had heretofore taken' had been necessarily simple. Force and violence were then the only means known to man by which a government could directly impel self-incrimination. It could compel the individual to testify—a compulsion effected, if need be, by torture. It could secure possession of his papers and other articles incident to his private life—a seizure effected, if need be, by breaking and entry. Protection against such invasion of 'the sanctities of a man's home and the privacies of life' was provided in the Fourth and Fifth Amendment by specific language.... But 'time works changes, brings into existence new conditions and purposes.' Subtler and more far-reaching means of invading privacy have become available to the government. Discovery and invention

have made it possible for the government, by means far more effective than stretching upon the rack, to obtain disclosure in court of what is whispered in the closet."

"Whenever a telephone line is tapped, the privacy of the persons at both ends of the line is invaded, and all conversations between them upon any subject, and although proper, confidential and privileged, may be overheard. Moreover, the tapping of one man's telephone line involves the tapping of the telephone of every other person whom he may call, or who may call him. As a means of espionage, writs of assistance and general warrants are but puny instruments of tyranny and oppression when compared with wiretapping."

"Unjustified search and seizure violates the Fourth Amendment.... [I]t follows necessarily that the Amendment is violated by the officer's reading the paper without a physical seizure, without his even touching it; and that use, in any criminal proceeding, of the contents of the paper so examined... any such use constitutes a violation of the Fifth Amendment."

"The protection guaranteed by the Amendments is much broader in scope. The makers of our Constitution undertook to secure conditions favorable to the pursuit of happiness. They recognized the significance of man's spiritual nature, of his feelings and his intellect.... They sought to protect Americans in their beliefs, their thoughts, their emotions and their sensations. They conferred, as against the government, the right to be let alone—the most comprehensive of rights and the right most valued by civilized man. To protect that right, every unjustifiable intrusion by the Government upon the privacy of the individual, whatever the means employed, must be deemed a violation of the Fourth Amendment. And the use, of evidence in a

> criminal proceeding, of facts ascertained by such intrusion be deemed a violation of the Fifth."

In 1934, the Federal Communications Act was signed into law. It established the Federal Communications Commission (FCC) and specifically prohibited the "interception and divulgence" of wire communications.

In 1937, the Supreme Court heard the case of another bootlegger, Frank Nardone, who had been convicted largely on the basis of information obtained by warrantless wiretaps. The Court held that information obtained through the wiretaps was inadmissible evidence, in effect reversing its previous decision in the Olmstead case.

Two years later, the Supreme Court upheld its 1937 decision when Nardone appealed another conviction based on information that was indirectly derived from wiretaps. As a result, Attorney General Robert Jackson ordered the FBI to stop its wiretapping activities.

When World War II began, FBI Director J. Edgar Hoover looked for any way possible to get around Attorney General Jackson's anti-wiretapping order. Hoover petitioned President Roosevelt to authorize wiretapping for purposes of national security, and President Roosevelt granted his consent. Under Hoover, wiretaps were customarily used for unlimited-time surveillance purposes rather than for criminal investigations. Records indicate that this practice continued until 1965 when a six-month time-limit on wiretap surveillance was instituted.

Hoover consistently and effectively resisted any legislation that would require warrants for wiretaps. Even after the war, Hoover obtained continued wiretapping authority from President Harry Truman. In fact, President Truman expanded the FBI's wiretapping authority to include wiretaps for purposes other than national security.

Records indicate that FBI Director J. Edgar Hoover went to extensive lengths to conceal any evidence of wiretapping and to hide any connections between executed wiretaps and their required logs.

In 1965, the use of wiretaps for surveillance purposes was restricted to require written approval from the attorney general. Wiretaps were limited to a period of no more than six months, at which time additional approval from the attorney general was required.

In 1967, President Johnson recommended that wiretapping authority be limited to federal authorities and limited to purposes of national security. Congress disagreed and passed Title III of the Omnibus Crime Control and Safe Streets Act in 1968, which legalized law enforcement wiretaps (with a search warrant) for investigative purposes in certain criminal cases including murder, kidnapping, extortion, gambling, counterfeiting, and the sale of drugs. Organized crime was clearly the primary target for Title III wiretaps.

Throughout the late 1960s and early 1970s, Presidents Kennedy, Johnson, and Nixon all used wiretaps for political purposes under the guise of national security. Of the three, President Nixon's wiretap transgressions were the most widely reported, if not the most egregious.

In May 1969, the *New York Times* reported that the United States had been bombing Cambodia for some time, contrary to the claims of the Nixon administration. President Nixon's national security advisor, Henry Kissinger asked FBI Director J. Edgar Hoover to find who was responsible for leaking the information. During Hoover's investigation, seventeen people's telephones were wiretapped, but the source of the leaks could not be found. At least one of the wiretaps was in place for twenty-one months.

In June 1971, the *New York Times* and *Washington Post* published portions of the classified "Pentagon Papers" that outlined the history of U.S. involvement in Vietnam. The government sued to block publication of the documents leaked by Daniel Ellsberg, and lost its case. The court found a clear case of prior restraint. Ellsberg was indicted as a spy. President Nixon's domestic affairs advisor, John Ehrlichman, authorized a burglary (and subsequent cover-up) of the office of Ellsberg's psychotherapist. Reports indicate that Ellsberg's telephone had been tapped, but the required wiretap authorization and all related logs could not be found.

Then, on June 17, 1972, President Nixon's campaign committee made a second attempt to break into the Watergate office building in an effort to wiretap the phone of Lawrence O'Brien, the Democratic party chair. Earlier in the year the Supreme Court had ruled that warrantless wiretapping was illegal, even for purposes of national security. The illegal activity ultimately led to the resignation of Nixon on August 9, 1974.

Reeling from the citizenry's lack of faith in government, the Senate convened an eleven-member committee in January 1975—the Senate Select Committee to Study Governmental Operations with respect to Intelligence Activities—to investigate "illegal, improper, or unethical activities" engaged in by government agencies under the guise of intelligence gathering. The committee uncovered regular and extensive presidential wiretapping dating from the Truman administration.

The committee's recommendation was that American citizens should not be subjected to illegal surveillance and specifically concluded "too many people have been spied upon by too many government agencies and [too] much information has been collected."

In 1986, the Electronic Communications Privacy Act (ECPA) updated the provisions of Title III of the 1968 Omnibus Crime Control and Safe Streets Act to include digital and electronic communications. Under the ECPA, wiretaps without specified locations could be used, so long as probable cause existed and the target of an investigation was switching telephones in order to evade surveillance. These unspecified location wiretaps are known as "roving" wiretaps.

Things on the wiretapping scene were relatively quiet until 1992 when the FBI announced its Digital Telephony proposal. If adopted, the proposal would mandate the inclusion of wiretapping capabilities in all telephone switching equipment. The FBI was clearly concerned that the use of strong encryption technologies would subvert its ability to gain information through intercepted telephone calls. Under the proposal, telephone companies would be given a year and a half to comply and would bear the costs of redesigning the system. (For more information about the FBI's Digital Telephony Proposal, see Security and Freedom Through Encryption Act on page 247.) The FBI's proposal found no congressional support, but served to get the FBI agenda's metaphorical foot in the door of the debate surrounding the use of strong cryptography.

Communications Assistance for Law Enforcement Act

In March 1994, the FBI trotted out a revised Digital Telephony proposal. This time FBI Director Louis Freeh provided secret documentation to the House and Senate Judiciary Committees outlining 180 cases in which court-authorized FBI wiretaps had been at least partially subverted. The FBI proposal became law as the Communications Assistance for Law Enforcement Act (CALEA).

CALEA mandated that all American telecommunications networks placed in service after 1994 be configured to enable complete and transparent interception by law enforcement agencies. The statute included a cryptography provision making telecommunications carriers responsible for any encrypted traffic on their networks that used encryption provided by the carrier. (For more information of the cryptography aspects of CALEA, see the Cryptography chapter beginning on page 237.)

One of the provisions of CALEA required the attorney general to accurately publish the maximum wiretap capacity required by law enforcement agencies. In October 1995, the capacity requirements were released, and the FBI claimed it would need wiretaps on approximately thirty thousand telephone lines simultaneously. There are about 160 million telephone lines in the United States, and the FBI's requirements were more than four times the total number of wiretaps executed in 1993.

Shortly after the release of the proposed wiretap capacity requirements, the FBI creatively interpreted CALEA, proposing that cellular carriers implement a standard that would allow law enforcement to determine the exact location of a cellular telephone within a half a second. Before CALEA was passed, FBI Director Louis Freeh testified before Congress, promising that the proposed legislation would not expand law enforcement's wiretapping abilities. The language of CALEA clearly precluded cellular location information:

> "... call-identifying information shall not include any information that may disclose the physical location of the subscriber...."

FBI Director Freeh also pressed for the ability to activate roving wiretaps without having to get individual court orders for each wiretap. At about the same time, President Clinton was also pressing for expanded electronic surveillance capabilities, including the bizarre idea that illegally obtained electronic surveillance information could be used in court, so long as it had not been obtained in "bad faith." For the most part, Congress kept a level head and rejected most of these proposals. Congress did, however, approve US$500 million for full implementation of CALEA and approved the use of subpoenas instead of search warrants to obtain telephone records.

Shortly after the explosion of TWA Flight 880 in August 1996, FBI Director Freeh and President Clinton renewed their efforts to expand the use of electronic surveillance on American citizens. Proposals included emergency wiretaps without warrants for forty-eight hours, airline passenger profiling, and roving wiretaps. The FBI and the Clinton administration clearly appeared to be leveraging widespread suspicion of terrorist responsibility for the airline explosion in order to fuel an effort for expanded surveillance powers. Again, Congress rejected the proposals.

The investigation of the TWA Flight 880 disaster was eventually closed; the cause of the explosion is now assumed to have been mechanical failure, not the act of terrorists.

In mid-February 1997, the FBI yet again revived its efforts to garner support from telephone companies and telecommunications trade associations for its plan to modernize and expand the agency's system for eavesdropping on telephone conversations. The telecommunications industry was near unanimous in its opposition to the FBI's expansion effort.

By October 1997, some members of Congress were beginning to question whether the FBI had overstepped the provisions of the CALEA legislation.

Three years after CALEA, not one dime had been spent on updating the nation's telephone switches and the FBI still hadn't provided specifications for the digital wiretapping system. The deadline of October 1998 was fast approaching. The FBI's CALEA implementation proposals had been strongly opposed by privacy advocates and the telephone companies. The privacy advocates were concerned about the increased wiretap capabilities. The telephone companies were concerned about the cost of implementation. The phone companies argued that they couldn't begin their upgrades until the FBI's specifications were approved. As of early July 1998, the stalemate continued.

The FBI plan would, for example, enable Los Angeles County, California law enforcement officials to expand surveillance capabilities by a factor of more than 100 times the current capacity of 1,360 simultaneous wiretaps. Additionally, it would be legal for law enforcement agencies to wiretap conference calls and continue to eavesdrop on the call even after the subject of the investigation had hung up.

The Cellular Telephone Industry Association calculated that the FBI's historical data shows that the highest number of simultaneous cellular telephone taps ever conducted—local, state, and federal combined—was 6,070. Now the FBI was proposing that it be given the ability to monitor a total of 103,190 simultaneous cellular calls. At the same time, most reported statistics tend to indicate that the crime rate is actually falling.

By February 1998, the FBI was riding the expansion of power hobbyhorse yet again; this time proposing that its wiretapping authority be expanded to include communications sent over Internet backbones and wireless devices. Civil liberties groups and privacy advocates responded swiftly by calling for a cut off in future funding and a Congressional investigation.

The FBI, as it had in the past, continued to deny any and all accusations that it was seeking to expand its wiretapping powers and specifically pledged it would not take advantage of packet-switching networks (like the networks that comprise the Internet) to secretly eavesdrop on or intercept communications.

Opponents of the FBI plan contend that the convergence of voice and data on packet-switched networks, including the Internet, would be included under CALEA as it is currently written and asked for changes to the statute.

In a packet-switched network, such as those that interconnect to form the Internet, data from multiple users are combined and sent along in packets across the network. Potentially, any information contained within the packets of a court-authorized wiretap target would be subject to interception. In effect, the conversations of many different, unrelated people could be simultaneously surveilled with a single wiretap order.

"It is our belief that CALEA has created an unworkable, impractical, and potentially unconstitutional surveillance scheme that threatens the privacy of citizens and the security of our nation's telecommunications infrastructure," wrote a consortium of advocacy groups in a letter to Congress. Among those groups were the Electronic Frontier Foundation, the Electronic Privacy Information Center, and the American Civil Liberties Union.

In late April 1998, just as this book was being finalized, the Cellular Telecommunications Industry Association together with the Personal Communications Industry Association filed suit in a Washington, DC federal court against the FBI and Justice Department. The suit alleged that the FBI and Justice Department are asking for a wiretapping system that is much more intrusive and significantly more expensive than the one provided for under CALEA.

EUROPEAN ECHELON NETWORK

In January 1998, a document purported to be an internal draft working paper of the European Parliaments Scientific and Technological Options Assessment group (STOA) was released detailing the European Echelon Network. The network allows the interception of voice and data traffic virtually anywhere on the continent. The report, entitled *An Appraisal of Technologies of Political Control*, is reported to be the result of an intensive study by the European Parliament but carries that organization's disclaimer.

The report expresses European Parliament fears that the regulatory controls necessary to prevent abuse by law enforcement agencies have been seriously eroded. Without appropriate regulatory control mechanisms and high-level accountability, the technologies of the Echelon Network "provide powerful tools of oppression," according to the report, and pose "a serious threat to civil liberties in Europe."

Instead of using the Echelon Network's underlying technologies to investigate crime, law enforcement agencies have reportedly begun increasingly to use the systems for surveillance: "tracking certain social classes and races of people... before any crime is committed."

The document points to alarming developments within some European countries. The British government, for example, has set up a DNA database to track certain classes of individuals based on their DNA, according to the report.

An Appraisal of Technologies of Political Control describes the enormous surveillance capabilities of the Echelon Network as "stretch[ing] around the world to form a targeting system on all of the key Intelsat satellites used to convey most of the world's satellite phone calls, Internet traffic, e-mail, faxes and telexes... designed primarily for non-military targets: governments, organisations and businesses in virtually every country." The report also alleges that all European electronic mail, telephone conversations, and fax transmissions are regularly intercepted by the United States' National Security Agency (NSA) which poses a significant economic threat to the continent.

The extensive report closes with a strong recommendation that the European Parliament (and presumably the European Union) actively and aggressively resist any attempt by the United States to make "private messages via the Internet accessible to U.S. intelligence agencies."

Cellular Phone Privacy

Even though a 1986 law makes interception of cellular telephone calls illegal, calls made from the devices are not private. Approximately one million radio scanners are in use throughout the country today and these same scanners can be used to eavesdrop on private cellular telephone conversations. The Washington Legal Foundation decided this posed a problem significant enough to request the Federal Communications Commission to require warning labels on cellular phones. The FCC denied the request.

Cellular telephones are in use by an estimated five million Americans. The cellular phone is a low-power radio that broadcasts over the FM band, but at a higher frequency than that used by commercial radio stations. Cellular communications rely on an array of ground antennae to pick up the signal and re-send, or relay, it toward its final destination. Each cell in a cellular service area is covered by a single antenna that is linked in a network with other antennas to blanket a local calling area.

The cellular telephone signal can be intercepted by an easily modified radio scanner available in electronics stores for a few hundred dollars. To intercept both sides of a conversation, two scanners are needed because each party transmits its signal on a different channel. Additionally, each time a cellular phone crosses between cells, the signal is automatically passed along or switched to another channel.

Sophisticated monitoring equipment is available that allows the interception of both sides of a cellular telephone call. They can be purchased in electronics stores for between US$1,000–US$6,000. Experts report that the most effective way to monitor telephone conversations is by placing a scanner within a half-mile or so of the person who is transmitting.

Secretly-made tape recordings of cellular telephone conversations were the central issue in an argument between a former governor of Virginia, Douglas Wilder, and Senator Charles Robb (R-Virginia). The recordings were reported to have been made by a Virginia Beach, Virginia businessman who is alleged to have made recordings of hundreds of calls by prominent Tidewater, Virginia residents. According to a report in the

Washington Post, the businessman "denied he taped Wilder but acknowledged he has 'intercepted phone calls.'"

Cellular companies have begun installing new technology that allows the location of cellular telephone users to be precisely tracked. Like most technology advances, this one has positive and negative aspects. It's a godsend to the family stuck in an overturned car during a winter blizzard. It's very helpful for emergency calls and ambulance drivers. On the negative side of the balance sheet, law enforcement agencies will likely want to apply the new technology to surveil suspects and other investigatory targets.

The question becomes whether the technology will be used for communication or surveillance, according to David Banisar of the Electronic Privacy Information Center, and other privacy advocates. From a purely technological perspective, the new systems appear to be capable of serving both purposes. The FBI has already made its intentions clear. Isn't it time for citizens to voice some concerns of our own?

TELEPHONE CALLER IDENTIFICATION PRIVACY

Your local telephone company's Caller ID service lets telephone customers see the number (and in most cases, the name) of the person calling before the telephone is answered. The Caller ID service can be linked to computer software programs to provide links between incoming telephone calls and a database. Additionally, telephone calls received can be saved for later retrieval or potential sale to mailing and telemarketing list vendors.

In December 1990, the Georgia Public Service Commission voted unanimously (5–0) to allow Southern Bell to offer Caller ID services without blocking the name and number of the caller. Only selected police agencies and social service hotlines that specifically request blocking were exempt from the ruling. The decision, however, made unlisted telephone numbers readily available to mailing and telemarketing list vendors, or to any individual or business the unlisted party might call. Southern Bell maintained that Caller ID without blocking would eliminate harassing and obscene telephone calls and enhance the privacy of customers.

According to a March 1998 *Washington Post* article, approximately half of all telephone subscribers in California (where Caller ID blocking is guaranteed by law) have disabled the Caller ID signal on their outgoing calls.

A related technology already in place throughout the country enables local telephone companies to itemize local calls in a manner identical to long distance calls. The government offices, businesses, organizations, and individuals you call provides remarkably complete information about your business, personal, social, political, and religious affiliations. This information can be potentially damaging if it falls into the wrong hands. AT&T has instituted voluntary guidelines that allow release of its long distance calling records only under subpoena or court order—except in the case of national security investigations. In that event the calling records are available on request.

Operation Sun Devil

In 1990, the United States Secret Service launched Operation Sun Devil. With guidance from regional telephone companies, the Secret Service attempted to put an end to the computer "hacker problem," once and for all. At the height of the operation's activity—early May 1990—28 raids were conducted in 14 cities over a 3-day period. Forty-two computers and 23,000 computer disks were confiscated and a grand total of 4 arrests were made.

The most widely known case was brought against a small Texas publishing company because of allegedly illegal activities by one of its employees. The case was quietly dropped when prosecutors learned that an allegedly stolen Southern Bell company document, claimed to be worth US$79,000, was available to customers for about US$25. Nevertheless, the publisher's legal fees grew to more than US$100,000 and its electronic publishing system—used exclusively to create product and manage the business—was confiscated. One has to wonder if the publishing system would have been so readily confiscated were it a traditional printing press instead of a network of computers.

Internet Privacy

In one instance of Internet privacy abuse, Microsoft, in 1997, brought a copyright infringement lawsuit against an individual for allegedly publishing instructions for circumventing Microsoft's copy-protection technology on a personal Web page. Microsoft's Minneapolis attorneys chose to pursue the records of the defendant's Internet service provider in order to track down anyone and everyone who downloaded the circumvention program (commonly referred to as a "crack"). According to a report in the Minneapolis *Star Tribune*, the Internet service provider complied with the demand from Microsoft without question and agreed to cooperate fully with the software giant's investigation.

The behavior of Microsoft and it's attorneys was obnoxious, if predictable. The compliant behavior of the Internet service provider is reprehensible. If a local copy shop were to offer free photocopies of one of my books or articles, would it be appropriate for me to go to the copy shop and insist on the personal information of everyone who received a copy of the material? If a book or magazine article is declared "illegal" by a government agency, is it appropriate to force libraries and bookstores to provide check-out and sales records? Is it appropriate to violate the privacy of all utility customers when illegal activity of a single customer is suspected?

Another recent incident of Internet privacy abuse occurred on April 2, 1997, when Texas Attorney General Dan Morales, served subpoenas on ten Internet service providers who did business with members of a secessionist group known as the "Republic of Texas." The subpoenas demanded copies of all Republic of Texas members' email, login information, and user identification as well as subscriber applications and billing information (including credit card and bank account numbers). Eight of the Internet service providers immediately complied with the subpoenas but two refused, citing a portion of the Electronic Communications Privacy Act that stipulates the information sought must be "relevant and material to an ongoing criminal investigation." The action by the Texas Attorney General against the Republic of Texas group was a civil, not criminal, investigation. Attorney General Morales responded by dropping the subpoenas for the civil investigation and said his office would file a criminal investigative demand.

The Social Security Administration had some problems of its own when, in early April 1997, it was forced to shut down its Web-based service that allowed American taxpayers to check their earnings records and social security eligibility estimates. Various members of Congress chastised the agency for poor security at the site that would conceivably let landlords, creditors, employers (and just about anyone else with a subject's social security number) browse records.

Proposed legislation, the Consumer Internet Privacy Protection Act of 1997, authored by Representative Bruce Vento (D-Minnesota), would prohibit an Internet service provider from disclosing personally identifiable information provided by a subscriber to such services without the subscriber's prior informed consent. Additionally, any subscriber could revoke consent at any time.

Unfortunately, Representative Vento's bill never made it to the full session of the House of Representatives.

Federal Trade Commission Internet Privacy Hearings

In early June 1997, the Federal Trade Commission (FTC) held Internet privacy hearings. Predictably, companies wanting to harvest consumer information for marketing purposes were in almost total disagreement with privacy advocates on the question of the role of government in the issue. Marketers insist that self-regulation is the best and only acceptable solution. Privacy advocates insist that government regulation of third-party use of personal information on the Internet is the only way to prevent continued abuse that is already out of control.

In preparation of the hearings, *Privacy & American Business* magazine surveyed 1,009 computer users in the United States:

- Eighty-seven percent of the surveyed computer users said that Web sites should not use cookies without permission;
- Eighty-five percent of the respondents said it was important for Web sites to tell visitors how cookies are used;
- Fifty-three percent of the users said they were concerned that site usage information would be linked to their email address and disclosed without permission.

In an early 1997 survey performed by the Georgia Institute of Technology, almost three-quarters of respondents said the surreptitious gathering of personal information online is illegal. Unfortunately, they're wrong; there is currently no guaranteed right to privacy online, and no restrictions on the use of personal information obtained online.

While many claim that the Fourth Amendment, limiting the government's power to conduct warrantless searches and invade private property, extends to include privacy invasions by governmental agencies, there is nothing that restricts the activities of private parties who collect and distribute information about any other private party.

Similarly, electronic communications are not given the same protection as postal mail. We continue to suppose that we have freedoms and rights that simply do not exist. Wiretapping, for example, in the past had to be physically carried out. The wiretapper—or at least a tape recorder—had to be physically near the person under surveillance to record or eavesdrop. With the advancement in telephone switching technology, this is no longer the case. Now your conversations can be easily eavesdropped upon simply by sending the proper signal tones down the telephone wire—from anywhere. (For more information, see Wiretapping on page 166.)

Many business advocates argue that if you take away the right of businesses to gather personal information, most businesses—especially new and small concerns—will fail. Privacy advocates, on the other hand, warn of the dissemination of compromising personal information, although most acknowledge there is no clear-cut right to privacy online.

For example, the Fair Credit Reporting Act restricts the information that credit bureaus can divulge, but has done nothing to prevent the dissemination of individual Social Security numbers. Similarly, the Privacy Act prohibits federal agencies from disclosing private information except for "routine use." The "routine use" exception renders the law virtually meaningless.

Prohibiting information that is gathered for one purpose from being used for other purposes—without the individual's informed consent—is one prevention for privacy abuse. This is nothing new; it's the underlying intent of almost all of the original privacy legislation. Intense lobbying efforts on behalf of marketing groups results in almost all of this underlying intent being stripped from proposed legislation before it passes.

The Direct Marketing Association was singled out by the Federal Trade Commission for not implementing a privacy policy. The Direct Marketing Association released its basic privacy principles in June 1996 but still didn't know how many of its member organizations were in compliance with the principles at the time of the FTC hearings a year later.

Marketing professionals are fond of believing that technology is the answer to privacy abuses, citing the Platform for Privacy Preferences (P3P) as an appropriate means of providing consumer protection. The Platform for Privacy Preferences was developed with the help of the World Wide Web Consortium (W3C). The P3P is designed to allow consumers to express how, when, and under what circumstances personal information can be released over the Internet. (For more information, see Open Profiling Standard on page 188.)

On one hand, Internet marketers emphasize that they can police themselves; no government regulation is needed. On the other hand, privacy advocates and civil libertarians argue that has clearly not been the case and that the abuses are only getting worse. The marketers continue to collect and redistribute more and more personal information about Internet users without restraint. Continued instances of unauthorized release of personal information raises legitimate questions and concerns about the effectiveness of self-regulation.

Privacy advocates note that the actions of marketers combined with those of law enforcement agencies are an explosive problem and that industry self-regulation is clearly inadequate. During the summer of 1997, the Electronic Privacy Information Center (EPIC) conducted a survey of 100 of the most popular Web sites. Of the 100 sites studied, only seventeen had explicit privacy policies. EPIC points to its study to support its demand that regulation is required to protect personal privacy on the Internet.

In March 1998, the Federal Trade Commission announced it would survey 1,200 commercial Web sites. The FTC wanted to look at Web site policies for collecting and disclosing personal information and whether or not users were being given any choice in how their personal information is ultimately used. The agency's report to Congress was delivered on June 1, 1998 and strongly suggested that industry self-regulation is inadequate for protecting personal privacy on the Net.

MICROSOFT'S INTERNET STOREFRONT

By August 1998, Microsoft plans to open an Internet storefront. Shoppers at Microsoft's Web store will be able to purchase products directly from Microsoft or from several authorized resellers. The actual transaction for any purchase however, will take place on Microsoft's server. All personal information provided to complete the transaction—name, address, telephone number, credit card number, etc.—will become the property of Microsoft, regardless of whether the purchase is made from Microsoft or one of its authorized resellers. All sales will be made *through* Microsoft, and Microsoft will receive a piece of *each* transaction.

Consider that Microsoft's non-sales-enabled Web site was serving approximately 1.5 million users each day in early 1998 to arrive at an estimate of the size and scope of the Microsoft Internet storefront problem.

Microsoft makes no attempt to conceal its intent to harvest personal information about its customers, claiming it's necessary in order to provide better, more personalized service through its New Interactive Technology for Reselling Online (NITRO) system. The position is more of the same old promises of better, faster, cheaper service. Better, faster, cheaper for Microsoft, but not necessarily for the rest of us.

Ironically, Microsoft apparently considers its customers' personal information to be of higher value than the products it sells. Microsoft announced it will keep its prices up to 20 percent higher than street prices charged by its reseller partners. Microsoft will instead make its profit by charging its resellers a mandatory referral fee for every order Microsoft directs through its NITRO system.

Even more disturbing, Microsoft will reportedly require its resellers to provide it with customer purchase information on all referral sales directed through NITRO.

MICROSOFT FIREFLY

Microsoft's record on privacy can charitably be called checkered. In April 1998, the software monolith did nothing to improve that record when it announced it had purchased a small software developer with a product that some experts consider to be very important for Web marketing and electronic commerce. This product can be used to protect personal privacy on the Internet. Microsoft's purchase of Firefly Network, Inc. for a reported US$40 million (or an amount equal to what one analyst called a "rounding error" on Microsoft's financial statements) marks the software giant's initial proactive foray into the online privacy fray.

Firefly's profiling technology allows users to control the information they disclose to Web sites. Privacy advocates point to Firefly technology as important in helping to protect personal privacy online. However, it also allows Web sites to gather huge amounts of users' personal information.

Firefly—both the company and the technology—grew out of the Massachusetts Institute of Technology's Media Lab. The original use for the technology was to provide collaborative filtering services that offered personalized recommendations for things like music, books, and movies, based on other users' preferences and behavior.

Marketing companies salivated at the potential for such pinpoint accuracy in advertising on the Internet with Firefly. Firefly, however, had adopted a set of strict privacy standards that permitted individual users control over the amount of personal information disclosed to the Web sites they visited.

Microsoft, in its acquisition announcements, downplayed the Firefly collaborative filtering technology and trumpeted the profiling technology. The profiling technology is an established standard that returns control of personal information to the user. In announcing the transaction, Microsoft executives stated that "information privacy is a basic right of computer users." The Firefly technology adheres to the World Wide Web Consortium's Platform for Privacy Preferences standard.

Reactions from privacy advocates were mixed. The Electronic Privacy Information Center's David Sobel was quoted in a *New York Times* article as saying, "Firefly and Microsoft have proposed standards that will make the world safe for data collection, and to that extent we have problems with these technologies." On the other hand, Deirdre Mulligan of the Center for Democracy and Technology, praised the Microsoft announcement in the same article: "We can't be Luddites and put our heads in the sand."

Given Microsoft's past behavior, it's very difficult to believe that the company might be concerned with protecting the privacy rights of its customers.

Open Profiling Standard

Microsoft, Netscape, and Firefly Network, Inc. (before its purchase by Microsoft) formed a consortium to develop a standard for exchanging personal information on the Web. The standard, called the Open Profiling Standard (OPS), was initially proposed by Netscape, Firefly, and VeriSign, Inc. in May 1997.

The Open Profiling Standard defines the creation of Personal Profiles that allow users to decide how much personal information they want to disclose to Web sites. OPS was submitted to the World Wide Web Consortium (W3C) in June 1997 and the proposal is included in the W3C's Platform for Privacy Preferences (P3P) standard. This standard will eventually provide a way for Web sites to delineate their privacy policies while simultaneously allowing users to control the release of their personal information. Internet users need an ownership position in the control and release of information that directly affects them, and most observers agree that the P3P standard holds the most potential.

DÉJÀ NEWS

Usenet's 50,000 newsgroups generate more than one gigabyte of new material on the Internet each day. Déjà News aggregates all of that material into its database. Users of the Déjà News service can search for articles by topic, specific newsgroup, author, and date. It's possible, for example, for anyone to note that you post frequently to the alt.support.aids newsgroup and draw what could be inaccurate conclusions.

An especially troubling search feature of the Déjà News service is something called "Author Profile." Users can aggregate posts made under a variety of identities or aliases if the original author didn't use an anonymous remailer or other similar technology. Selecting the Author Profile on myself, for example, yielded the following:

Author: mfraase@farces.com (Michael Fraase)

- 13 unique articles posted.

- Number of articles posted to individual newsgroups (slightly skewed by cross-postings):
    - 7 comp.dcom.isdn
    - 2 rec.music.gdead
    - 1 comp.infosystems.www.html
    - 1 comp.os.ms-windows.nt.misc
    - 1 comp.society.privacy
    - 1 comp.text.frame

It's interesting what can be learned from my posting habits even though most of my posts can be accounted for by activity on mailing lists that I forgot were cross-posted to associated Usenet newsgroups. If anyone cared, it could be deduced that I'm interested in ISDN, the Grateful Dead, HTML, Microsoft Windows NT, Privacy, and FrameMaker. Although severely limited in that it produces a very narrow profile of my interests, it is eerie in its accuracy.

Déjà News' principals recognize that the service can be used negatively to build dossiers on individuals. Déjà News addresses the problem by honoring the "x-no-archive" header standard. If a post to a newsgroup (or cross-posted mailing list) contains the "x-no-archive" entry in the message header information, it will not be archived. Most users are unaware of this option.

According to reports, Déjà News averages more than 100 million searches each month.

One of the things that bothers me about services like Déjà News is that they manage to change the very nature of the medium. Usenet (and mailing lists) were designed to be fleeting and transitory, not permanent and searchable. Now, we're collectively confronted with the fact that any opinion we've ever expressed online can potentially come back and haunt us in the most peculiar ways. This is simply impossible in any other medium. Conversely, Usenet newsgroups and the cross-posted mailing lists hold vast stores of incredibly useful information, and in that regard, services like Déjà News provide a remarkably useful tool.

Unsolicited Bulk Email ("Spam")

Unsolicited bulk email is widely known as spam in deference to a comedy sketch by Monty Python's Flying Circus in which the characters chant "Spam, Spam, Spam, Spam, Spam, Spam, Spam, Spam, Spam.... in response to every statement or question. For those who are unfamiliar with Monty Python, envision the contents of a can of the trademarked potted meat product hurled into the blades of a common house fan.

In its June 1997 Internet privacy hearings, the Federal Trade Commission made it clear that it already possessed the authority to restrict junk emailers who "engage in unfair or deceptive practices." The FTC can shut down anyone participating in fraudulent mass marketing with a court order. The agency can also levy fines of up to US$11,000 for each act after an agreement has been reached to cease the fraudulent activities.

Restrictions on commercial speech, like telemarketing phone calls and unsolicited commercial faxes, have traditionally survived First Amendment challenges. Direct mail and door-to-door solicitations have been found to enjoy greater protection. When the Supreme Court overturned the Communications Decency Act, most legal experts agreed that online messages and publications should receive the same constitutional protections granted print media. What remains to be determined, however, is if spam is more analogous to direct mail or to unsolicited commercial faxes.

In April 1997, World Research published a survey of more than one thousand Internet users regarding the question of unsolicited bulk email. The responses from the user community were enlightening:

- Twenty-eight percent called the amount of junk email they received "moderate."
- Thirty-nine-and-a-half percent felt the amount of junk email they received was "heavy to very heavy."
- Forty-three percent of the respondents said they "hate" unsolicited commercial email.
- Sixty-eight-and-a-half percent of those surveyed considered spam to be "not useful at all."
- Sixty-six-and-a-half percent of the users said junk email should be regulated.

By June 1997 at least seven states—California, Colorado, Connecticut, Massachusetts, Nevada, New York, and Rhode Island—were considering the regulation of unsolicited commercial email. On the national level, three proposed bills were introduced in Congress and are discussed below.

NETIZENS PROTECTION ACT

Introduced by Representative Chris Smith (R-New Jersey), the Netizens Protection Act of 1997 (HR 1748) would mandate an "opt-in" system for commercial email. Such a system would prohibit the sending of unsolicited commercial email to anyone who had not *previously* agreed to receive it.

This bill was crafted to extend the ban on junk faxes—provided in the Telephone Consumer Protection Act of 1991—to include unsolicited bulk email. Exceptions would be provided for existing business relationships. The Netizens Protection Act of 1997 would require bulk emailers to accurately identify themselves and provide a valid return email address.

Under the proposed legislation, consumers or Internet service providers could bring suit against a bulk emailer for US$500 per message or actual damages whichever is higher. Treble damages would be allowed where willful disregard could be proven.

Representative Smith's bill would require consumers to opt-in to receive bulk email. An opt-in system places the burden of managing a spam distribution list on the bulk emailer rather than placing the perennial burden of getting off such lists on the consumer. Of all the proposed legislation, this is the only one that places the burden of unsolicited bulk email on the originator of the material instead of the recipient.

Electronic Mailbox Protection Act

Senator Robert Torricelli's (D-New Jersey) Electronic Mailbox Protection Act of 1997 (S. 875) would regulate bulk email by requiring an "opt-out" system for all bulk email including commercial, religious, or political messages. Such a system would prohibit sending bulk email to anyone who had specifically requested not to receive it.

Initially the opt-out system would operate on a case-by-case basis but would include a provision for a global opt-out (or opt-in) system, if it is imposed by an Internet standards body.

Under the Electronic Mailbox Protection Act of 1997, consumers would be able to sue a bulk emailer for US$500 per message or the Federal Trade Commission could levy statutory fines of US$5,000 per violation.

The statute would prohibit bulk emailers from harvesting email addresses from Internet service providers and would require accurate routing information in each email message header.

Senator Torricelli's proposed legislation would allow bulk emailers to send a single message to an individual. If the individual responds with a request to be removed from the spammer's distribution list, the removal request would have to be honored. The problem is that each individual would still be required to respond to each solicitation, placing the responsibility on the recipient of spam instead of the originator, where it belongs.

UNSOLICITED COMMERCIAL ELECTRONIC MAIL CHOICE ACT

The Unsolicited Commercial Electronic Mail Choice Act of 1997 (S. 771), authored by Senator Frank Murkowski (R-Alaska), would institute an opt-out system similar to the one proposed by Senator Robert Torricelli's Electronic Mailbox Protection Act of 1997. In addition, Senator Murkowski's proposed bill would require commercial email messages to be clearly labeled with the word "Advertisement" appearing as the first word in the Subject line. The proposed legislation would also require Internet service providers to filter unsolicited bulk email upon customer request.

Under the terms of the proposed law, a consumer could sue a bulk emailer for up to US$5,000 and the Federal Trade Commission could levy statutory fines up to US$11,000.

Senator Murkowski's bill doesn't really address the problem: spam is still spam regardless of how it is labeled. It may be easier to recognize and filter, but it is still wasteful of limited bandwidth and a recipient's time. Spam is particularly offensive for those Internet users who still pay for connectivity based on the amount of time they are connected. Like the Torricelli proposal, it does nothing to place the responsibility for unsolicited bulk email where it belongs—on the sender.

In February 1998, the Federal Trade Commission announced it had notified more than one thousand bulk emailers that government agencies would immediately begin monitoring bulk email for fraud. The United States Postal Inspection Service agreed to aid the FTC in its monitoring program. Unsolicited email believed to be fraudulent can be forwarded to a special FTC email address, <uce@ftc.gov>, where it will be examined.

Bulk emailers and the Direct Marketing Association quickly reacted to the threat of government regulation by promising to offer programs that allow consumers to opt-out of receiving spam. As of early July 1998, no such program has materialized.

Privacy advocates warn that some of the proposals to regulate bulk email might create databases of consumer preferences. None of the proposed legislation would protect those databases from misuse. First Amendment scholars contend that while bulk email can probably be Constitutionally regulated, it may lead to a slippery slope of regulating other content on the Internet.

Meanwhile, individuals are growing increasingly frustrated at the volume of junk email they receive—at their own expense. Internet service providers are seeing their costs rise as a result of the actions of irresponsible spammers who use resources they do not even own to wreak their havoc. Responsible businesses are shying away from using email in certain ways under the fear that they might be falsely labeled as spammers.

Of all these arguments, the fact that spam transfers the cost of a marketing message from the marketer to the consumer is the most compelling. The cost to send one million unsolicited commercial email messages is negligible while the cost to transport and process those one million email messages is quite significant. More importantly, the costs are borne by someone other than the originator of the message, the seller.

There are also hidden costs. It's not uncommon for large Internet service providers to receive several thousand complaints about junk email each day. Someone has to field those complaints and respond to them. Receipt of unsolicited bulk email is the number one complaint received by Internet service providers of any size; more than busy signals and more than service outages. Industry estimates indicate that many Internet service providers spend US$150,000 or more each year to deal with spam, including personnel, hardware, and software. Most Internet service providers have also been victimized by bulk emailers forging email message headers so spam appears to have been sent from somewhere other than where it actually originated.

In late March 1998, Washington became the first state to regulate unsolicited bulk email. While not outlawing spam, the Washington statute makes it illegal for anyone to forge email header information or "misrepresent the messages' point of origin." Because the law applies to anyone within Washington state that *sends* or *receives* email, the ramifications could ripple beyond the state's borders; it's often difficult and sometimes impossible to identify the geographic location of an email recipient.

FURTHER...

Small indications are beginning to surface that the citizenry is fed up with their privacy being invaded in the name of streamlined commerce without tangible benefit. We are tired of being interrupted by telemarketing calls. We are refusing to give our phone numbers to store clerks. We are demanding unpublished telephone numbers. We are becoming cautious about providing Social Security numbers. A few are going so far as to sort their trash. A handful are using encryption tools for secure email on the Internet.

It's possible, if difficult, to stop telemarketers cold in their tracks. The Telephone Consumer Protection Act of 1991 allows you to demand that telemarketers remove you from their call lists. If telemarketers continue to call you after you've requested to be removed from their call lists, they can be subject to substantial fines.

At least that's the theory. In reality, the Telephone Consumer Protection Act was weakened by lobbying groups representing telemarketers. The statute doesn't even apply to telemarketing calls to businesses, for example. According to the law, if you demand to be put on a do not call list and the calls continue, you can file suit for US$500. Even if you sue, however, the statute provides what's called an "affirmative defense" for telemarketers. Currently, all the telemarketer has to do is tell the judge that it has implemented appropriate procedures to prevent violation of the law. Unless you can prove otherwise, the case is automatically dismissed.

My wife and I have found that much better results can be obtained simply by demanding to be added to the telemarketer's "do not call" list and sending invoices for subsequent infractions at our standard billing rate. Our invoices aren't always paid, but the calls stop very quickly.

When the rights of personal privacy and the rights of information access begin to overlap into an information eclipse, a wide variety of possible results appears. The darkest area of the eclipsing bodies—the portions that actually overlap—forms an area ripe for censorship. And make no mistake; censorship occurs in all spheres, both public and private. The Constitution only prohibits censorship in the public sphere. Could it be that it's time for that to change?

Resources

- Acxiom Corporation: <www.acxiom.com>
- Amazon.com: <www.amazon.com>
- American Bankers Association: <www.aba.com>
- American Library Association: <www.ala.org>
- America Online Inc.: <www.aol.com>

- An Appraisal of Technologies of Political Control: <jya.com/atpc.htm>
- California Bankers Association: <www.calbankers.com>
- CDNow: <www.cdnow.com>
- Coalition Against Unsolicited Commercial Email (CAUCE): <www.cauce.org/>
- Computer Professionals for Social Responsibility: <www.cpsr.org>
- Decision Strategies: <www.tmn.com/dsi/>
- Déjà News: <www.dejanews.com>
- Direct Marketing Association: <www.the-dma.org>
- Electronic Frontier Foundation: <www.eff.org>
- Electronic Privacy Information Center: <www.epic.org>
- Federal Bureau of Investigation: <www.fbi.gov>
- Federal Trade Commission: <www.ftc.gov>
- Firefly Network, Inc.: <www.firefly.net>
- Georgia Tech personal information survey: <www-survey.cc.gatech.edu>
- Griswold v. Connecticut: <laws.findlaw.com/US/381/479.html>
- Hertz Corp.: <www.hertz.com>
- Microsoft Corp.: <www.microsoft.com>
- Nardone v. United States (1937): <laws.findlaw.com/US/302/379.html>
- Nardone v. United States (1939): <laws.findlaw.com/US/308/338.html>

- Netscape Corp.: <www.netscape.com>
- Office of Technology Assessment Archives: <www.ota.nap.edu>
- Olmstead v. United States: <laws.findlaw.com/US/277/438.html>
- Open Profiling Standard: <www.firefly.net/OPS/>
- Platform for Privacy Preferences: <www.w3.org/P3P/>
- Privacy & American Business: <hudson.idt.net/~pab/>
- Public Interest Research Group credit bureau study: <www.pirg.org/pirg/consumer/credit/mistakes/>
- Quicken: <www.quicken.com>
- Social Security Administration: <www.ssa.gov>
- TRUSTe: <www.truste.org>
- United States Secret Service: <www.ustreas.gov/usss/>
- World Wide Web Consortium: <www.w3.org>

CHAPTER

8

CENSORSHIP

The First Amendment to the United States Constitution clearly precludes the government from censoring most forms of speech and guarantees a press free of government interference:

> "Congress shall make no law respecting an establishment of religion, or prohibiting the free exercise thereof; or abridging the freedom of speech or of the press; or of the right of the people peaceably to assemble and to petition the Government for a redress of grievances."

No mention is made, however, in any of the founding documents about non-governmental censorship. We have depended heavily upon the remarkable insight of our Founding Fathers. Yet how could they be forewarned of overriding corporate interests when such entities simply were not deployed to the spectacular degree seen in this century?

Censorship issues, like personal privacy issues, are impacted by both government and the private sector. The 1990s saw the ascension of the private sector's censorship and privacy invasion activities eclipse those of the government. Unfortunately, the word censorship has become so overused and in such a wide range of contexts, it is fast becoming meaningless. We no longer agree, as a culture, what constitutes censorship.

An era bombarded with endless streams of information, parallels endless attempts to ban it.

CORPORATE CENSORSHIP

In the United States, corporations are chartered by and exist solely at the pleasure of the citizenry. Corporations are, at least in theory, under the authority of the citizens and the charter of incorporation is a revocable privilege granted by the people. Incorporation is not an inalienable right. Corporations were intended to be accountable to society, but they are now answering, for the most part, only to their shareholders. Too many shareholders only want to hear "20 percent annualized growth curves." Reasonable people quickly recognize such a high level of sustained growth is potentially cancerous for society. If we remember that cancer cells grow in total disregard of the cells that surround them, such disregard is what makes cancer—late 20th century style and corporatism—so insidious.

Intentionally and forcefully limiting the free flow of information and a diversity of opinions has become a full-contact sport in the 1990s. In April 1997, The *Wall Street Journal* reported that *Esquire* magazine killed an article when Chrysler threatened to withdraw its advertising from the magazine. What had managed to ruffle Chrysler's corporate feathers was a description of gay sex in a work of fiction. Edward Kosner, then *Es-*

quire's editor-in-chief, killed the story and Will Blythe, the magazine's literary editor, resigned in protest over what was cited as Kosner's caving in to corporate concerns.

It turns out that Chrysler's media buyer—Pentacom, a subsidiary of BBDO Worldwide, which itself is a subsidiary of Omnicom Group, Inc.—demanded that 100 publications carrying Chrysler advertising alert it "in advance of any and all editorial content that encompasses sexual, political, social issues or any editorial that might be construed as provocative or offensive. Each and every issue that carries Chrysler advertising requires a written summary outlining major theme/articles appearing in upcoming issues."

According to an April 1997 *New York Times* article, most recipients of the Pentacom letter—which demanded a signature of acknowledgment—denied acquiescing to Chrysler's demands. But the article went on to quote a Chrysler spokesperson as saying that "...everybody agreed."

That same month, *Fortune* magazine ran a cover story about IBM's chairman and chief executive officer, Louis Gerstner Jr., in its April 14 issue. While overall, the article was positive in tone, Gerstner was described as not being nice and having a "career-long obsession with money, status, and a desire to get ahead." Shortly after the article appeared, IBM and its subsidiaries began pulling all of its estimated US$6 million per year advertising from *Fortune*. IBM reportedly refused to return telephone calls from Fortune reporters at the time.

Predictably, five months later, the American Society of Magazine Editors (representing editors of more than 850 magazines) and the Magazine Publishers of America (representing more than one thousand magazines) issued a joint statement prompting magazines not to submit editorial to advertisers for review prior to publication. Doing so, the statement advised, may "at the very least create the appearance of censorship and ultimately could undermine editorial independence." Of course, without editorial independence, readers have less cause to perceive any publication's content as credible.

The general perception—right or wrong—is that modern magazines have a single purpose for existing: to deliver subscribers to advertisers and in so doing to reap the largest revenues possible from advertisers. Magazine industry insiders contend that they derive revenue in almost equal parts from subscribers and advertisers.

The existence of an impenetrable wall between advertising and editorial functions may be arguable for general interest magazines, but it is not true for trade publications—especially those with controlled circulation—like those that cover the computer industry. A controlled circulation magazine is distributed free of charge to "qualified" readers and made available at a high subscription rate to anyone else. In my experience as a freelance writer for controlled circulation publications, I can point to more than a few instances of pressure to appease an advertiser. The most outrageous example was the controlled circulation newspaper that printed a retraction of a criticism I had made of a highly advertised product in a rumor column.

As more publications are available online, it becomes ever more problematic and time consuming for a reader to differentiate between advertising and editorial content. The American Society of Magazine Editors has issued a set of standards for online publications, entitled the "ASME Guidelines for New Media." Recognizing the growing difficulty in discerning between editorial and advertising content, the ASME Guidelines offer a simple solution: online publishers should more clearly label what is editorial material and what is sponsored content or advertising. The ASME Guidelines are strictly voluntary and offer several additional suggestions:

- On editorial Web pages, associative links to external sites should not be sold or traded.

- Search engines that carry a publisher's branding identity should not give preferential treatment or prominence to advertisers.
- The use of a sponsor's logo is acceptable only when the publisher controls the content and in no way endorses the sponsor or its product(s).
- Advertising links should not appear in a table of contents for editorial content.

Relatively few Internet users are aware that the Net itself has a sort of institutional memory that is both organic and infallible. Newsgroup postings, for example, are archived and can be searched by author, date, or content. Net-literate journalists regularly trawl archive services and search engines like Déjà News and Alta Vista when researching any news story with an Internet "hook." The Net's institutional memory helps keep any attempt at censorship at bay.

In March 1998, seventeen-year-old Christopher Marquis opened a UPS package containing a homemade explosive device that killed him and injured his mother. About a week prior to the bombing, two newsgroup postings carrying an America Online return address threatened Marquis' life. After Marquis' death, even more threatening messages addressed to the teenager appeared.

When the FBI announced it had a suspect in custody, newsgroup readers were surprised to learn the suspect was not the author of the threatening messages.

Within three days of the bombing, most of the threatening messages were nowhere to be found in the archives. Those who looked for these messages found only "cancel" messages in their place. The messages were deleted by America Online representatives, who cited violations of its terms of service.

Newsgroup posting cancellations are a regular occurrence on the Internet, but the overwhelming majority of cancellations are a result of spam or technical malfunctions, like multiple reposting accidents. Almost never are messages cancelled based on content, as in the America Online case. Nevertheless the "cancel" messages provided irrefutable proof that *something* on the topic had originally been published and that an audit trail existed indicating who had removed the material.

Book publishing is apparently no more immune from corporate censorship than magazine publishing. In late February 1998, HarperCollins Publishers dropped plans to publish a book written by Chris Patten, the last British governor of Hong Kong. HarperCollins corporate head, Rupert Murdoch, reportedly determined that the work was too negative in its view of China. HarperCollins, in a prepared statement released to the media, said, "Rupert Murdoch did not agree with many of Patten's positions in Hong Kong, which he thought abrogated promises made by the previous government."

The incident could have easily gone unnoticed, given the large number of books and authors being dropped daily by the large, consolidated, New York publishing houses. But it was precisely that the statement was made that makes such an apparent and total disregard of the author's intimate knowledge of China an obvious threat to Murdoch. HarperCollins however, alluded that the book was a "politically incorrect" tome. Politically incorrect for whom, we might ask.

To make matters worse, various media outlets reported that when Patten's editor, Stuart Proffitt, was told HarperCollins was dropping the book and was asked to concur with the decision, Proffitt refused. Reports indicate that Adrian Bourne, managing director of News Corporation's trade book division, handed Proffitt a "gagging letter" threatening Proffitt with termination of employment without compensation for gross misconduct if he discussed the matter with anyone.

Chris Patten is suing HarperCollins for damages and breach of contract. His book has been picked up by Macmillan. Stuart Proffitt, Patten's editor, is suing HarperCollins for breach of contract.

Rupert Murdoch, through his News Corporation, has extensive business holdings throughout China and would appear to have a history of kowtowing to the Chinese government. In 1994, the Chinese government protested BBC documentaries on Chinese dissidents and Murdoch removed the BBC news service from STAR TV, his Hong Kong-based satellite television service.

Even our schools, it appears, are not exempt from corporate censorship. In March 1998, a Georgia teenager was suspended from school for a day for refusing to wear a Coca-Cola shirt, instead donning a shirt emblazoned with the Pepsi logo. The Coca-Cola Company sponsors a national contest with a US$10,000 prize for the school that comes up with the best plan for distributing discount coupons.

In the small town one hundred miles from Coca-Cola's Atlanta headquarters, the school's students were encouraged to wear clothes in Coca-Cola's corporate red-and-white colors and line up on the athletic field to spell out the word "COKE" for a picture. A dozen Coca-Cola Company executives were on hand to watch the activity.

Mike Cameron, a high school senior, instead wore a Pepsi-Cola shirt while standing in the middle of the group. Cameron claims he wore his Pepsi shirt all day, but the school's principal insists Cameron wore another shirt on top of the Pepsi shirt and removed it just before the picture was shot.

The school's principal, Gloria Hamilton, suspended Cameron for one day. Hamilton was quoted in the *Washington Post* as saying that Cameron was suspended for a "being disruptive and trying to destroy the school picture," not for wearing the Pepsi shirt. Tom Dorhmann, superintendent of the Columbia County

Board of Education, corroborated Hamilton's account and "accused Cameron of manipulating the news media," according to the *Washington Post* story.

Pepsi spokesman Brad Shaw, recognizing an opportunity, reportedly complimented Cameron's taste in shirts and supplied the teenager with several more.

That any school in America would need to resort to such corporate-sponsored contests and exhibitions seems to have gone over the collective head of mainstream media. It is the domain of advertisers and marketers to arrive at a merchandising plan for discount coupons. Distracting the nation's schools and students seems dangerously close to using a public resource for private gain. The merchandising of our schools may not be something to which we want to aspire.

Platform for Internet Content Selection

"Self-regulation" is the rallying cry of free-market libertarians that seem to populate cyberspace in inordinate numbers. "Let the market decide," the online industry mantra goes, and "keep Big Government off our backs." Until the late 1990s most civil rights advocates were either silent on the issue or willing to ride along on the self-regulation bandwagon.

Toward the end of 1997, free-speech and civil rights advocates began questioning the wisdom of self-regulation in an out-of-control market, pointing to what *New York Times* columnist Denise Caruso describes as "a new, insidious form of censorship—untouchable in a court of law—that abdicates to private industry the government's traditional role of protecting free speech."

The self-regulating focal point around which the free-marketers dance is a technology called the Platform for Internet Content Selection (PICS). PICS is simply software that can be used to filter and block content on the Web through a consistent rating system. Initially at least, PICS was embraced as an alternative to the Communications Decency Act. PICS allows virtually anyone to create a customized content filtering and blocking system. Within a year, however, PICS found a lot of opponents who argued that the filtering and blocking technology turned the Web into a powerfully automated censorship tool, a veritable global censorship engine.

Users—ranging the political gamut from the National Organization of Women to the Christian Coalition—could use PICS to create their own special flavor of censorship, based on their own worldview. But so could a whole range of other organizations we wouldn't ordinarily think of as censors. Imagine, for example, if Microsoft Corp. used PICS to prevent its users access to information from or about its competitors. What if Martha Stewart or the government of the People's Republic of China did the same? What if Disney became the sole determinant of the type of information to which children could have access?

A variety of different Internet content filtering systems and services have existed since the mid-1990s. What differentiates PICS from its predecessors is that PICS filters and blocks surreptitiously. A PICS user has no way of knowing that access to any sites are being blocked, let alone which ones or why.

What most concerns PICS opponents is that corporate or private regulation of content on the Web, through technologies like PICS, is a greater threat than any currently realistic threat posed by government. As Lawrence Lessig, a visiting professor at the Harvard Law School said in a *New York Times* article, "The problem with PICS is if Microsoft uses it, it's a private action, not testable under the U.S. Constitution. You can't go into court and complain about what they do."

One of the most pernicious aspects of PICS is that any type of material *deemed* to be objectionable can be filtered. The technology is much more flexible than the term "content filter" would imply. Filtering can be done at virtually any level; from the individual user, the organization, the Internet service provider, or even, presumably, at the state level. With a true information filter, the user determines what sort of information is rejected. In the case of PICS, the choice to reject certain information would not, necessarily, be yours. In any case, you would not even know what information was being suppressed.

Critics of PICS point out the Orwellian nature of the suppression of certain types of information without informed consent. When a school board decides to take another crack at removing Salinger's *Catcher in the Rye* from library shelves, they have to actually vote, *in public*, to do so. The fear of facing potential public embarrassment has always been an effective tool for communities. PICS, however, allows such actions to take place behind the scenes, undetected, by remote control. And it is as if the material never even existed at all.

(For more information about PICS in relation to information access issues, see Platform for Internet Content Selection on page 121.)

OTHER FILTERING SOFTWARE

Several commercial filtering software options are available on the market, and almost all of them work the same way. The corporation that markets the filtering software defines—by hand—on a case-by-case basis, which Internet sites to filter, based on a subjective assessment of the content contained within the site.

In late 1996, an eighteen-year old Vanderbilt University student was accused by Solid Oak Software—maker of the Cybersitter commercial filtering software program—of illegally obtaining the list of sites blocked by the Cybersitter software. The student, Bennett Haselton, who also founded the anti-censorship group Peacefire, claimed that he merely ran the Cybersitter software on his computer and kept track of the sites that were blocked. The list of sites Cybersitter blocked raised more than a few eyebrows and included The Well, the National Organization of Women, and *Mother Jones* magazine.

Solid Oak Software, for its part, added Peacefire to its list of blocked sites. Solid Oak Software went even further and told Peacefire's Internet service provider that the sites of all of the service provider's content customers (almost 2,500 domain names) would be added to the blocked sites list if the Peacefire site wasn't removed from service.

There's an old saw about censorship on the Internet: "the Net interprets censorship as damage and simply routes around it." In April 1997, Haselton put that theory into action when he posted a software program on the Peacefire site that could be used to decrypt Cybersitter's blocked sites list.

Among the sites Haselton discovered to be blocked by Cybersitter—in addition to those mentioned above—included several regional Internet service providers, the Gay and Lesbian Alliance Against Defamation, Peacefire, Godiva Chocolatier, and Ethical Spectacle, which had criticized the blocking policies used in the Cybersitter software.

But Haselton wasn't done yet. In July 1997, he announced his suspicions that Solid Oak Software may be surveilling its user's Web browsing activities. When Haselton received email from his readers indicating that they had tried to download the Cybersitter software from the Solid Oak Software Web site and were denied access, he set out to investigate.

Haselton claimed he discovered that the Solid Oak Software site would scan users' hard drives for evidence that they had accessed the Peacefire site. If so, access to the Cybersitter software was denied.

Solid Oak Software and its Cybersitter product is not the only filtering software to come under fire as censorware. In December 1997, the Censorware Project was formed by six founding members: Seth Finkelstein, Bennett Haselton, Jamie McCarthy, Michael Sims, James Tyre, and Jonathan Wallace. The six activists spent some seventy hours going through the five thousand-plus domain names in the Learning Company's Cyber Patrol software's CyberNOT list. The group came up with 200 examples of inappropriately blocked sites including the MIT Project on Mathematics and Computation and The National Academy of Clinical Biochemistry.

It is one thing for parents to use censorware with minors in their homes. It's quite another to censor university students who are required to conduct comprehensive research and to learn to think for themselves.

School and Library Filtering

In 1996, fewer than one-half of the nation's public libraries were connected to the Internet. As of mid-1998, more than three-quarters of the country's libraries enjoy Internet connectivity and for many Americans, provide their only Internet access. Loudoun County, Virginia and its six-branch public library emerged as the first test case for Internet filtering.

The Loudoun library policy requires that all computers in the library that have a connection to the Internet contain filtering software designed specifically to block pornographic Web sites. Children are not allowed to use any of the computers without parental permission. If a library user is caught viewing what the library staff considers to be inappropriate material on the Web, the user is requested to stop. If the user continues, he or she is asked to leave. If the user doesn't leave upon staff request, they are subject to criminal trespassing charges.

The software used in all of Loudoun County's six library branches is Log-On Data Corp.'s X-Stop. The X-Stop software filters sexually explicit content, but like most other competing products, the software also denies access to information on topics ranging from breast cancer to sex education and gay rights. Library patrons can submit a written request to the library staff, requesting that a particular site be unblocked.

It's difficult to imagine long lines of citizens in the library with requests for unblocked sites. Imagine the breast cancer patient who must access "sexually explicit" material in an effort to better educate herself about her condition. She routinely stands in such a line and consequently becomes a target of suspicion, simply because she would rather not discuss her health challenges with friends and neighbors who might be curious. Etiquette is too seldom followed these days and such library lines would require a whole new behavior code.

In a lawsuit filed in the Federal District Court, a group called Mainstream Loudoun alleges that the county library policy is a government activity infringing the First Amendment rights of library patrons. The county, for its part, argues that the local library cannot be forced to carry a particular kind of material.

History may be on the side of Loudoun County. In 1982, the United States Supreme Court ruled in Board of Education v. Pico that a school district may not remove certain books from public school library shelves simply because it dislikes the ideas contained in the books. But Justice William J. Brennan Jr. wrote in his opinion that the Supreme Court's ruling affected only the discretion to remove books from library shelves, not a library's decision about which books to acquire for their collections.

Loudoun County considers accessing a Web site to be the digital equivalent of requesting a certain book via inter-library loan. The county argues that a library is not under any First Amendment obligation to fill an inter-library loan request. Similarly, libraries cannot be forced to purchase any particular material it does not want. Advocates of the library policy add that the federal government's failure to craft legislation to regulate indecency on the Internet puts the onus to do so on local governments.

The Mainstream Loudoun group contends that the library's filtering policy was a form of removal and has nothing to do with library acquisitions, because the software used by the library is designed solely to exclude certain content and doesn't acquire anything. The attorney representing the plaintiffs, Robert Corn-Revere, likened the library's censorship policy as analogous to "subscribing to a magazine and after the fact razoring out articles [thought to be] offensive." Mainstream Loudoun also takes exception to the library's policy of having librarians monitor what materials patrons view on the Internet-connected computers.

In early April 1998, U.S. District Judge Leonie Brinkema ruled that the civil liberties lawsuit against the Loudoun County Public Library could proceed and that the use of filtering and blocking software by public libraries may constitute censorship of protected speech. Judge Brinkema flatly rejected Loudoun County's request to dismiss the case, and concluded that filtering Internet access in a library is not the equivalent of a library branch selecting books to place on library shelves. Loudoun County will have to prove, in a full trial, that its library system is not censoring patron's access to material on the Internet.

In her ruling, Judge Brinkema drew an analogy between the filtering of Internet content to blacking out passages in books. Citing the Supreme Court's rejection of the Communications Decency Act, Judge Brinkema said the library system could not, "in the interest of protecting children, limit the speech available to adults to what is fit for 'juveniles.'"

Some libraries take a decidedly low-tech approach to preventing patrons from accessing questionable material on the Internet. They require Internet using patrons to sign a form agreeing not to access pornographic material on the Net.

In March 1998, a group of eleven adult residents of Ventura County, California filed a lawsuit in Los Angeles federal court challenging the local library system's policy that requires computer-using patrons to sign a form agreeing not to access "sexually explicit" material on any of the computers in library system's fifteen branches.

Denying that the lawsuit is about the merits of pornography, the attorney for the library patrons, William Weilbacher, was quoted in the *New York Times* as saying, "I don't believe that my clients would have any objection to requiring children to sign the user agreement. But here we have adults that are essentially being parented by the local library agency. That's not a proper role for the government."

According to the *New York Times*, Richard Rowe, the Ventura County library agency administrator said the agreement containing the rule against accessing sexually explicit material was created because pornography "is perceived to be offensive to the community." Rowe acknowledged that he wasn't aware of any complaints from patrons whose sensibilities were offended by the Web browsing activities of others.

Most observers agree that the Ventura County situation is especially troubling because adults have a right to access constitutionally protected materials, including sexually explicit images that are not legally obscene.

In a plan announced in early 1998, American schools are being offered subsidies to pay for various Internet services. Senator John McCain (R-Arizona), chairman of the Senate Committee on Commerce, Science, and Transportation, called for restricting the availability of indecent material to classrooms in order for schools to be eligible for the subsidy offer.

Opponents to McCain's plan say the decision to limit access to materials should rest solely with the individual schools, school districts, and parents; not the Federal government. After all, the argument goes, education is traditionally run at the local level and administered according to community standards. Activists pointed out that, if McCain's plan relies on filtering and blocking software, it could run into First Amendment problems.

In late March 1998, Vice President Al Gore announced his support for filtering Internet content in schools and libraries stating, "As we connect every school and classroom to the Internet, we must protect our children from the red-light districts in cyberspace." Gore said, in his statement, that Congress should tie the requirement to protect minors from "inappropriate" content on the Internet to the US$2.5 billion annual Internet access discounts made available to public schools and libraries. The discounts, known as "e-rates" are administered by the Federal Communications Commission (FCC).

Vice President Gore, confusingly, denied that he was supporting Senator John McCain's (R-Arizona) Internet School Filtering Act. McCain's bill requires libraries and schools participating in the e-rate program to install blocking software on their computers. A Gore spokeswoman was widely quoted in the media as saying, "We do not support the McCain bill. The legislation [Vice President Gore] would support would not require blocking, it would just require that schools and libraries put a plan in place regarding their students and patrons accessing inappropriate material." But Gore's prepared statement read, in part, "We must bring the combined power of parents, teachers, and technology together if we are going to protect our students in a way that will work in every community and reflect the values of each community."

Coming down squarely on the middle of the filtering fence, Gore's spokeswoman said, "If their local values dictate that [allowing open access to all material, including "inappropriate" content] then it is up to the school and community."

COMMUNICATIONS DECENCY ACT SEQUELS

Less than six months after the United States Supreme Court overturned the Communications Decency Act (CDA) as unconstitutional, the key Republican sponsor of the legislation in the Senate, Senator Dan Coats (R-Indiana), introduced a bill many are referring to as CDA II. The proposed law would make it illegal for commercial Web sites to distribute material that is "harmful to minors." Coats points out that commercial pornography providers can easily prevent children from accessing their sites by requiring credit cards or personal identification numbers. Unlike the original CDA legislation that applied to all content on the Internet—Web sites, newsgroups, email, and chatrooms—the new Coats proposal applies only to Web sites.

In a new twist, the targeted material would not be limited to pornographic images. The proposed legislation would apply to "any communication, article, recording, or writing depicting in a patently offensive way with respect to what is suitable for minors, an actual or simulated sexual act or sexual contact, actual or simulated normal or perverted sexual acts, or a lewd exhibition of the genitals."

This wrinkle would apply the "harmful to minors" test and its attendant penalties to "adult-oriented" Web sites, even though the term is not clearly defined. Regardless of terminology and definitions, the proposed law would probably impact decidedly mainstream sites like Web-based bookstores and music vendors.

Under the proposed law, violators could face a fine up to US$50,000 and six months imprisonment.

A rather odd component of the Coats proposal requires the Federal Communications Commission (FCC) to create a "method of restricting access" to the sites found to contain offensive material.

In yet another step through the looking glass, the Coats legislation would require both the FCC and Department of Justice to publish—on their respective Web sites—a definition of the term "material that is harmful to minors."

The United States has had obscenity laws since 1842. In 1973, the Supreme Court threw up its collective hands about trying to reach a clear definition of obscenity and tossed the "contemporary community standards" can of worms to the individual states. In 1987, the Supreme Court refined the standard, stating that offensive material was not obscene if it was found to have social value from the viewpoint of a "reasonable person." By now—especially after the Supreme Court overturned the Communications Decency Act—it should be clear that the obscenity laws that govern physical space can also be applied to the virtual space of the Internet.

Nevertheless, on March 12, 1998, the Senate Commerce Committee passed both pieces of legislation proposed by McCain and Coats. Most observers agreed that several senators would likely put "holds" on the proposed bills, preventing consideration in the full Senate. The American Civil Liberties Union (ACLU), the Center for Democracy and Technology (CDT), and the Electronic Privacy Information Center (EPIC) all pledged legal challenges if the bills pass Congress. (For more information on the CDA with regard to the press, see Communications Decency Act on page 77.)

STATE RESTRICTIONS

The United States Supreme Court overturned the Communications Decency Act as overly broad and restrictive, but as of mid-1998, seventeen states have CDA-equivalent laws on their books.

Tennessee, for example, calls for Congress to create a special top-level domain on the Internet for adult-oriented sites. Commercial Internet sites in the United States are aggregated under the .com domain. Tennessee's position, apparently, is that a new top-level domain—such as .xxx or .sex—be created for adult-oriented Internet sites.That state also requires schools to use blocking software and criminalizes teachers and librarians who fail to do so.

Illinois and New Mexico both criminalize the electronic distribution of "indecent" (New Mexico) or "harmful" (Illinois) material to minors. Proposed legislation in Rhode Island would make it illegal to use a computer for "immoral or illegal" activities involving children.

FURTHER...

Censorship threats have become a regular feature of the American landscape. Perhaps the threats are the result of citizens' growing awareness of both the global exploitation of children and of corporate "self-preservation." In everything from advertising to corporate mergers, corporations have increased their power base exceptionally during the past several decades, and the attempt by commercial entities to control information has continued to increase proportionately. Children, however, appear to be forgotten as the battle rages, and the battle seems to be less about real values than it does about economics. Can we afford to allow corporate interests to surpass and eclipse those of our nation's children?

What are parents to do? Educating children to respect the difference between right and wrong is a good starting point, but is it enough? Voicing concern about children and about censorship while *participating* in our schools, our neighborhoods, activist groups, and all those places that children first learn the operating mores of a society, will always be a better alternative than some technological panacea. The current state of affairs can best be described as government and corporations both struggling to determine what content adults and children alike should have a right to access.

Reactionary legislation, like the Communications Decency Act and its spawn, are as commonplace as they are predictable. However, government, citizens and the corporate sector will always try to control what they fear or do not understand. Similar fear-based reactions have occurred in the area of computer crime as well.

RESOURCES

- Alta Vista: <www.altavista.digital.com>
- American Civil Liberties Union (ACLU): <www.aclu.org>
- BBC: <www.bbc.co.uk>
- Center for Democracy and Technology: <www.cdt.org>
- Déjà News: <www.dejanews.com>
- Department of Justice: <www.usdoj.gov>
- Electronic Privacy Information Center (EPIC): <www.epic.org>
- Ethical Spectacle: <www.spectacle.org>
- Federal Communications Commission (FCC): <www.fcc.gov>
- Fortune magazine: <www.pathfinder.com/fortune/>
- Gay and Lesbian Alliance Against Defamation: <www.glaad.org>
- Godiva Chocolatier: <www.godiva.com>

- HarperCollins Publishers: <www.harpercollins.com>
- Learning Company (Cyber Patrol): <www.learningco.com>
- MIT Project on Mathematics and Computation: <www-swiss.ai.mit.edu>
- Mother Jones: <www.motherjones.com>
- National Academy of Clinical Biochemistry: <www.nacb.org>
- National Organization for Women (NOW): <www.now.org>
- News Corporation: <www.newscorp.com>
- New York Times: <www.nytimes.com>
- Peacefire: <www.peacefire.org>
- Solid Oak Software (Cybersitter): <www.cybersitter.com>
- STAR TV: <www.startv.com>
- WELL: <www.wenet.net/hooked/services/well.html>
- X-Stop: <www.xstop.com>

CHAPTER

9

COMPUTER CRIME

Jack Kerouac and Neal Cassady hitchhiked the highways of America during the 1940s and 1950s. Computer hackers of the 1980s, 1990s, and beyond are now travelling the byways of the electronic frontier. Computer hackers, with their determination to know and understand the vast recesses of the net, are creating the beat generation of the new millennium.

A 1986 study by the Office of Technology Assessment found that, while much attention is focused on computer hackers, more significant security problems are posed by individuals who are authorized to access compromised systems. Similarly, the National Telecommunications and Information Security Committee found that most of the crimes against government computers were committed not by hackers, but by people with authorized access to those computers.

A May 1996 report from the Senate's Permanent Investigations Subcommittee states that banks and large corporations lost an estimated US$800 million due to hackers in 1995. Citing "fear of the marketplace," most losses were not reported to law-enforcement agencies.

Because it is impossible for any computer system to be free of risk of potential intrusion, our society's cultural norms and mores emerge as critical components in computer crime. As you review the three following accounts of high-profile computer crimes, consider which of our laws and cultural norms are best applied.

The "Hollywood Hacker"

Steve Goldman's apartment was raided on March 8, 1990 by the U.S. Secret Service and Los Angles police. Goldman, a freelance investigative reporter, was reportedly working on an exposé of "tabloid" television shows like Current Affair and Hard Copy. Goldman had been a contributor to these programs in the past. According to accounts in the *Los Angeles Times* and elsewhere, Goldman was caught attempting to access Fox Television network computers in New York and Los Angeles without authorization. He was charged under Section 502(c)(2) of the California Penal Code.

From the reports, it appears that access to the Fox computers required no password, only a login id. Tracey Miller, of Los Angeles radio station KFI, described Goldman as someone who "had managed to infiltrate the world of tabloid journalism and then got caught up in a sting operation involving Fox Television computers."

The search warrant indicated that Fox employee Paul Smirnoff noticed unsuccessful login attempts on the Fox computer in New York used by Current Affair writers. Smirnoff ordered a "bait" story to be placed in the Los Angeles computer. Investigators gathered evidence for their allegations against Steve Goldman—who allegedly took the bait—and made the raid on Goldman's apartment on March 8, 1990. What makes this raid different from others, however, is that the Secret Service and Los Angles police were accompanied on the raid by a Fox Television reporter and camera crew.

Traditionally, the Secret Service has been consistently quiet about their procedures and maintains that the times and dates of raids are "secret." Not only were the Fox Television reporter and crew present, but reports indicate that they seemed to have the full cooperation from the law enforcement officials at the scene. The question must be asked: Did collusion between law enforcement and the media occur in this event?

Fox Television's dramatic report opened with law enforcement agents in bullet-proof vests and guns drawn outside Goldman's Los Angeles apartment. Were Charles Keating, Michael Milken, or Oliver North arrested in a similar manner? Computer raids similar to the Goldman case had become almost commonplace in the early 1990s.

There are some serious questions inherent in this case that call for further examination:

- Does the mainstream media inflame our perceptions of hacking, especially in instances like the Goldman case above?
- Where was the "objectivity" of the news crew in this case? Was it merely coincidence that the Fox television crew was included in the raid of this investigative journalist? (Goldman was working on an exposé of the kind of television pseudo-journalism Fox helped popularize.)
- Do computer crime victims regularly grossly overstate or understate their "losses?" Why did Bell South claim a US$74,449 "loss" on an allegedly

"stolen" document that was available to the public—via a toll-free order number—for less than US$30?

- Did the Secret Service become involved in the Goldman case because of asserted claims that a "federal interest computer" was being compromised? The Secret Service withdrew from the case almost immediately after the raid. This is most interesting in light of the tenacity exhibited by the Secret Service in other computer crime cases.(For more information, see Computer Fraud and "Federal-Interest Computers" on page 230.)

James Fallows, the Washington editor of *The Atlantic Monthly*, in his book, *Breaking the News: How the Media Undermine Democracy* (1996, Pantheon) examines how the "enraging habits" inherent in the media's current practices have caused Americans to "distrust journalists even more than they do government officials. Unless journalism changes, it will destroy itself and severely damage American democracy."

Fallows goes on to remind us that there are many responsible beat reporters who are extremely knowledgeable and dedicated, especially in their area of expertise. But they are today being replaced by—and having to compete with—"star" journalists who may or may not exhibit the same level of expertise or dedication.

KEVIN MITNICK

In early 1995, Kevin Mitnick was seen as the most dangerous and notorious of all computer hackers. Mitnick was captured in mid-February 1995 after having come close to bringing a handful of West Coast Internet service providers—including the WELL and Netcom—to their electronic knees. Or at least that's the story portrayed in the mainstream and trade press.

On Christmas Day, 1994, Kevin Mitnick managed to break into the computer system of one of America's most prominent computer and network security experts, Tsutomu Shimomura. An over-hyped "hacker war" ensued in the national press as security expert Shimomura set out to catch Mitnick, the wily hacker. The hacker war had all the elements of a good cyber-Western, complete with good guys and bad guys. Look below the surface however, and it becomes murky as to just how good and bad the players were in this high-tech soap opera.

Shortly after Christmas 1994, Tsutomu Shimomura was made aware that the computer system in his San Diego office had been compromised. Shimomura returned to San Diego and began to analyze the break-in with his team.

In mid-January 1995, Shimomura brought the hacker attacks to the attention of John Markoff, a *New York Times* journalist, who had profiled Mitnick and his hacking exploits in an earlier book he co-authored. About a week later, Markoff wrote a front-page account of the break-in and a profile of Tsutomu Shimomura. Throughout the first two weeks of February 1995, Shimomura and Markoff secretly helped the federal government and Sprint Cellular track Kevin Mitnick. On February 15, 1995, Kevin Mitnick was captured by the FBI—with the help of Shimomura and Markoff—in Raleigh, North Carolina.

Within a year, the great hacker war erupted into a catfight between two journalists—each publishing a book on the same day—telling a wildly different story of the events leading to the capture of Kevin Mitnick. For many observers, this battle over the truth became the greater story.

If you believe the account in *Takedown: The Pursuit and Capture of Kevin Mitnick, America's Most Wanted Computer Outlaw—by the Man Who Did It*, Mitnick was a hard-boiled criminal intent upon destroying Tsutomu Shimomura's reputation as a security expert, while simultaneously wreaking havoc on the nation's computer networks. The book's author, Tsutomu

Shimomura and co-author, *New York Times* journalist John Markoff, gave a first-hand account of the techniques used to foil the sly hacker's subsequent break-in attempts and the events that led to his capture. John Markoff is widely respected as one of the country's best technology journalists and was the writer who first broke the Mitnick story in his January 23, 1995 front-page story in the *New York Times*.

If, on the other hand, you believe the account presented by Jonathan Littman in his book, *The Fugitive Game: Online With Kevin Mitnick*, the computer hacker was little more than a somewhat unstable—but mostly harmless—trickster who fell victim to Shimomura and one of the country's most highly respected technology journalists in their quest to cash in on a huge book advance. Littman, a Mill Valley, California author and journalist, spent almost a third of his book portraying the Mitnick myth as created from almost-whole cloth by John Markoff's coverage in the *New York Times*.

Shimomura and Markoff say that Littman is distorting the truth. According to published accounts, Littman feels the same about Shimomura and Markoff. The truth probably lies somewhere between the two poles.

The more disturbing aspect of the involvement of Shimomura and Markoff in the hunt for Kevin Mitnick is the capacity in which they operated. In various parts of *Takedown*, Shimomura and Markoff reveal that they actively participated in the eavesdropping of cellular telephone conversations with the help of Sprint Cellular engineers.

The only way Shimomura and Markoff would have had *legal* access to the cellular communications was in the event they were acting as agents for the federal government or Sprint Cellular. For John Markoff in particular, the question is especially dicey. Had Markoff overstepped the bounds of a journalist as participant observer? After all, it was his front-page stories in the *New York Times* that helped focus international attention on Kevin

Mitnick as criminal computer hacker. Markoff was involved to the extent that he was listed as a victim in an FBI affidavit, alleging his email account had been broken into by Mitnick. (For more information about journalists as participant observers, see Online Journalism on page 122.)

And where is Kevin Mitnick in all of this? He was convicted of breaking into Tsutomu Shimomura's computer, computer systems owned by two California-based Internet service providers, and of illegal possession of telephone access codes. Mitnick has denied in numerous accounts that he broke into Shimomura's computer.

Julio Cesar Ardita

On March 29, 1996, United States Attorney General Janet Reno announced on national television that the Federal Bureau of Investigation had successfully conducted its first "Internet wiretap" resulting in an arrest warrant for Julio Cesar Ardita.

Reno, the FBI, and the Clinton administration were all intent on using the Ardita case to illustrate the U.S. government's need to be able to conduct wiretaps on the Internet.

Several aspects of the story were not immediately reported:

- It is significantly less expensive and more effective to protect vulnerable computers with strong cryptography than to chase hackers.
- The computer hacked by Ardita could have easily been protected with strong cryptography.
- Ardita did virtually nothing to hide his identity or his hacking activities.
- Computer hacking isn't an extraditable crime in Argentina.

- Julio Cedar Ardita, at the time the arrest warrant was issued, was somewhere in Buenos Aires.

The Ardita case is typical of the way mainstream media portray hacking and computer crime incidents. The full story is rarely told and any semblance of fairness is gone as soon as the word "hacker" or "Internet" appear.

An important reason for such unbalanced reporting is that a majority of mainstream journalists simply do not often understand computers, networks, or the dynamic that attracts a hacker.

Computer Fraud and "Federal-Interest Computers"

In 1986, Congress revised Title 18 of the United States Code, Section 1030, empowering the Secret Service and other law enforcement agencies to investigate fraud and related activities in connection with "federal-interest computers." Specific prohibitions are included for:

- Knowingly accessing a computer to obtain certain information, protected for reasons of national security, with intent to injure the United States.

- Intentionally accessing a computer to obtain, without authorization, financial record information from a financial institution.

- Intentionally accessing a computer used exclusively by the United States government.

- Intentionally accessing a computer to affect, without authorization, the government's use of any computer used by the United States government.

- Knowingly and intentionally accessing a federal-interest computer to fraudulently obtain anything of value other than the use of the computer.
- Intentionally accessing a federal-interest computer to alter, damage, or destroy information, or prevent authorized use of any such computer, and thereby:
    - causing a monetary loss of US$1,000 or more; or
    - modifying or impairing a medical examination, medical diagnosis, medical treatment, or the medical care of an individual.
- Knowingly and intentionally accessing a computer to traffic in any password through which a computer can be accessed without authorization, where such trafficking affects interstate or foreign commerce, or such computer is used by or for the Government of the United States.

Terrorist Infrastructure Attacks

In mid-1996, the Clinton administration formed a commission to study the United States' vulnerability to terrorist attacks on the country's digital telecommunications infrastructure. This infrastructure includes the Internet, long distance telephone switches, local telephone service, and ancillary services like the New York Stock Exchange's networked computers.

The President's Commission on Critical Infrastructure Protection released a summary of its classified report in mid-October 1997. The summary stated that the country is unprepared to defend its infrastructure from terrorist attacks. According to the summary, the commission recommends that the country prepare for an attack on critical industries including electrical power, telecommunications, and transportation, among others.

The commission's chair, retired Air Force General Robert Marsh, recommended that government computer systems begin using strong encryption. Because this recommendation came at about the same time the Clinton administration began to realize that its attempt to regulate domestic use of strong cryptography technologies was failing, it is surprising.

The use of strong encryption by American citizens has been hotly debated since the mid-1990s. Various members of the country's law enforcement and intelligence communities have forcefully and consistently contended that allowing the use of unbreakable encryption would enable criminals—including terrorists—to hide their illegal activities. The only acceptable solution, according to law enforcement, is to mandate government possession of all keys needed to decrypt any encrypted communication. (For information on the government's attempt to regulate the domestic use of strong encryption, see Government Cryptography Control on page 246.)

Ironically, the commission's summary strongly suggested that widespread use of strong encryption—in both public and private sectors—is the United States' single best defense against attacks by terrorists and spies. Reportedly, various members of the commission had been pressured to support the FBI's demand for a key recovery or key escrow system. Although the commission ultimately endorsed key recovery, it did so for a very different reason. The commission specified the necessity of such systems to allow the recovery of data by businesses and other organizations in the event of lost encryption keys. The commission specifically did not recommend key recovery for use by law enforcement.

In February 1998, the Pentagon announced that at least eleven of its computer systems had been attacked by a small group of individuals launching a "highly organized and systematic" attack. Deputy Secretary of Defense John Hamre said that only unclassified information had been accessed.

Critics almost immediately began to question Hamre's motivation for releasing information about a series of attacks on the Pentagon's computers, especially any "highly organized and systematic attack." Speculation tended to revolve around Hamre's attempt to garner support for increased funding of the Defense Department.

Until early 1997, any attempt to open a telnet connection to a government system was considered an "attack" on the remote system. Telnet is an Internet protocol used to establish a remote terminal emulation connection to a host over a network. Typing **telnet hostname** at any command-line prompt on a computer connected to a network attempts to open a terminal emulation connection to that host. Upon connection, the user is, in most cases, prompted for a username and password. Most computer and network security experts agree that attempted break-ins are fairly common while successful security breaches are relatively uncommon.

According to reports in the *New York Times* and *Washington Post*, Hamre's announcement was made to a select group of national journalists. Pentagon officials reportedly refused to provide a transcript of the announcement or comment on what was said at the meeting.

Regardless of the level of sophistication of system attacks, most networked organizations regularly employ a technique known as "compartmentalizing" information on any system accessible on the Internet. By isolating—compartmentalizing—sensitive information on those systems that are not connected to any public network, any attack is rendered virtually harmless, even if successful. Any exposure of sensitive information to attacks over a public network would be clearly negligent.

Within two weeks of the Pentagon announcement of systematic attacks on its computer systems, the FBI managed to locate and seize the computer equipment of two teenaged suspects located in Cloverdale, California.

Within days of the FBI's locating the suspects, the Justice Department announced it was creating a government center to crack down on computer intrusion crimes. The center, called the National Infrastructure Protection Center, will initially cost US$64 million to fight computer crime and attacks on the country's infrastructure.

Computer and network security experts were virtually unanimous in dismissing the center as short-sighted and ineffective. *Wired* Magazine's online publishing venture quoted Peter Neumann, SRI International's principle computer scientist as saying, "Perhaps this is a con game. You put out a system with miserable protection and hope that someone breaks it. Then you can ask for millions of dollars more to perform further palliative protections, rather than getting to the core of the problem—significantly ratcheting up the security of the infrastructure."

Most experts agreed that a better approach would be to hold the vendors of software and hardware systems accountable for their products. This could easily be accomplished by changing the law to prohibit vendors from waiving security responsibilities. Today, any liability for security problems is specifically disclaimed by most vendors' license agreements.

Ironically, while the Justice Department is proposing exorbitant spending to make the country's computing and networking infrastructure more secure, it is also telling us that the same systems that are subject to "the most organized and systematic [attacks]… the Pentagon has seen to date" are secure enough to protect the cryptography keys in the key escrow or key recovery system favored by the Clinton administration. (For more information about the Clinton administration's infatuation with key escrow and key recovery, see Government Cryptography Control on page 246.)

At the same time, security experts agree that the overwhelming majority of security breaches are internal, usually the work of a current or former employee. Experts say it's hard to put an exact number on internal security breaches, but most agree that the range is somewhere between 70 percent and 90 percent.

In early February 1998, the Computer Security Institute released its third annual computer crime survey. According to the survey, 64 percent of respondents reported computer security breaches within the past year, an increase of 16 percent over the previous year's survey and a 22 percent increase compared with the original 1996 survey. Almost one-half of the respondents cited the Internet as the most frequent point of attack.

At first glance it would appear that the Computer Security Institute survey contradicts the views of computer and network security experts. Nothing in the survey indicates that the Internet-based attacks were not the work of employees or former employees. In fact, more than two-thirds of the survey respondents said it was "not likely" that attacks were the work of foreign governments or foreign competitors. Almost one-half of the respondents consider U.S. competitors to be a "likely source of attack."

The survey respondents did, however, mention independent hackers as posing significant security threats. The survey questions were provided by the San Francisco office of the FBI's International Computer Crime Squad.

FURTHER...

The simplest yet most effective way to deal with computer crime is to encourage the use of strong cryptography products. Criminals will always be able to use encryption tools, but we will all sleep better knowing we have access to the tools necessary to protect ourselves.

RESOURCES

- California Penal Code: <www.ljextra.com/practice/criminal/calpenal.html>
- Computer Security Institute: <www.gocsi.com>
- FBI Infrastructure Protection Task Force: <www.fbi.gov/programs/iptf/iptf.htm>
- Los Angeles Times: <www.latimes.com>
- Office of Technology Assessment Archives: <www.ota.nap.edu>
- President's Commission on Critical Infrastructure Protection: <www.pccip.gov>

Chapter 10

Cryptography

Soon we will all be using nearly transparent data encryption techniques for everything from electronic mail to digital voice communications. How will law enforcement agencies deal with this? The criminal element in society will be quick to jump on this new technology. Will public policy forbid encrypted communication? Will electronic mail services refuse to accept encrypted messages? Will courts be able to force us to reveal our encryption keys—under what circumstances? Would such disclosure of our encryption keys be considered self-incrimination under the Bill of Rights? Data encryption has the power to render all wiretaps useless. What then?

In order to even begin addressing these questions, we need to understand a little bit about the history of cryptography and how it is currently being used.

The Data Encryption Standard (DES) was developed in the mid-1970s under sponsorship of the National Institute of Standards and Technology (NIST). DES was designed for individual, commercial, and governmental users who did not require military-level encryption. The DES algorithm is conventional in nature; anyone holding the single cryptographic key can encrypt or decrypt messages.

Public key cryptography systems evolved about the same time as DES. Public key systems use a pair of keys—a public key and a private key—and messages encrypted in one key can be decrypted only with the other key. It doesn't matter which key is used for encryption, only that its companion key must be used for decryption. Public keys are widely distributed, allowing messages to be encrypted and decrypted without either originator or recipient ever revealing their private keys.

Digital signatures can be used to "sign" or authenticate an electronic message or document using a public key encryption system like PGP. The recipient is given the digitally signed material and is informed that it came from the originator. The recipient uses the originator's public key to verify the digital signature. If the verification is successful, the recipient knows that the message did, indeed, come from the originator and hasn't been altered in any manner since it left the originator.

Current law in the United States forbids the export of software or hardware products that provide cryptographic protection using keys larger than 40 bits. 40-bit key cryptographic systems have been demonstrated to be vulnerable to attack. In practice, this tends to prevent strong cryptographic tools from being used in the United States as well, since almost all manufacturers find it economically unfeasible to produce two versions of the same product: one with strong cryptography for domestic use and a separate product with weak cryptography for export.

In mid-February 1997, a team of programmers based in Switzerland cracked a 48-bit encryption code in thirteen days in response to a challenge sponsored by cryptography vendor RSA Data Security. Previously, a 40-bit encryption code was cracked in less than four hours by a Berkeley graduate student. The 48-bit encryption code was approximately 256 times more difficult to crack than the 40-bit code because the number of possible key combinations increases by a factor of two for each bit.

In June 1997, a 56-bit encryption code was cracked. By the time you read this, a 64-bit key will likely have been cracked. And so on, and so on. Commonly available public key cryptography systems currently use keys as large as 4,096-bits.

Not content to wait for the U.S. legal system to catch up with technology, RSA Data Security has licensed its strong cryptographic technology to Japan's Nippon Telegraph and Telephone Corporation (NTT). NTT built a strong cryptographic system around RSA technology, based on a two-chip set and began selling the system in early June 1996.

Article 21 of the Japanese Constitution specifically forbids wiretapping and NTT has already sold its chipset to customers in fifteen countries, including the United States. It's reasonable, therefore, to assume that access to strong cryptography is available to virtually anyone on the planet with a computer and an Internet connection.

The NTT system uses a 1,024-bit public key system.

Clipper Chip

In mid-April 1993, President Clinton approved a directive on "Public Encryption Management." The government had developed an encryption microcircuit—the Clipper chip—that was more robust than the then current government standard. The Clipper chip also permitted the escrowing of encryption keys; allowing the government to access encrypted information through the use of an escrowed private key.

Key escrow and key recovery are interchangeable names for a system that allows third party—including government law enforcement and intelligence agencies as well as businesses and other organizations—access to private encrypted communications. Law enforcement and intelligence agencies traditionally demand mandatory key escrow and key recovery systems for all use of strong cryptography tools in the United States. Toward the end of the 1990s, some cryptograph vendors joined in the call for key recovery.

The government generally claims it needs access to encrypted communications to prevent crime and terrorism. Businesses argue they need access to encrypted employee communications to prevent unauthorized encryption by disgruntled employees.

The Clipper chip itself was designed by Mykotronx of Torrance, California. According to the National Institute for Standards and Technology (NIST), the underlying encryption technology had already been developed by the National Security Agency (NSA). President Clinton's public cryptography initiative was built around the NSA technology and the technical specifications of that encryption technology are classified.

President Clinton directed Attorney General Janet Reno to request manufacturers of communications hardware employing encryption to install the Clipper chip in their products. President Clinton stated that his intention was not to prevent other encryption methods from being developed, but also stated, "In making this decision, I do not intend to prevent the private sector from developing, or the government from approving, other microcircuits or algorithms that are equally effective in assuring both privacy and a secure key escrow system." Reasonable readers will deduce that President Clinton intended the key escrow system to be mandatory.

President Clinton went on to say, "The administration is not saying, 'since encryption threatens the public safety and effective law enforcement, we will prohibit it outright' (as some countries have effectively done); nor is the U.S. saying that 'every American, as a matter of right, is entitled to an unbreakable commercial encryption product.'"

With the Clipper chip design, each device that contains the chip would have two private keys deposited in two distinctly separate key escrow databases established by the Attorney General at the time of manufacture. Access to the encryption keys would be limited to government officials with legal wiretap authorization. The two key escrow databases would be controlled by two to-be-determined government agencies.

A second encryption chip, called Capstone, was also under development by the NSA. Capstone is a superset of the Clipper chip, designed to implement the Digital Signature Standard (DSS) to provide authentication through digital signatures.

In April 1993, Computer Professionals for Social Responsibility (CPSR) filed eleven Freedom of Information Act requests for information related to President Clinton's encryption initiative, the Clipper chip itself, and the underlying technology developed by the NSA. CPSR suspected that the NSA and NIST violated the Computer Security Act of 1987, legislation that limits the NSA's role in the development of public encryption technologies to providing "advice and assistance."

The NSA has publicly stated that it had actively developed both the Clipper and Capstone chips.

Pretty Good Privacy

In June 1991, Phil Zimmerman's Pretty Good Privacy (PGP) public key cryptography software was posted to the Internet. PGP almost immediately became the standard cryptographic system used on the Internet. The U.S. government claimed that posting the software to the Internet violated the ban on exporting cryptographic technology and launched an investigation of Zimmerman and his software.

In January 1996, after an extensive four-and-a-half year investigation, federal prosecutors informed Zimmerman's lawyers that the investigation was closed—no charges would be filed.

In early March 1996, bills were introduced in both the House and Senate that would loosen the rules that govern the use and export of cryptographic technology. Sponsored in the Senate by Patrick Leahy (D-Vermont), the legislation would have let businesses and individuals use any kind of encryption system they choose instead of the easily-cracked systems currently mandated by the federal government. A surprise supporting witness of the bill was FBI Director Louis Freeh. Freeh acknowledged that American businesses are put at a disadvantage by the current restrictions and are vulnerable to industrial espionage. Freeh's support was probably a direct result of Leahy's inclusion of support for government key escrow within his bill.

Two months later, in May 1996, competing legislation was introduced in the Senate by Conrad Burns (R-Montana) called the Promotion of Commerce Online in the Digital Era Act. The competing legislation would not only encourage the use of cryptographic technology (like PGP) but would prohibit the implementation of a mandatory key escrow or recovery system. Burns' proposal called for the promotion of electronic commerce, competitiveness among American software companies, the protection of intellectual property, and privacy. Leahy agreed to endorse the Burns bill, including the provision that would specifically prevent the creation of a government key escrow system.

Shortly thereafter, the U.S. State Department distributed a warning to several domestic companies producing software designed to make PGP easier to use.These domestic products make PGP easier to use but they do not contain cryptographic technology in themselves. The companies were warned not to export their software products even though the products contained no cryptographic elements. Companies ignoring the warning, according to the State Department, could be prosecuted under the federal arms export restrictions.

Specifically, Sunnyvale, California-based Network TeleSystems was warned by the State Department not to export an email program the company was developing because it contained PGP "hooks" that make it easier to send and receive encrypted email messages. At the same time, San Diego-based Qualcomm, Inc. received State Department export approval for its Eudora 3.0 email product that also has hooks for external programs. The difference? Eudora's hooks are not PGP-specific.

In a situation similar to Phil Zimmerman's, University of Illinois-Chicago research professor Daniel Bernstein fought long and hard against the United States government for his right to post his cryptography research to the Internet. On December 6, 1996, U.S. Northern California District Court Judge Marilyn Hall Patel ruled that the government's restriction of Bernstein's distribution of his research on the Internet was unconstitutional. Judge Patel found that the U.S. State Department exercised prior restraint on Bernstein's speech when, in 1992, it labeled his cryptography research a "munition" under export law and required Bernstein to obtain an export license.

While Judge Patel's ruling protects computer software source code as a form of speech, commercial cryptography programs are still considered to be a munition and subject to the State Department's export license requirement. Computer software *source* code is considered a form of speech, but computer software *object* code (the actual software program that you run on your computer) is not. This is roughly analogous to allowing the use of the alphabet, but prohibiting the speech produced by using the alphabet.

In early December 1997, PGP, the company Phil Zimmerman formed to sell commercial versions of his widely used cryptography software, was sold to Network Associates, Inc. for US$35 million. At first blush, one would have to cheer Phil Zimmerman's fortune: for years he was harassed by various agencies of the U.S. government and never knew from one day to the next whether he would face criminal charges. On closer examination, however, the acquisition is problematic for users of the popular cryptography program. Phil Zimmerman actively campaigned against any sort of key escrow or key recovery system proposed by the government and testified before Congress that key recovery would "strengthen the hand of a police state."

Network Associates, on the other hand, has actively promoted nearly any incarnation of key escrow and key recovery. Network Associates is a member of the Key Recovery Alliance, a trade association with about sixty corporate members that lobbies for mandatory key escrow and key recovery systems that would allow businesses to recover the cryptographic keys of employees used to make information private. Zimmerman carries the title of "fellow" at Network Associates, but as of this writing it is too soon to tell what responsibilities he will have at the company.

Some high technology companies, such as Network Associates, support key recovery because it would allow them to export products that contain elements of strong cryptography that are currently forbidden. The Commerce Department prohibits the export of products that contain strong cryptography unless the manufacturer promises to develop key recovery features.

Within months of the PGP acquisition, Network Associates had resigned its membership in the Key Recovery Alliance, under pressure from Zimmerman and other PGP principals. In an apparent contradiction to Phil Zimmerman's philosophy, the most recent version of PGP for Business Security—release 5.5.5 as of this writing—includes an option that allows employers to retain a "master" key that can be used to access any employee's encrypted materials. PGP for Business Security ships with its key recovery option disabled by default. Some corporate users support the option for key recovery because it would allow them to recover encrypted information when an employee leaves the organization.

At a cryptography conference in February 1998, Zimmerman defended the inclusion of the key recovery option in the PGP software:

> "Right now, a subpoena can be used to get at a recipient's key, and there are a variety of ways to get the plaintext content of a message. In the grand scheme of things, I think our solution doesn't affect the outcome of any investigation."

Two months after Network Associates resigned its membership in the Key Recovery Alliance, the company acquired Trusted Information Systems for more than US$300 million and announced that it would probably rejoin the Key Recovery Alliance. Trusted Information Systems makes RecoverKey, a software product that allows corporations to escrow the private keys of employees. Trusted Information Systems has major consulting engagements with U.S. government agencies, especially in the intelligence sector and specifically with the National Security Agency.

Some privacy advocates view this turn of events as indicative of Phil Zimmerman's reduced status and level of responsibility within the Network Associates corporate hierarchy, although Zimmerman staunchly continues to defend Network Associates and the "master" key functionality of his PGP software.

In late February 1998, Network Associates announced that it would integrate RecoverKey, the Trusted Information Systems key recovery system, into its corporate security products, including PGP for Business Security. Network Associates said it would not, however, use the RecoverKey or any other key recovery technology in its PGP for Personal Privacy product targeted for use by individuals.

(For information about using the PGP software, see Using Pretty Good Privacy on page 276.)

National Research Council Cryptography Report

In late May 1996, a report prepared for the National Research Council of the National Academy of Sciences called for the United States government to immediately relax export controls on cryptography and let industry set data security standards. The report, which was commissioned by Congress, directly opposed existing Clinton administration proposals and called for businesses to adopt technologies to prevent illegal wiretapping of computer data, telephone, cellular, and other electronic communications.

Specifically, the report takes issue with Clinton administration efforts to require the use of a key escrow system that would let law enforcement and intelligence agencies unlock encrypted information.

Recanting the position of U.S. law enforcement agencies—that cryptography makes it easier for criminals to conceal their activities from law enforcement—the report specifically notes that cryptography would help prevent crime by shielding electronic communications and transactions from criminals.

Government Cryptography Control

In the early 1990s, the Clinton administration proposed using a key escrow system to enable government to have access to information encrypted by American citizens. An appropriate court order would be required to recover the key(s) necessary to decrypt a suspect message, but control of secure communication would be removed from the citizenry. With the proposed key escrow system, users of encryption technologies would be required to deposit a key to access their information to an authorized third party, certified by the government.

President Clinton's key escrow system was met with disdain by industry experts and privacy advocates, who mostly focused on the Orwellian nature of the system's intrusiveness. Law enforcement officials, on the other hand, were quick to support the plan because it would allow them easy access to information that might prove useful in solving crimes.

In the meantime, government agencies began encrypting their own information. By mid-1997, the Clinton administration was faced squarely with the dilemma of not only who gets the keys, but the more important problem of who *decides* who gets the keys. In a pilot program that implemented key recovery systems in ten federal agencies, all ten participating agencies eliminated the centralized key registry. It's clear that federal agencies—just like citizens—don't want anyone else to have control over their cryptography keys.

Security and Freedom Through Encryption Act

In 1992 the Federal Bureau of Investigation announced its Digital Telephony Proposal. The proposal would require the design of all telephone switching equipment to include technology that would allow authorized wiretapping. Telephone companies would have a year and a half to comply with the proposal. Organizations that operated private branch exchange (PBX) equipment would be allowed three years to bring their equipment within compliance. All of the costs inherent in adding the eavesdropping technology would be borne solely by the manufacturing companies and organizations. (For information about wiretapping, see Wiretapping on page 166.)

The FBI asserted that technological advances, such as cellular telephone service and call forwarding features, had made it much more difficult to obtain results from authorized wiretaps. When pressed to provide evidence supporting these claims, the agency was unable to do so. In fact, a Freedom of Information Act suit filed by Computer Professionals for Social Responsibility revealed no known instance of a failed wiretap as a result of any new telecommunications technology.

Most government agencies and both houses of Congress opposed the FBI proposal. No Congressional sponsor came forward in support of the FBI proposal. Interestingly, another Freedom of Information Act action—this one initiated by the Electronic Privacy Information Center (EPIC)—uncovered internal FBI memos that indicated the law enforcement agency itself gave the proposal less than 3:1 odds of being adopted.

What seemed to matter to the FBI wasn't whether or not its proposal was adopted. What apparently mattered to the FBI was that its position—that wiretapping was essential to effective law enforcement—be adopted. However, the overwhelming majority of the American citizenry disapproved (and continues to disapprove) of most wiretapping efforts.

Traditionally, the question of use regarding wiretaps has been very slippery. In the late 1960s, wiretapping was proposed as a way to target gambling and put a dent in organized crime. In the late 1970s through the mid-1980s—after gambling had been legalized in every region of the country—the wiretapping target shifted to investigations surrounding illegal drugs.

The FBI maintained its anti-strong cryptography position throughout the 1990s. In September 1997, the agency redoubled its effort to challenge any legislation that would relax controls on strong cryptography tools. The FBI's modified proposal would mandate a digital surveillance system capable of allowing real-time access to all encrypted communications. The updated proposal would require all encryption products to have a key recovery feature, including products sold in the domestic market. This is a reversal of previous positions held by the law enforcement community that sought restrictions only on products intended for export.

The latest FBI proposal is seen by privacy advocates as a direct attempt to undermine the Security and Freedom Through Encryption (SAFE) Act, sponsored by Representative Robert Goodlatte (R-Virginia). The SAFE Act would relax current export controls on encryption technology and would prohibit any mandatory domestic key recovery or key escrow system. The SAFE Act was passed by the House International Relations and Judiciary committees in the summer of 1997 and attracted more than 250 co-sponsors.

Around the same time, the Clinton administration modified its position on strong domestic cryptography to support a voluntary key recovery system.

Within days of the FBI's push for cryptography restrictions, and after classified briefings, the House National Security Committee voted to strengthen, rather than relax, export restrictions on encryption technology. On a 45-to-1 vote, the committee added an amendment—proposed by Representative Curt Weldon (R-Pennsylvania) and Representative Ronald Dellums (D-California)—to the SAFE Act that would grant the President and the Secretary of Defense control over cryptography exports. The only opposing vote was made by Representative Adam Smith (D-Washington).

Many political observers criticized the FBI's demand of instantaneous decryption of secure communications. The consensus was perhaps summed up best by Jerry Berman, the director for the Center for Democracy and Technology: "[The FBI's proposal] is not the first step towards the surveillance society; it is the surveillance society."

The classified national-security briefings by the law enforcement and intelligence communities have become notorious for reversing the strong cryptography positions of America's political representatives. Those who have participated in the presentations refer to them simply as "The Briefing." Representative Patrick Kennedy (D-Rhode Island) was widely quoted shortly after the House National Security Committee vote as saying, "I'll tell you, I attended one of those classified briefings by the National Security Agency, and I could not be more impressed with the threat to national security posed to our men and women in uniform. What this bill will end up doing is overwhelm our national security."

Two days after the House National Security Committee vote, the House Select Committee on Intelligence voted to support the FBI's proposal to restrict strong cryptography technology. The National Security Committee has no jurisdiction over the key escrow aspects of the FBI proposal, but the Select Committee on Intelligence does—and it used that jurisdiction to propose the establishment of the first governmental controls on the use of strong cryptography tools within the borders of the United States by American citizens.

One of the proposed changes to Representative Goodlatte's original SAFE Act would specifically make it illegal to make or sell any strong encryption product without a trap door for law enforcement: "After 31 January 2000, it shall be unlawful for any person to manufacture for distribution, distribute, or import encryption products intended for sale or use in the United States, unless that product includes features or functions that provide an immediate access to plaintext capability."

Civil libertarians, privacy advocates, and technologists were all dumbfounded at the momentum the FBI, and its director Louis Freeh, managed to amass. Three months earlier, the SAFE proposal had more than 250 co-sponsors and was virtually assured of passage. Now it had been turned completely on its head.

Representative Porter Goss (R-Florida), when quoted in the *New York Times*, cast some light on The Briefing cited by many committee members as the reason for changing their votes:

> "American citizens have a right to their privacy and their access to the freest possible markets. But they also have a right to their safety and security. Terrorist groups that plot to blow up buildings, drug cartels that seek to poison our children and those who proliferate in deadly chemical and biological weapons are all formidable opponents of peace and security in the global society. These bad actors must know that the United States' law enforcement and national security agencies, working under proper oversight, will have the tools to frustrate."

Because The Briefing is classified, attendees are sworn to secrecy. But several representatives have questioned the secretive nature of the briefings and their very necessity. "There is nothing being said that couldn't be or hasn't been said in public. But in closed meetings, misleading statements aren't always corrected," said Representative Zoe Lofgren (D-California), a cosponsor of the original SAFE Act.

A 1996 National Research Council report questioned the compelling nature of The Briefing. Reportedly, the authors of the report were exposed to the same information as Briefing attendees, yet felt the issue could be discussed publicly—without compromising either the information or the source of the information. The National Research Council report concluded that domestic controls on strong cryptography were unnecessary and, perhaps more importantly, that wiretapping technologies should be proven effective before they are adopted.

With regard to the specifics of the proposed measure passed by the House Select Committee on Intelligence, privacy advocates, civil libertarians, and software manufacturers all likened the domestic cryptography provisions to being required to turn over your spare house key to the FBI. Jerry Berman, executive director of the Center for Democracy and Technology, was widely quoted as saying, "This one would have to be available to the FBI and they could use it without you knowing about it. This is setting up a massive bureaucracy. It is setting up a whole search and seizure regime where there is no notice."

Because The Briefing held by the law enforcement and intelligence communities is classified, we'll never know how a piece of legislation designed to enhance American citizens' privacy—through the creation and use of strong cryptography tools—was turned on its head. Nor will we likely ever know how the original proposal, prohibiting any type of mandatory domestic key recovery system, morphed into requiring such a system.

The final nail in the SAFE Act's coffin was seemingly hammered by two members of the House Commerce Committee. Within a day of the House Select Committee on Intelligence vote to gut SAFE, two members of the Commerce Committee announced they were prepared to follow suit. An amendment authored by Representative Tom Manton (D-New York), a former New York City police officer, and Representative Michael Oxley (R-Ohio), a former FBI agent, would ban the production and use of encryption technology that precluded immediate access by law enforcement officials.

Oxley, the former FBI agent, was obviously privy to The Briefing at the hands of the law enforcement and intelligence communities. He was quoted at length in the *New York Times*: "Indeed, I would find it difficult to believe that a member who heard the briefing could walk away not committed to addressing security issues. Frankly, I wish everyone interested in this issue could have heard for themselves the alarming briefing that members of our committee heard."

Somewhat surprisingly, Assistant Commerce Secretary William Reinsch spoke out against the various House amendments and FBI director Louis Freeh—even though Reinsch currently supports both restraints on strong cryptography exports and a national key recovery system.

Computer Professionals for Social Responsibility identified six key problems with the proposed legislation:

1. Bans on strong cryptography products are violations of free speech. More specifically, courts have already ruled that encryption is a constitutionally protected form of communication (Bernstein v. U.S. State Department).

2. All current Internet sites would be required to purchase compliant systems.

3. Restricting the export of strong cryptography tools will not benefit law enforcement since strong encryption tools already exist outside of the United States.

4. Restricting the export of strong cryptography tools seriously hurts the competitiveness of American technology vendors.

5. The technology required to comply with the proposed legislation has never been tested.

6. The proposed legislation unduly expands the powers of the government and would eliminate the probable cause requirement for legal wiretaps.

Within a week of the announcement of the Oxley-Manton amendment to the SAFE Act, a group of more than twenty-five law professors wrote an open letter to the members of the House Commerce Committee. The letter expressed alarm at the unconstitutional nature of the proposed legislation, citing the government's unprecedented attempt to monopolize a single form of communication and to require "a license to exercise the right to speak."

Obviously the law professors had not been subjected to The Briefing.

Ironically, the Defense Department insists that strong encryption technologies are crucial for its responsibility to protect both the Internet and American citizens. Similarly, members of the President's Commission on Critical Infrastructure Protection have privately expressed concern about the ability to protect the keys held in any key recovery or key escrow system. According to a *New York Times* report, however, several members of the commission have said they have been ordered to follow the FBI's lead with regard to a key recovery system.

On September 24, 1997 the House Commerce Committee surprisingly rejected the FBI-backed proposal with a 35–16 vote, leaving the SAFE Act, as originally proposed by Representative Robert Goodlatte (R-Virginia), intact. Specifically, the Oxley-Manton amendment that would have required a key recovery system for domestic cryptography was defeated.

Representative Michael Oxley (D-Ohio), the former FBI agent, predictably beat a dead horse while simultaneously showing his ignorance of the very nature of strong cryptography. He was widely quoted as stating, "law abiding citizens have no reason to fear this" and "If these cryptographers are so smart, why don't they invent some decryption devices for law enforcement?"

A provision of the bill, as adopted by the Commerce Committee, would establish a National Encryption Technology Center (NET Center) within the Department of Justice that would work to decrypt encrypted materials used in crimes. Another provision called for a six-month study of the impact of mandatory key escrow by the department of Commerce's National Telecommunications Information Agency. The provision doubled the criminal penalties—to ten years imprisonment—for the use of strong encryption in the commission of a felony. Yet another provision of the bill would require a five-member panel of representatives from government, industry, and law enforcement to study the issues and make recommendations within a year and a half.

If nothing else, one thing that became apparent after the four-hour argument in the House Commerce Committee was just how cleanly the privacy advocates and the key recovery advocates cleaved. The vast majority of those seeking to impose strict controls on strong cryptography work for the government, while most of those seeking to make encryption technology available to the American citizenry work in the private sector.

FBI director Louis Freeh, clearly articulated the government's position when he testified before a Congressional committee in September 1997, saying, "All of law enforcement is also in total agreement on one aspect of encryption. The widespread use of uncrackable encryption will devastate our ability to fight crime and prevent terrorism."

But just how accurate is this statement?

By late October 1997, it was clear that the tide was turning against the FBI's position on domestic encryption. Senate majority leader Trent Lott (R-Mississippi) called the FBI's attempt to regulate domestic use of strong cryptography tools "simply wrong." Lott went on to suggest clearly that any attempt to control the use of encryption by American citizens was probably unconstitutional.

In an October 21, 1997 letter to President Clinton, Lott wrote:

> "The FBI wants to require that any company that produces or offers encryption security products or services guarantee immediate access to plain text information without the knowledge of the user. Their proposal would subject software companies and telecommunications providers to prison sentences for failure to guarantee immediate access to all information on the desktop computers of all Americans. That would move us into an entirely new world of surveillance, a very in-

> trusive surveillance, where every communication by every individual can be accessed by the FBI."
>
> "Where is probable cause? Why has the FBI assumed that all Americans are going to be involved in criminal activities? Where is the Constitution?"
>
> "While we are restricting our own international commerce, foreign companies are now manufacturing and selling stronger, more desirable encryption systems, including the top-end 128-bit systems, anywhere in the world they want. Clearly, our policy doesn't make sense."

Lott had good bit of technological coaching in drafting his letter, acknowledging the influence of Jim Barksdale, CEO and president of Netscape Communications.

Secure Public Networks Act

Meanwhile, the Senate, learning from the House's missteps, tried a different tack. Instead of trying to use The Briefing to beat the opposition into submission, the Senate decided to try an old reliable: "bribery."

The Secure Public Networks Act, introduced in mid-June 1997 by Senators John McCain (R-Arizona) and Bob Kerrey (D-Nebraska), would provide commercial incentives for participating in domestic key recovery. The proposed legislation would also establish a system of key certificate authorities who would be authorized by the government to hold encryption keys.

This bill was designed to derail competing legislation that would loosen government encryption policy, specifically the Security and Freedom Through Encryption (SAFE) Act, proposed by Representative Robert Goodlatte (R-Virginia) and Pro-CODE, proposed by Senators Conrad Burns (R-Montana) and

Patrick Leahy (D-Vermont). Both SAFE and Pro-CODE would ban mandatory key recovery systems.

Under the Secure Public Networks Act, fifteen new federal crimes dealing with encryption technology and key recovery would be created, with penalties of up to five years in prison. The bill would also reinforce the Clinton administration's policy of limiting encryption exports to no stronger than 56-bit keys, a key length that was cracked in mid-June 1997.

The bill would make key recovery mandatory for all products purchased by the government, and for any product used over any network even partially funded by the federal government. Law enforcement would need only a simple subpoena to access private keys; current federal regulations require a court order.

Perhaps more importantly, the McCain-Kerrey Secure Public Networks Act would, for the first time, tie digital signature certificates to the key recovery system and put digital signature certificate licensing under the auspices of the United States government. Digital signature certificates establish and verify the identity of the author of an encrypted communication message or electronic document and are a crucial part of electronic commerce (ecommerce). The proposed legislation would prohibit an individual from obtaining a digital signature certificate without storing their private key with a government-authorized third party.

Privacy advocates oppose the legislation as a violation of the basic right to keep one's personal communications and papers private. Not only would the bill mandate government-approved key recovery systems, it would allow law enforcement agencies access to cryptographic keys without a search warrant, requiring only a subpoena.

In mid-January 1998, Senator John Ashcroft (D-Missouri) announced that he would convene hearings before the Senate Judiciary subcommittee to discuss Constitutional issues regarding the encryption debate. Critics of the government's position on strong cryptography have consistently argued that limiting the use of strong encryption tools violates the First (free speech) and Fourth (freedom from unreasonable search and seizure) Amendments of the U.S. Constitution.

Senator Ashcroft made his announcement via satellite address to a cryptography conference. "While national security and law enforcement ought to be discussed," Ashcroft stated, "the discussion clearly should include the public interest in privacy, the business interest in privacy, and the interest in the public and business community about unlawful search and seizure in the Bill of Rights," the Missouri Democrat concluded.

Representative Robert Goodlatte (R-Virginia), author of the original Security and Freedom Through Encryption (SAFE) Act also addressed the cryptography conference by satellite. Goodlatte pointed out that strong cryptography is needed to fight crime, turning the tables on the law enforcement and intelligence communities and putting an anti-crime spin on the pro-encryption position.

PRESIDENT CLINTON'S MARKET-DRIVEN APPROACH

Having seen all attempts to mandate a key recovery or key escrow system defeated—sometimes narrowly and sometimes roundly—the Clinton administration set off on an entirely new tack in early October 1997. Apparently abandoning its demand for a mandatory key recovery system, the Clinton administration began to take a market-driven approach.

The Clinton administration's new market-driven concept is simple. Although key recovery will not be mandatory, the United States government will begin purchasing new technology that will only communicate with key recovery systems. If you want to communicate securely with any government agency, you'll have to use an encryption system that allows key recovery.

"If private parties want, they can ignore key recovery," said Assistant Commerce Secretary William Reinsch, "unless they want to communicate with us in an encrypted fashion."

This approach is reminiscent of the government's attempt to seed the Clipper chip market by purchasing Clipper-chip enabled telephones (which were just about the only Clipper-chip telephones purchased at all).

While the Clinton administration was waiting for the other shoe to drop, the European Commission flatly rejected proposals that would ensure American law enforcement agency access to encrypted material transmitted over telephone and computer networks. According to the European Commission view, the United States' electronic cryptography plans would:

1. Threaten privacy and weaken existing European data-privacy laws.
2. Stifle electronic commerce. Strong encryption is currently produced by more than 840 companies.
3. Be ineffective; hackers would simply find new ways to override any limitations and criminals would use existing strong encryption options.
4. Prevent law-abiding companies and citizens from protecting themselves from criminal attacks and economic damage from industrial espionage, credit-card fraud, cellular telephone fraud, etc.

The Clinton administration's response was as predictable as it was transparent (and amusing). It was also rudely U.S.-centric: "I am a little surprised," said Assistant Commerce Secretary William Reinsch. "My question to the European Commission is, where do they think the market is going? Our sense is that corporations engaged in electronic commerce want key recovery in some form, because they want to recover their own records and to monitor their own employees."

The Clinton administration hasn't completely abandoned its attempts to demand a centralized key recovery system, however. On November 5, 1997, the President's Commission on Critical Infrastructure Protection (commonly referred to as President Clinton's commission on cyber-terrorism) released a report that recommended mandatory key recovery that would allow the decryption of encrypted messages by law enforcement agencies with the appropriate court order.

Robert Marsh, a retired Air Force general, is chair of President Clinton's cyber-terrorism commission. Marsh testified before a Senate panel that same day, saying that if a voluntary key recovery plan didn't work, a mandatory system would be necessary. Marsh was asked by Senator Jon Kyl (R-Arizona)—the chair of the Senate Judiciary Committee's Subcommittee on Technology, Terrorism and Government Information—if mandatory key recovery was necessary. Marsh responded, "We think businessmen will find it in their best interest to incorporate these controls. Of course, in due time, [mandated key recovery] may be an option if they are not willing to accept them." In other words, if they don't make the proper choice, we'll be forced to make it for them.

Not content with recommending that American citizens be required to submit their encryption keys to the government, the President's commission on cyber-terrorism also recommended exemptions to the Freedom of Information Act. Specifically, the commission said in its report, effective protection of the United State's infrastructure—including telecommunications, energy, and other "core services"—requires that currently unclassified information related to infrastructure be classified and exempted from FOIA requests. FOIA became effective on July 4, 1967 and was strengthened in 1974, largely as a result of Watergate. In 1996, FOIA was expanded to include electronic documents.

The commission on cyber-terrorism report recommends that a new bureaucracy—the Office of National Infrastructure Assurance—be created within the president's National Security

Council. The new office would determine what infrastructure information should be classified. Many found it disturbing that the proposed agency would have an unprecedented reach within government, "coordinating cyber-support to existing and planned decision-making processes in the law enforcement, national security, counter-terrorism, and intelligence areas," according to the commission's report. Critics railed that the proposal would make government even less accountable for its activities in these areas.

In response to President Clinton's less dogmatic approach to mandatory key escrow, an alliance of high technology companies was established to wage its own public relations battle in the great American cryptography wars. The alliance, named Americans for Computer Privacy, formed in February 1998 to make the average American citizen aware of the dangers inherent in government- or corporate-controlled key escrow and key recovery. The organization's stated goal is legislation that will remove export restrictions on strong cryptography and prohibit mandatory key escrow or key recovery.

Jack Quinn, the alliance's legal advisor and a former counsel to President Clinton, was widely quoted as succinctly stating the Americans for Computer Privacy position: "I think people will understand that the FBI director's [Louis Freeh] proposal for domestic encryption controls is really like asking them to make a duplicate of their front door key and leave it at the post office in case he wants to get inside."

Another analogy that Americans for Computer Privacy likes to use is that of the PIN code associated with your ATM card. Imagine if you had to provide your ATM card's PIN code to the government so it could check on your bank account balance from time to time, without your permission or knowledge.

Other analogies include having to keep a spare key to your front door at the local police station and government installation of surveillance cameras in your home, with a promise that they wouldn't be used unless it became necessary to investigate an alleged crime. Americans for Computer Privacy believes examples like these are immediately understood by the citizenry.

The Americans for Computer Privacy organization is led by Ed Gillespie, a former communications director for the Republican National Committee and spokesperson for the Republican Contract with America. More than twenty-five trade organizations—both inside and outside of the technology industry—and more than seventy corporations have joined the organization. Members of Congress supporting strong cryptography without key escrow include Senators John Ashcroft (R-Missouri), Conrad Burns (R-Montana), Patrick Leahy (D-Vermont). Also lending their support to the alliance are Representatives Sam Gejdenson (D-Connecticut), Robert Goodlatte (R-Virginia), Zoe Lofgren (D-California), and Rick White (R-Washington).

The Americans for Computer Privacy coalition's financial backers are heavy-hitters in the high-technology industry—including Microsoft, Oracle, Netscape, the Software Publishers Association, and the Business Software Alliance—who managed to raise about US$15 million before the organization was even officially announced.

Privacy advocates and civil liberties organizations are working with the Americans for Computer Privacy group but will not likely join the organization. At the Americans for Computer Privacy launch in early March 1998, the American Civil Liberties Union, the Electronic Frontier Foundation, and the Electronic Privacy Information Center, released a prepared statement in support of the alliance's goals.

The same day Americans for Computer Privacy formally announced its existence, Vice President Al Gore sent a letter to Senator Tom Daschle (D-South Dakota), Senate Democrat leader, stating that the administration wanted to address the cryptography question through cooperation with industry, not legislation.

In mid-March 1998 both the Clinton administration and the FBI appeared to have retreated—at least temporarily—from mandatory key escrow.

On March 17, 1998, Robert Litt, the principal associate deputy attorney general, told the Senate Judiciary subcommittee on the Constitution that the Clinton administration was interested in finding a cooperative solution to the debate surrounding the use of strong cryptography. "We are all looking at this point not to impose mandatory legislation and will work cooperatively with industry to find whatever solutions are available," Litt testified. Litt also indicated that he was representing the FBI position when he was questioned on the matter by Senator Russell Feingold (D-Wisconsin). "The Administration is not wedded to key recovery, or any single technological approach. We are flexible, provided that the resulting solutions and arrangements preserve the nation's ability to protect the public safety and defend our national security," continued Litt.

Clearly hedging the administration's bets, Litt emphasized repeatedly that his testimony is representative of the Clinton administration and FBI positions "at this time" and would surely change if pro-encryption legislation was offered that would prohibit any type of mandatory key escrow or key recovery.

Most privacy advocates remained skeptical of any basic position shift by the Clinton administration or the FBI. A *voluntary* key escrow solution that would create a *de-facto* key recovery standard is a central provision of the Clinton administration-crafted Secure Public Networks Act. The act was sponsored by Senators Bob Kerrey (D-Nebraska) and John McCain (R-Arizona) in mid-June 1997. (For more information, see Secure Public Networks Act on page 256.)

In a surprising move, Network Associates announced on March 19, 1998 that it would bypass U.S. export restrictions on strong cryptography and allow its Dutch subsidiary to sell an international version of the company's Pretty Good Privacy (PGP) encryption product. The international version of the software does not include any kind of key escrow or key recovery facility and is said to have been developed independently by a group of cryptographers at Switzerland's Cnlab Software. At the time of this writing (early July 1998), the U.S. government had not determined whether Network Associates had violated any U.S. law but were actively investigating the situation. (For more information about PGP, see Pretty Good Privacy on page 241; for information about using PGP, see Using Pretty Good Privacy on page 276.)

To add insult to injury, On March 25, 1998 the Electronic Privacy Information Center (EPIC) obtained a November 1996 government memo in which Assistant Commerce Secretary William Reinsch acknowledged that key recovery systems were considered to be "costly and less efficient" by non-American users. Reinsch was clear in his November 1996 memo to other government officials:

> "Police forces are reluctant to use 'escrowed' encryption products (such as radios in patrol cars). They are more costly and less efficient than non-escrowed products. There can be long gaps in reception due to the escrow features—sometimes as long as a ten second pause. Our own police do not use recoverable encryption products; they buy the same non-escrowable products used by their counterparts in Europe and Japan,"

Ironically, the President's Commission on Critical Infrastructure Protection released a summary of its classified report in October 1997, strongly suggesting that *widespread use of strong encryption is the United States' single best defense against attacks by terrorists and spies*. (For more information about the Commission and its summary, see Terrorist Infrastructure Attacks on page 231.)

The appropriate solution seems almost painfully obvious to an informed observer. Use of strong cryptography by American citizens should be encouraged as a front-line crime prevention measure. Simultaneously, severe mandatory sentences should be imposed on anyone who uses strong cryptography in the commission of a felony.

Authentication and Digital Signatures

In the ongoing feud between the government and privacy advocates, the one thing that gets lost is the common ground on digital signatures. Both sides agree that verified authentication—the ability to determine that you are who you say you are or that I am who I say I am—is a crucial part of electronic commerce. What government apparently forgets at times, however, is that *verified authentication is best accomplished through strong, non-escrowed, public key cryptography.*

United States bankers have requested a federal law to standardize digital signatures and at least thirty-six states have enacted some sort of legislation covering digital signatures. Bankers have pointed out that there are currently more than 1.1 million online banking users in America and that number is expected to grow to 2.1 million users in the United States (about forty million worldwide) by the new millennium.

Senator Bob Bennett (R-Utah), chair of the Senate Banking subcommittee on Financial Services and Technology, introduced legislation that would standardize all authentication technologies, including digital signatures. Bennett's bill will probably reopen the great American cryptography wars.

FURTHER...

Now that we know the threats and dangers inherent in an information eclipse we might again ask ourselves the same questions posed at the beginning of this chapter. Next, let's take a look at some specific actions we can all take to protect ourselves.

RESOURCES

- Americans for Computer Privacy: <www.computerprivacy.org>
- Center for Democracy and Technology: <www.cdt.org>
- Computer Professionals for Social Responsibility (CPSR): <www.cpsr.org>
- Computer Security Act of 1987: <www.rdc.noaa.gov/~security/csa-1987.html>
- Electronic Privacy Information Center (EPIC): <www.epic.org>
- Federal Bureau of Investigation (FBI): <www.fbi.gov>
- Freedom of Information Act (FOIA): <www.seas.gwu.edu/nsarchive/nsa/foia.html>
- Key Recovery Alliance: <www.kra.org>
- Mykotronx: <www.rnbo.com/mykoweb/index.htm>
- National Academy of Sciences: <www.nas.edu>
- National Institute for Standards and Technology (NIST): <www.nist.gov>

- National Research Council: <www.nas.edu/nrc/>
- National Security Agency (NSA): <www.nsa.gov>
- Network TeleSystems: <www.nts.com>
- Nippon Telegraph and Telephone (NTT): <www.ntt.co.jp>
- President's Commission on Critical Infrastructure Protection: <www.pccip.gov>
- Pretty Good Privacy (PGP): <www.nai.com/default_pgp.asp>
- Qualcomm, Inc.: <www.qualcomm.com>
- RSA Data Security: <www.rsa.com>
- Security and Freedom Through Encryption (SAFE): <www.house.gov/goodlatte/encryption.htm>
- Secure Public Networks Act: <www.senate.gov/~kerrey/inits/encrypt/encrypt1.html>
- Senate Judiciary Committee: <www.senate.gov/committee/judiciary.html>
- State Digital Signature Legislation: <www.steptoe.com/digsig.htm>
- Trusted Information Systems: <www.tis.com>

CHAPTER

11

IN REAL LIFE...

What can we, as American citizens, do to maintain a modicum of control over—and privacy in—our work and personal lives? We can begin by applying the following real life tips and information. When you find or develop more of your own, be sure to share them with me.

1. Giving your social security number to anyone, unless it is absolutely required, is reckless. When you have doubts about providing your social security number, ask the inquirer to be specific about the need for the information. Also ask what other agencies or businesses the information will be shared with, and with whom the information might be shared in the future. Government benefits cannot be denied for refusal to provide a social security

number. Some states still use your social security number as your drivers license number. This is unconscionable, but you don't have much choice if you want to drive.

2. With any request for information, decide whether or not you are prepared to release that information to every individual, organization, or business that has contact with the inquirer. That universe of "networking" is much bigger than any of us could ever imagine.

3. Your credit card is at less risk for abuse when you use it to make purchases on-line than when your waiter disappears with it in your favorite restaurant. Which do you think is easier—capturing a valid credit card number from a diner or decoding an encrypted on-line transaction? While you might want to make a point of retrieving your credit card as quickly as possible in restaurants you do not frequent regularly, you do not need to be afraid of transacting business on-line. Hopefully, restaurants and waiters will also become more sensitive to this fact and provide "quick" check out solutions for their clientele while protecting patron's cards.

4. Consumers are not obligated to disclose their zip code or telephone number when making a purchase with a credit card.

5. Cookie technology enables your Web browser software to create a record of the Web sites you visit, as well as the specific pages you click through (access) at each site—called the "clickstream." Cookies can be used for malevolent purposes, such as surreptitiously surveilling your browsing habits in order to construct a digital dossier on your interests without your knowledge or consent. But cookies can also be used to make your Web browsing expe-

rience more efficient, such as maintaining login identification and password information. Arts & Farces *internet* (the Arts & Farces Web site), for example, uses cookies to maintain the contents of your shopping basket during an ecommerce session. At the end of the session, however, the cookie expires. Reputable Web sites state specifically what they use cookie technology for and usually publish an explicit privacy policy. Current versions of Web browser software allow you to refuse cookies on a site-by-site basis. Use this feature to refuse cookies from any site that doesn't clearly state its policies.

6. Ask your political representatives to strengthen the Telephone Consumer Protection Act of 1991 to curb excessive telemarketing calls. Telemarketing calls are too easily abused to procure information regarding your household by stealthy individuals, businesses, and even criminals.

7. Teach your young children to use the telephone responsibly. It's alarming how many children use the telephone as a toy, dialing random numbers in an attempt to emulate adult behavior. Dialing random numbers can be dangerous for children. Teach your children very early (they will learn best by your example) to immediately identify themselves when placing a call *and to expect incoming callers to do the same*. This is simple telephone etiquette, yet it is surprising to observe the number of otherwise well-mannered individuals and professionals who fail to exercise this simple courtesy.

8. Try to determine the true purpose of all telemarketing calls. If you are not immediately aware of the caller's purpose, by all means interrupt to inquire (it is *your* time a caller is spending, after all). Are

the questions being asked true to that purpose? If not, politely—but firmly—end the call.

9. Be aware of the manner in which you answer your telephone. It's entirely appropriate to answer anonymous requests such as "what number is this?" with a simple, "what number did you dial, please?"

10. The telephone book lists your street address. The county registrar of deeds holds the assessed valuation and the amount of tax on the property for that address—and it is public information. Determine whether it's in your interest to use a P.O. Box rather than your residential address for your telephone listing, newspaper and magazine subscriptions, mail order purchases, automobile registrations, and the like.

11. Consider modifying the spelling of your name on each subscription you hold. Your initials, formal name, informal versions, etc. are all valid. This strategy allows you to tell at a glance who is selling or renting your personal information to third parties without your consent.

12. If you have a complaint about the handling of your records by a financial institution, contact the appropriate regulatory agency:

    - Banks are regulated by the Federal Deposit Insurance Corporation (FDIC), Consumer Affairs Division, 550 17th Street N.W., Washington, DC 20429.

    - Savings and loans are regulated by the Federal Home Loan Bank Board, Office of Community Investment, 1700 G Street N.W., Washington, DC 20552.

    - Credit unions are regulated by the Federal Credit Union Association (FCUA), and letters should be addressed to the National Credit Union Association (NCUA), Department of Supervision and Examination, 1776 G Street N.W., Washington, DC 20456.

13. Applications for insurance sometimes require individuals to sign an authorization statement that allows the insurer to obtain information from virtually any source. Privacy experts refer to this as a search warrant without due process. Many of these authorization statements do not specify limits on the scope of the investigation or the information sources employed. Even more disturbing, many of these authorization statements do not specify an expiration date. It is obviously in everyone's best interest to help prevent fraudulent insurance claims. Nevertheless, limits to such searches should be explicit and stated. When asked to sign such an authorization statement, strike out statements that permit unlimited access to and dissemination of information unrelated to the service sought. Also make sure that an expiration date is specified.

14. If you have been denied credit, the creditor is required to disclose the nature of the information on which it based its decision. If the denial was because of a report from a credit bureau or credit reporting agency, the creditor must supply the name and address of the credit bureau or reporting agency. Upon receipt of a written request, the reporting agency must supply you with the nature and substance of all information (except medical information) about you in its file. The reporting agency must also supply you with the sources of its information and all recent recipients of the credit report. If you challenge the report, the credit bureau must reinvestigate and eliminate any information

that cannot be confirmed. Unfortunately, there are all too many reports of this simply not being the case. The Fair Credit Reporting Act prohibits the reporting of adverse information that is more than seven years old. If you are still not satisfied, write a statement of less than one hundred words to be included in your report.

15. If you have been improperly billed for a credit transaction, contact the creditor as soon as possible *in writing*. The creditor must acknowledge your letter unless the error has already been corrected. After receipt of your letter, the creditor has ninety days to either correct the error or explain why it believes the billing to be correct. Once the creditor has received your letter, it cannot try to collect any amount questioned, and it cannot report you as delinquent.

16. Periodically review copies of your medical records and insist on the deletion of anything not directly related to health care or anything that might be misconstrued. *This is especially important if your employer subscribes to a managed-care plan.* In most of these cases, you must sign a release form that allows your health care provider to divulge your information to anyone within the managed care or your employer's organizations. You might also inquire of your physician whether or not any information in your files has been forwarded to the Medical Information Bureau. Physicians are required to file certain information with this bureau but the majority of the population seems largely unaware of its very existence.

17. If you suspect your mail has been opened, contact the postmaster general and the attorney general in your state. A search warrant must be obtained in order for domestic, first-class mail to be opened

and a court order is required to detain mail. It's a crime for anyone to open or destroy mail which is not addressed to him or her.

18. Obtain copies of all records about you held by the federal government by writing to each agency you think may have information about you, citing the Privacy Act of 1974. Make each request as specific as you can. If you are required to pay a fee for this service, it must be limited to the actual costs of search and duplication. If you are denied access, you can file a civil action against the agency. You can also request to make an amendment to any record that concerns you. Submit the request to the appropriate agency in writing. If the agency refuses your request, it must inform you of the procedures for an administrative appeal. Finally, if your request under the Privacy Act is unsuccessful, request the records under the Freedom of Information Act (FOIA). Exemptions for disclosure are different under the FOIA, so your request may be successful in certain cases.

    - The United States Government Manual lists all federal agencies and their functions. It is available in most libraries or can be purchased directly from the Superintendent of Documents, U.S. Government Printing Office, Washington, DC 20402.

19. Obtain copies of all records about you held by the state governments of any states in which you have resided. Ten states—Arkansas, California, Connecticut, Indiana, Massachusetts, Minnesota, New York, Ohio, Utah, and Virginia—have Fair Information Practice laws on the books that mirror the federal Privacy Act of 1974 on the state level. If your state doesn't have specific privacy laws,

contact your state's attorney general and ask what information is available to you under the state's public records laws. You might also ask if this information is shared with other agencies, and if so, which ones.

20. Ask to see and to copy your records from any private sector organization that keeps a file on you. Try to correct information that is inaccurate.

21. The Fourth Amendment offers protection from unreasonable searches and seizures. Be careful not to inadvertently waive this protection by voluntarily opening your premises to intruders.

USING PRETTY GOOD PRIVACY

Did you know that the encryption software you may be using is classified as a weapon by your government? Well, if you're a citizen of the United States, it's sad but true. The exporting of some types of encryption software may be illegal in the United States. Never mind that *these tools have been widely available internationally for years*. The use of strong cryptography, like PGP, in America—by the citizenry—is perfectly legal. At least for now. Trying to stop the flow of information is like trying to push a river.

If you want to conduct business over the Internet or transfer sensitive information to your friends and associates, encryption software is a vital and necessary tool. And of all the encryption software available, Phil Zimmerman's Pretty Good Privacy (PGP), now published by Network Associates, Inc., is among the most powerful and widely used. Best of all, the price is right. PGP is distributed for noncommercial individual use free of charge. Commercial users are required to purchase the software. The commercial product for individual use is identical to the freeware version with the addition of technical support and a commercial use license. No technical support is provided for the freeware version of PGP.

PGP allows you to communicate securely with people you've never even met. If you find that unimportant, I'd invite you to think for a moment about the amount of information you transfer across unsecured channels that could do serious damage if it was intercepted by the right (or wrong) person.

Important: *Under no circumstances should you ever disclose your private key to anyone else*. Don't worry, it's virtually impossible to accidentally disclose your private key.

Obtaining the PGP Software

You can obtain the freeware version of PGP software directly from Network Associates, Inc.'s Web site. As of this writing (early July 1998), the current version is 5.5.5.

Important Note: Versions of the PGP software are available for Macintosh, UNIX, and MS-Windows operating systems. This section assumes you know how to use a Web browser and manage files you've downloaded from the Internet.

Use these instructions to download the PGP software.

1. Launch your favorite Web browser.
2. Navigate to the following URL: <http://www.pgp.com:8001/freeware/>
    - The PGP freeware download page should be displayed. If not, try to navigate to the appropriate page from the Network Associates, Inc. home page <www.nai.com>.
3. Click on the link associated with the software for your operating system. The software will be down-

loaded to your local hard disk drive. You may need to decode and decompress it.

4. Locate the downloaded file and decode and decompress it if necessary.

INSTALLING THE PGP SOFTWARE—MACINTOSH

When you have successfully downloaded and decompressed the software, you can use these steps to install PGP on your computer.

1. Launch the PGP installer software by double-clicking its icon. The PGP freeware banner screen appears, as shown below.

Figure 11-1: PGP Freeware Banner Screen.

2. Click the **Continue...** button. The PGP freeware license appears.

3. Click the **Accept** button if you agree to the license terms. The release notes for this version of the PGP software appear.
4. Click the **Continue** button. The Installation Window appears, like the example shown below.

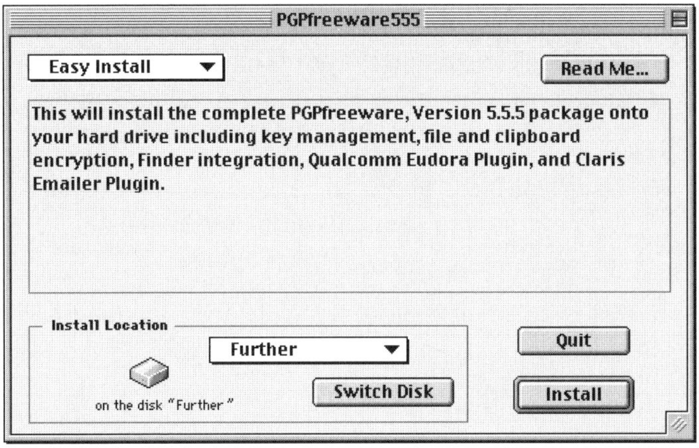

Figure 11-2: PGP Freeware Installation Window.

5. Click the **Install** button. The PGP software will be installed on your hard disk drive.
   - If you're an expert user, select the Custom Install option and the appropriate items for installation.
6. Click the **Restart** button. Your computer will reboot and the PGPmenu icon will appear in the Menu Bar.

Generating a Key Pair—Macintosh

When the PGP software is properly installed on your computer, use these steps to generate a key pair consisting of a public key that you will distribute freely, and a private key that you will keep secret.

1. From the PGPmenu, select the PGPkeys... command. The PGPkeys program launches and the PGPkeys Window appears.
2. From the Keys menu, select the New... command. The Key Generation Wizard Window appears, providing overview information about public and private keys.
3. Click the **Next** button. The Key Generation Wizard prompts you to enter your name and email address.
4. Enter your full name and email address in the provided fields.
5. Click the **Next** button. The Key Generation Wizard prompts you to select the number of bits for your key pair.
6. Select the number of bits to use for your key pair. Alternatively, enter a custom key size in the provided field.
   - Remember that larger key sizes result in more secure keys, but take longer to generate. On a modern computer it should only take a few minutes to generate even a 4096-bit key.
7. Click the **Next** button. The Key Generation Wizard prompts you for the optional expiration date for your key pair.
8. Enter the expiration date for your key pair in the provided field. Alternatively (and in most cases), accept the default option to generate a key pair without an expiration date.

- *Important Note*: If your key pair expires you will no longer be able to encrypt or sign documents, but you will still be able to decrypt and verify the signatures of documents you receive.

9. Click the **Next** button. The Key Generation Wizard prompts you for the passphrase for your key pair.

10. Enter your passphrase in both fields.

    - If your passphrase is considered to be inadequate, a warning message will appear when you click the **Next** button to continue. You have the option of entering a more secure passphrase or continuing with the one you specified.

11. Click the **Next** button. The key pair generation process will begin. It may be necessary for you to type random keystrokes or move your mouse around to provide additional random data. In this event, follow the on-screen instructions.

12. Click the **Next** button. The Key Generation Wizard reports that the key generation was successful and prompts you to send your public key to a key server.

13. Select the appropriate option reflecting your preferences for sending your public key to a key server and click the **Next** button.

    - The Key Generation Wizard indicates that your key was sent successfully (if you selected that option) and reports that the key generation process is complete.

14. Click the **Done** button. A pair of keys appears in the PGPkeys Window, as shown in the following example showing two private keys and multiple public keys.

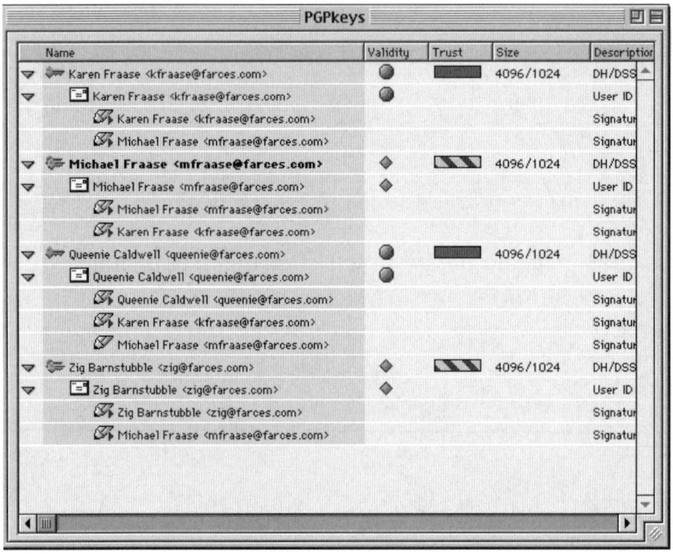

Figure 11-3: PGP PGPkeys Window with Example Key Pairs.

ENCRYPTING DOCUMENTS—MACINTOSH

When you have generated a key pair you can use these steps to encrypt a document from within the Macintosh Finder.

1. In the Finder, select the document(s) you want to encrypt.

2. From the PGPmenu, select the Encrypt... command. The PGP Recipients dialog box appears,

containing a list of the public keys available on your keyring, as shown in the following example.

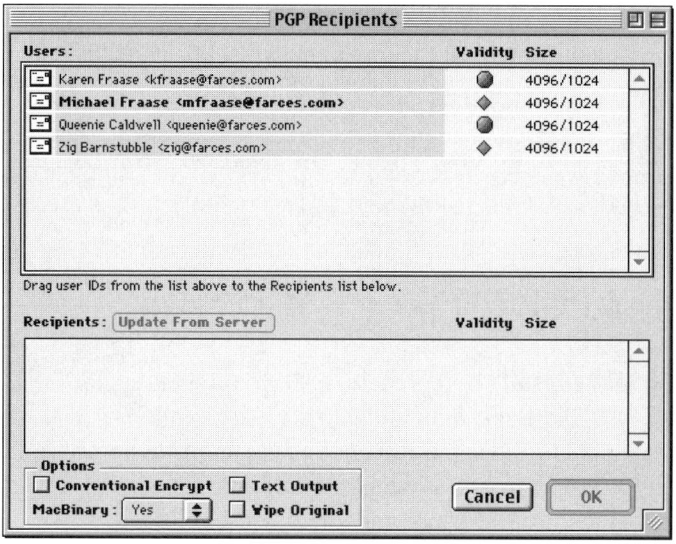

Figure 11-4: PGP Recipients Dialog Box with Available Public Keys.

3. Drag the public key of the recipient whom you will want to be able to decrypt the document from the top pane in the PGP Recipients dialog box to the lower pane.

4. Click the **OK** button. The document(s) you selected in step 1 will be encrypted using the public key of the recipient you specified in step 3.

Decrypting Documents—Macintosh

Use these steps to decrypt documents you receive from your friends and associates.

1. In the Finder, select the document(s) you want to decrypt.
2. From the PGPmenu, select the Decrypt/Verify... command. The Passphrase dialog box is displayed.
3. Enter your passphrase.
4. Click the **OK** button. The document will be decrypted.

USING PGP FOR EMAIL—MACINTOSH

During the installation process, encryption plug-ins for the Eudora and Claris Emailer programs were installed, if you have those email programs installed on your computer before you install PGP. When you have generated a key pair you can use these steps to send encrypted email within Claris Emailer.

1. Compose a new email message within Claris Emailer as you would ordinarily.
2. Within the Claris Emailer Message Window, click the appropriate encryption action button, referring to the following figure. The passphrase dialog box will be displayed.

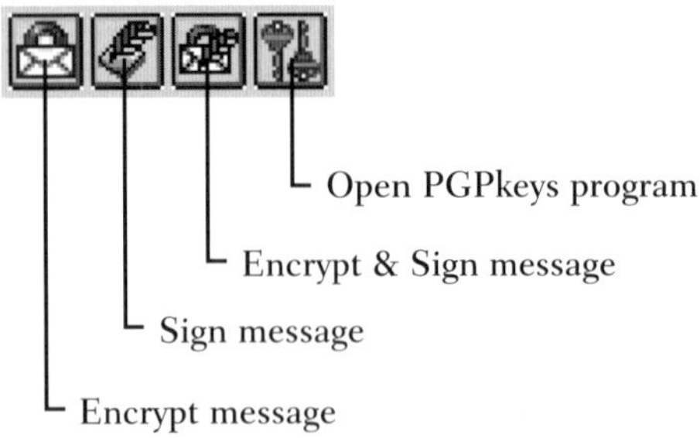

Figure 11-5: PGP Encryption/Decryption Options within Claris Emailer.

- Click the **Lock** button to encrypt the message.
- Click the **Quill** button to digitally sign the message.
- Click the **Lock + Quill** button to encrypt and digitally sign the message.
- Click the **Keys** button to launch the PGPkeys program.

3. If the recipient's public key is available on your keyring, the message will be encrypted using that key. If, on the other hand, the recipient's public key is not on your keyring, the PGP Recipients dialog box appears, as shown in the example below.

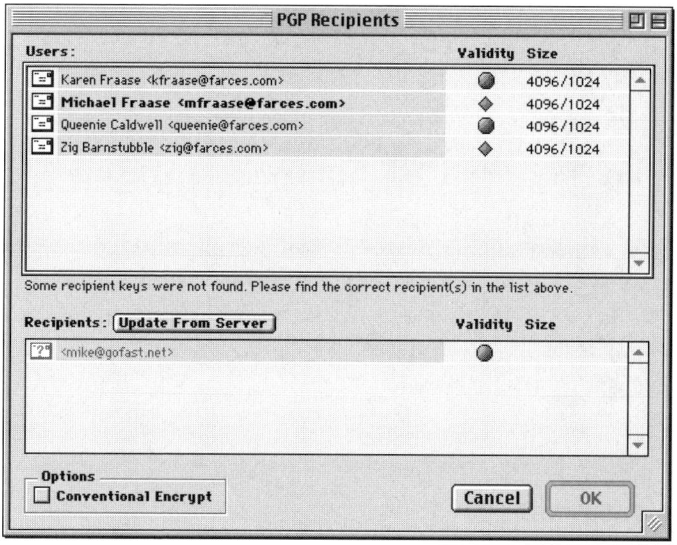

Figure 11-6: PGP Recipients Dialog Box with Unknown Recipient.

4. Click the **Update From Server** button to retrieve the recipient's public key from the key server.

5. Enter your passphrase in the dialog box (for digital signatures only).
6. Click the **OK** button. The selected action will be applied to your email message.
7. Click the **Send Now** button within Claris Emailer. Your encrypted email will be sent.

Use these steps to decrypt email messages that you receive that have been encrypted with your public key.

1. Open the encrypted email message in Claris Emailer. It will appear scrambled.
2. Click the **Unlock** button in the Message Window. The Passphrase dialog box is displayed.
3. Enter your passphrase.
4. Click the **OK** button. The message will be decrypted.

INSTALLING THE PGP SOFTWARE—WINDOWS

When you have successfully downloaded and decompressed the software, you can use these steps to install PGP on your computer running Microsoft Windows 95, Microsoft Windows 98, or Microsoft Windows NT.

1. Launch the PGP installer software by double-clicking its icon. The PGP setup screen appears, as shown below.

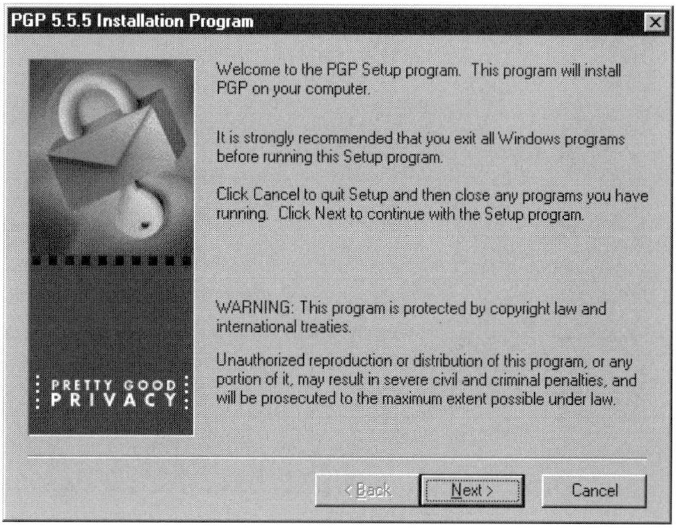

Figure 11-7: PGP Setup Screen.

2. Click the **Next** button. The PGP freeware license appears.
3. Click the **Yes** button if you agree to the license terms. The User Information Window appears.
4. Enter your full name in the appropriate field.
5. Enter your company name in the appropriate field.
6. Click the **Next** button. The Destination Directory Window appears.
   - If you want to install the PGP software in a directory other than the default selection, click the Browse button and navigate to the directory in which you want to install the software.

7. Click the **Next** button. The Select Components Window appears, like the example shown below.

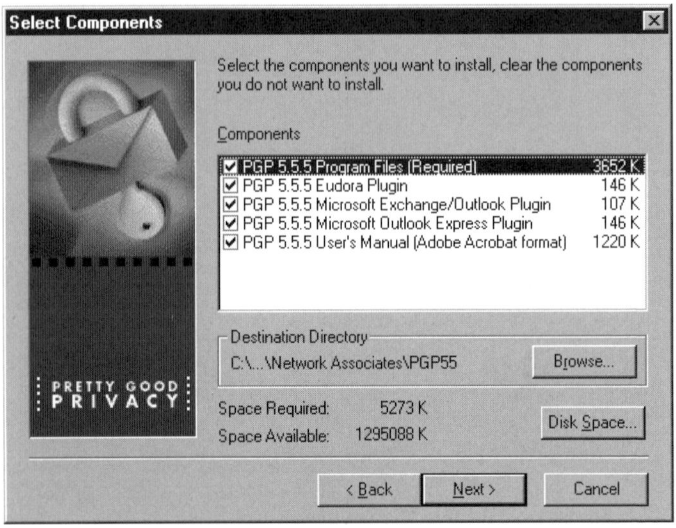

Figure 11-8: PGP Select Components Window.

8. Select the components you want to install.

9. Click the **Next** button. The Check Setup Information Window appears.

10. Click the **Next** button. The PGP software will be installed on your hard disk drive and the Setup Complete Window is displayed.

11. Click the **Finish** button. The PGP Tray icon is installed in the status area of the Windows Taskbar. Depending upon your selections in the Setup Complete Window, the software version release notes may be displayed and the PGPkeys program may be launched.

Generating a Key Pair—Windows

When the PGP software is properly installed on your computer, use these steps to generate a key pair consisting of a public key that you will distribute freely, and a private key that you will keep secret.

1. From the PGP Tray icon in the status area of the Windows Taskbar, select the Launch PGPkeys... command. The PGPkeys program launches and the PGPkeys Window appears.
2. From the Keys menu, select the New... command. The Key Generation Wizard Window appears, providing overview information about public and private keys.
3. Click the **Next** button. The Key Generation Wizard prompts you to enter your name and email address.
4. Enter your full name and email address in the provided fields.
5. Click the **Next** button. The Key Generation Wizard prompts you to select the number of bits for your key pair.
6. Select the number of bits to use for your key pair. Alternatively, enter a custom key size in the provided field.
    - Remember that larger key sizes result in more secure keys, but take longer to generate. On a modern computer it should only take a few minutes to generate even a 4096-bit key.
7. Click the **Next** button. The Key Generation Wizard prompts you for the optional expiration date for your key pair.

8. Enter the expiration date for your key pair in the provided field. Alternatively, (and in most cases) accept the default option to generate a key pair without an expiration date.

   - *Important Note*: If your key pair expires you will no longer be able to encrypt or sign documents, but you will still be able to decrypt and verify the signatures of documents you receive.

9. Click the **Next** button. The Key Generation Wizard prompts you for the passphrase for your key pair.

10. Enter your passphrase in both fields.

    - If your passphrase is considered to be inadequate, a warning message will appear when you click the **Next** button to continue. You have the option of entering a more secure passphrase or continuing with the one you specified.

11. Click the **Next** button. The key pair generation process will begin. It may be necessary for you to type random keystrokes or move your mouse around to provide additional random data. In this event, follow the on-screen instructions.

12. Click the **Next** button. The Key Generation Wizard reports that the key generation was successful and prompts you to send your public key to a key server.

13. Select the appropriate option reflecting your preferences for sending your public key to a key server and click the **Next** button.

- The Key Generation Wizard indicates that your key was sent successfully (if you selected that option) and reports that the key generation process is complete.

14. Click the **Done** button. A pair of keys appears in the PGPkeys Window, as shown in the following example showing three private keys and multiple public keys.

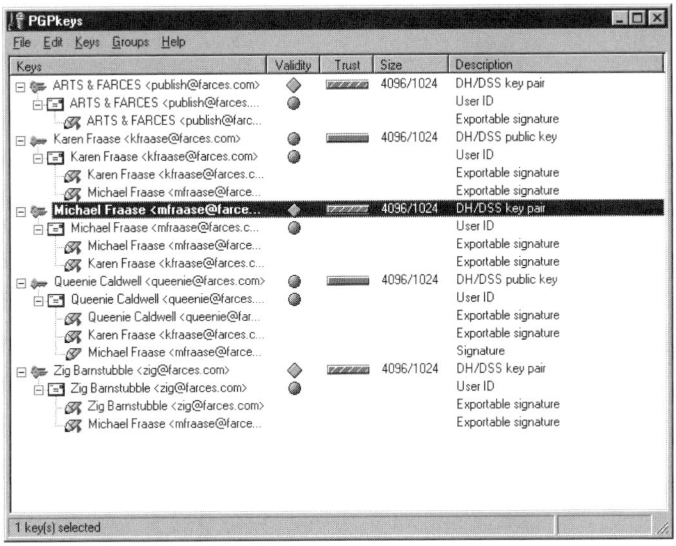

Figure 11-9: PGP PGPkeys Window with Example Key Pairs.

ENCRYPTING DOCUMENTS—WINDOWS

When you have generated a key pair you can use these steps to encrypt a document from within the Windows Desktop.

1. Using the right mouse button in the Windows Desktop, right-click the document(s) you want to encrypt. The shortcut menu appears.

2. From the PGPmenu, select the Encrypt… command. The PGP Recipients dialog box appears, containing a list of the public keys available on your keyring, as shown in the following example.

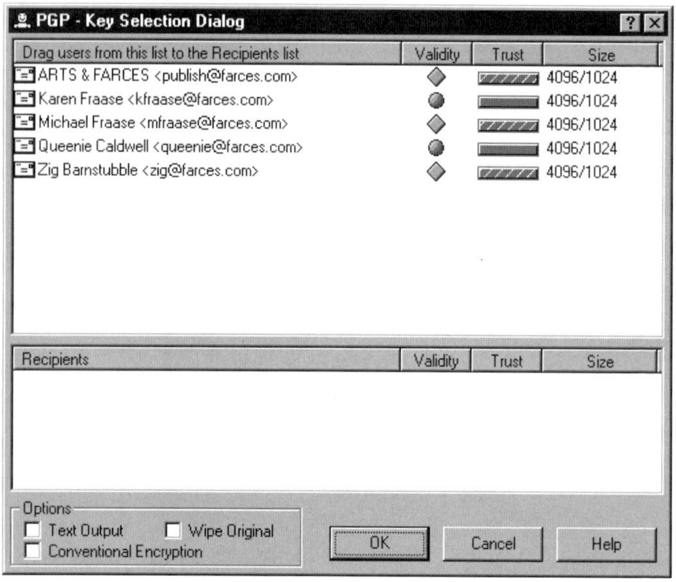

Figure 11-10:PGP Recipients Dialog Box with Available Public Keys.

3. Drag the public key of the recipient whom you will want to be able to decrypt the document from the top pane in the PGP Recipients dialog box to the lower pane.

4. Click the **OK** button. The document(s) you selected in step 1 will be encrypted using the public key of the recipient you specified in step 3.

Decrypting Documents—Windows

Use these steps to decrypt documents you receive from your friends and associates.

1. Using the right mouse button in the Windows Desktop, right-click the document(s) you want to decrypt. The shortcut menu appears.
2. From the PGPmenu, select the Decrypt/Verify... command. The Passphrase dialog box is displayed.
3. Enter your passphrase.
4. Click the **OK** button. The document will be decrypted.

Using PGP for Email—Windows

During the installation process, specialized encryption plug-ins for the Eudora, Outlook, and Outlook Express programs were installed if you have those email programs installed on your computer before you install PGP. When you have generated a key pair you can use these steps to send encrypted email within Outlook.

1. Compose a new email message within Outlook as you ordinarily would.
2. From the PGP menu, select the appropriate encryption action. Alternatively, within the Outlook Message Window, click the appropriate encryption

action button, referring to the following figure. The passphrase dialog box will be displayed.

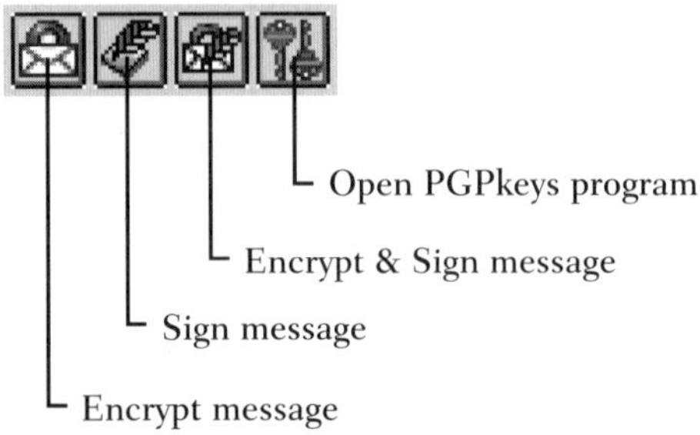

Figure 11-11:PGP Encryption/Decryption Options within Outlook.

- Click the **Lock** button to encrypt the message.
- Click the **Quill** button to digitally sign the message.
- Click the **Lock + Quill** button to encrypt and digitally sign the message.
- Click the **Keys** button to launch the PGP-keys program.

3. If the recipient's public key is available on your keyring, the message will be encrypted using that key. If, on the other hand, the recipient's public key is not on your keyring, the PGP Recipients dialog box appears.
4. Click the **Update From Server** button to retrieve the recipient's public key from the key server.
5. Enter your passphrase in the dialog box (for digital signatures only).
6. Click the **OK** button. The selected action will be applied to your email message.

7. Click the **Send Now** button within Outlook. Your encrypted email will be sent.

Use these steps to decrypt email messages that you receive that have been encrypted with your public key.

1. Open the encrypted email message in Outlook. It will appear scrambled.
2. Click the **Unlock** button in the Message Window. Alternatively, use the Decrypt command on the PGP menu. The Passphrase dialog box is displayed.
3. Enter your passphrase.
4. Click the **OK** button. The message will be decrypted.

RESOURCES

- Federal Deposit Insurance Corporation (FDIC): <www.fdic.gov>
- Federal Home Loan Bank Board: <www.fhlbanks.com>
- National Association of Federal Credit Unions: <www.nafcunet.org>
- Network Associates, Inc.: <www.nai.com>
- PGP freeware: <www.pgp.com:8001/freeware/>

Bibliography

Agre, Philip E. and Marc Rotenberg. *Technology and Privacy: The New Landscape*. Cambridge, MA: MIT Press, 1997.

Alderman, Ellen and Caroline Kennedy. *The Right to Privacy*. New York: Alfred A. Knopf, 1995.

Bagdikian, Ben H. *The Media Monopoly*. 5th ed. Boston: Beacon Press, 1997.

Bamford, James. *The Puzzle Palace*. Boston: Houghton Mifflin, 1982.

Bender, Gretchen and Timothy Druckrey, eds. *Culture on the Brink: Ideologies of Technology*. Seattle: Bay Press, 1994.

Birkerts, Sven. *The Gutenberg Elegies: The Fate of Reading in an Electronic Age*. Boston: Faber and Faber, 1994.

Boyle, James. *Shamans, Software, and Spleens: Law and the Construction of the Information Society*. Cambridge, MA: Harvard University Press, 1996.

Branscomb, Anne Wells. *Who Owns Information? From Privacy to Public Access*. New York: BasicBooks, 1994.

Brill, Alida. *Nobody's Business*. Reading, PA: Addison-Wesley, 1990.

Brodie, Richard. *Virus of the Mind: The New Science of the Meme*. Seattle: Integral Press, 1996.

Brook, James and Iain A. Beal, eds. *Resisting the Virtual Life: The Culture and Politics of Information*. San Francisco: City Lights, 1995.

Burnham, David. *Above the Law: Secret Deals, Political Fixes, and Other Misadventures of the U.S. Department of Justice*. New York: Scribner, 1996.

———. *A Law Unto Itself: Power, Politics and the IRS*. New York: Random House, 1989.

———. *The Rise of the Computer State*. New York: Vintage Books, 1983.

Cavazos, Edward A. and Gavino Morin. *Cyberspace and the Law: Your Rights and Duties in the On-line World*. Cambridge, MA: MIT Press, 1994.

Danaher, Kevin, ed. *Corporations are Gonna Get Your Mama: Globalization and the Downsizing of the American Dream*. Monroe, ME: Common Courage Press, 1996.

Dertouzos, Michael. *What Will Be: How the New World of Information will Change Our Lives*. New York: HarperCollins, 1997.

Dery, Mark. *Escape Velocity: Cyberculture at the End of the Century*. New York: Grove Press, 1996.

———, ed. *The South Atlantic Quarterly* 92, no. 4 (Fall 1993).

Diffie, Whitfield and Susan Landau. *Privacy on the Line: The Politics of Wiretapping and Encryption*. Cambridge, MA: MIT Press, 1998.

Donner, Frank J. *The Age of Surveillance*. New York: Alfred A. Knopf, 1980.

Ellul, Jacques. *The Technological Society*. New York: Vintage Books, 1964.

Fallows, James. *Breaking the News: How the Media Undermine American Democracy*. New York: Pantheon Books, 1996.

Fricker, Richard L. "The INSLAW Octopus: What's Really Behind the Scandal at Justice." *Wired*, March/April 1993.

Garson, Barbara. *The Electronic Sweatshop: How Computers are Transforming the Office of the Future into the Factory of the Past*. New York: Simon & Schuster, 1988.

Ginsberg, Benjamin. *The Captive Public: How Mass Opinion Promotes State Power*. New York: BasicBooks, 1986.

Grossman, Lawrence K. *The Electronic Republic: Reshaping Democracy in the Information Age*. New York: Viking, 1995.

Hagel, John III and Arthur G. Armstrong. *Net Gain: Expanding Markets Through Virtual Communities*. Boston: Harvard Business School Press, 1997.

Hendricks, Evan, Trudy Hayden, and Jack D. Novik. *Your Right to Privacy*. 2d ed. New York: Bantam Books, 1990.

Hentoff, Nat. *Free Speech for Me—But Not for Thee: How the American Left and Right Relentlessly Censor Each Other*. New York: HarperCollins, 1992.

Herman, Edward S. and Noam Chomsky. *Manufacturing Consent: The Political Economy of the Mass Media*. New York: Pantheon Books, 1988.

Katz, Jon. *Media Rants: Postpolitics in the Digital Nation*. San Francisco: HardWired, 1997.

———. *Virtuous Reality: How America Surrendered Discussion of Moral Values to Opportunists, Nitwits and Blockheads like William Bennett*. New York: Random House, 1997.

Kelly, Kevin. *Out of Control: The Rise of Neo-Biological Civilization*. Reading, MA: Addison-Wesley, 1994.

Korton, David C. *When Corporations Rule the World*. West Hartford, CT: Kumarian Press, 1995.

Larson, Erik. *The Naked Consumer: How Our Private Lives Become Public Commodities*. New York: Henry Holt, 1992.

Lewis, T.G. *The Friction-Free Economy: Marketing Strategies for a Wired World*. New York: HarperCollins, 1997.

Linowes, David F. *Privacy In America: Is Your Private Life in the Public Eye?* Chicago: University of Illinois Press, 1989.

Littman, Jonathan. *The Fugitive Game: Online with Kevin Mitnick*. Boston: Little, Brown, 1996.

Mander, Jerry and Edward Goldsmith, eds. *The Case Against the Global Economy: And For a Turn Toward the Local*. San Francisco: Sierra Club Books, 1996.

Marwick, Christine M. *Your Right to Government Information*. New York: Bantam Books, 1985.

Mitchell, William J. *City of Bits: Space, Place, and the Infobahn*. Cambridge, MA: MIT Press, 1995.

Mosco, Vincent and Janet Wasko, eds. *The Political Economy of Information*. Madison, WI: University of Wisconsin Press, 1988.

Negroponte, Nicholas. *Being Digital*. New York: Alfred A. Knopf, 1995.

Neumann, Peter G. *Computer-Related Risks*. New York: Addison-Wesley, 1995.

Postman, Neil. *Amusing Ourselves to Death: Public Discourse in the Age of Show Business*. New York: Penguin, 1985.

———. *Conscientious Objections: Stirring Up Trouble About Language, Technology, and Education*. New York: Vintage, 1988.

———. *Technopoly: The Surrender of Culture to Technology*. New York: Alfred A. Knopf, 1992.

Reich, Charles A. *Opposing the System*. New York: Crown, 1995.

Robins, Natalie. *Alien Ink: The FBI's War on Freedom of Expression*. New Brunswick, NJ: Rutgers University Press, 1992.

Roszak, Theodore. *The Cult of Information: The Folklore of Computers and the True Art of Thinking*. New York: Pantheon Books, 1986.

Rothfeder, Jeffrey. *Privacy for Sale*. New York: Simon & Schuster, 1992.

Schneier, Bruce and David Banisar. *The Electronic Privacy Papers: Documents on the Battle for Privacy in the Age of Surveillance*. New York: John Wiley & Sons, 1997.

Schwartau, Winn. *Information Warfare: Chaos on the Electronic Superhighway*. New York: Thunder's Mouth Press, 1994.

Schweizer, Peter. *Friendly Spies: How America's Allies are Using Economic Espionage to Steal Our Secrets*. New York: Atlantic Monthly Press, 1993.

Shenk, David. *Data Smog: Surviving the Information Glut*. New York: HarperCollins, 1997.

Shimomura, Tsutomu and John Markoff. *Takedown: The Pursuit and Capture of Kevin Mitnick, America's Most Wanted Computer Outlaw—By the Man Who Did It*. New York: Hyperion, 1996.

Slouka, Mark. *War of the Worlds: Cyberspace and the High-Tech Assault on Reality*. New York: BasicBooks, 1995.

Smith, Robert Ellis. *Privacy: How to Protect What's Left of It*. Garden City, NY: Anchor Press, 1979.

Stack, Jack. and Bo Burlingham. The *Great Game of Business*. New York: Currency Doubleday, 1992.

Toffler, Alvin. *The Third Wave*. New York: Bantam Books, 1981.

Wagman, Robert J. *The First Amendment Book: Celebrating 200 Years of Freedom of the Press and Freedom of Speech*. New York: Pharos Books, 1991.

Wurman, Richard Saul. *Information Anxiety*. New York: Doubleday, 1989.

———. *Information Architects*. Zurich: Graphis Press Corp., 1996.

In addition to the above publications, the following newspapers, magazines, and online publications were instrumental in the research for this book.

Alta Vista <www.altavista.digital.com>
HotBot <www.hotbot.com>
HotWired <www.hotwired.com>
Los Angeles Times <www.latimes.com>
Minneapolis Star Tribune <www.startribune.com>
New York Times <www.nytimes.com>
Salon <www.salon1999.com>
Saint Paul Pioneer Press <www.pioneerplanet.com>
San Jose Mercury News <www.sjmercury.com>
Village Voice <www.villagevoice.com>
Washington Post <www.washingtonpost.com>
Yahoo <www.yahoo.com>

Web Resources

2600 Magazine: The Hacker Quarterly: <www.2600.com>

Acxiom Corporation: <www.acxiom.com>

Alta Vista: <www.altavista.digital.com>

Amazon.com: <www.amazon.com>

America Online Inc.: <www.aol.com>

American Bankers Association: <www.aba.com>

American Civil Liberties Union (ACLU): <www.aclu.org>

American Library Association: <www.ala.org>

American Reporter: <www.american-reporter.com>

Americans for Computer Privacy: <www.computerprivacy.org>

An Appraisal of Technologies of Political Control: <jya.com/atpc.htm>

John Perry Barlow: <www.eff.org/~barlow/>

BBC: <www.bbc.co.uk>

BGH Bulletin: <www.foxbghsuit.com>

Bibliothèque nationale de France (French National Library): <www.bnf.fr>

Boston Spa Library: <www.leeds.gov.uk/library/branches/bs.html>

Stewart Brand: <www.gbn.org/staff/sbb/brand.html>

Business Software Alliance: <www.bsa.org>

California Bankers Association: <www.calbankers.com>

California Penal Code:
<www.ljextra.com/practice/criminal/calpenal.html>

CDNow: <www.cdnow.com>

Center for Democracy and Technology (CDT): <www.cdt.org>

Central Intelligence Agency: <www.odci.gov/cia/>

Church of Scientology: <www.scientology.org>

Coalition Against Unsolicited Commercial Email (CAUCE):
<www.cauce.org/>

Communications Decency Act: <www.fcc.gov/telecom.html>

Computer Professionals for Social Responsibility (CPSR):
<www.cpsr.org>

Computer Security Act of 1987:
<www.rdc.noaa.gov/~security/csa-1987.html>

Computer Security Institute: <www.gocsi.com>

Copyright Clearance Center (CCC): <www.copyright.com>

Copyright Licensing Agency (CLA): <www.cla.co.uk>

Corporation for National Research Initiatives (CNRI):
<www.cnri.reston.va.us>

C|Net news.com: <www.news.com>

Decision Strategies: <www.tmn.com/dsi/>

Déjà News: <www.dejanews.com>

Department of Housing and Urban Development (HUD):
<www.hud.gov>

Department of Justice: <www.usdoj.gov>

Digital Future Coalition: <www.ari.net/dfc/>

Direct Marketing Association: <www.the-dma.org>

Electronic Frontier Foundation (EFF): <www.eff.org>

Electronic Privacy Information Center (EPIC): <www.epic.org>

Ethical Spectacle: <www.spectacle.org>

Federal Bureau of Investigation (FBI): <www.fbi.gov>

FBI Infrastructure Protection Task Force: <www.fbi.gov/programs/iptf/iptf.htm>

Federal Communications Commission (FCC): <www.fcc.gov>

Federal Deposit Insurance Corporation (FDIC): <www.fdic.gov>

Federal Home Loan Bank Board: <www.fhlbanks.com>

Federal Trade Commission (FTC): <www.ftc.gov>

Firefly Network, Inc.: <www.firefly.net>

Fortune magazine: <www.pathfinder.com/fortune/>

Fox Television: <www.fox.com/tv.html>

Freedom of Information Act (FOIA): <www.seas.gwu.edu/nsarchive/nsa/foia.html>

Freedom of Information Act (FOIA): <www.aclu.org/library/foia.html>

Gay and Lesbian Alliance Against Defamation: <www.glaad.org>

General Accounting Office (GAO): <www.gao.gov>

Georgia Tech personal information survey:
<www-survey.cc.gatech.edu>

Global Business Network: <www.gbn.org>

Godiva Chocolatier: <www.godiva.com>

gofast.net, Inc.: <www.gofast.net>

Griswold v. Connecticut:
<laws.findlaw.com/US/381/479.html>

HarperCollins Publishers: <www.harpercollins.com>

Hertz Corp.: <www.hertz.com>

History Channel: <www.historychannel.com>

House Oversight Committee: <www.house.gov/cho/>

"Inslaw Octopus" (Richard L. Fricker):
<www.wired.com/wired/1.1/features/inslaw.html>

Internal Revenue Service (IRS): <www.irs.ustreas.gov>

International Data Corporation: <www.idc.com>

Internet Content Coalition: <www.netcontent.org>

Key Recovery Alliance: <www.kra.org>

Learning Company (Cyber Patrol): <www.learningco.com>

Library of Congress: <www.loc.gov>

Los Angeles Times: <www.latimes.com>

Microsoft Corp.: <www.microsoft.com>

Microsoft Sidewalk: <sidewalk.com>

Minneapolis StarTribune: <www.startribune.com>

Minnesota Data Practices Act:
<www.revisor.leg.state.mn.us/stats/13/>

MIT Project on Mathematics and Computation:
<www-swiss.ai.mit.edu>

Mother Jones: <www.motherjones.com>

Mykotronx: <www.rnbo.com/mykoweb/index.htm>

Nardone v. United States (1937):
<laws.findlaw.com/US/302/379.html>

Nardone v. United States (1939):
<laws.findlaw.com/US/308/338.html>

National Academy of Clinical Biochemistry: <www.nacb.org>

National Academy of Sciences: <www.nas.edu>

National Association of Federal Credit Unions:
<www.nafcunet.org>

National Crime Information Center (NCIC):
<www.fbi.gov/2000/ncicinv.htm>

National Institute for Standards and Technology (NIST):
<www.nist.gov>

National Organization for Women (NOW): <www.now.org>

National Research Council: <www.nas.edu/nrc/>

National Security Agency (NSA): <www.nsa.gov>

Netscape Corp.: <www.netscape.com>

Network Associates, Inc.: <www.nai.com>

Network TeleSystems: <www.nts.com>

New York Times: <www.nytimes.com>

News Corporation: <www.newscorp.com>

Newsbytes: <www.newsbytes.com>

Nippon Telegraph and Telephone (NTT): <www.ntt.co.jp>

No Electronic Theft Act:
<dev.abanet.org/intelprop/hr2265.html>

Office of Management and Budget (OMB):
<www.whitehouse.gov/WH/EOP/OMB/html/ombhome.html>

Office of Technology Assessment: <www.ota.nap.edu>

Olmstead v. United States:
<laws.findlaw.com/US/277/438.html>

Online Journalism Review <www.ojr.org>

Open Profiling Standard (OPS): <www.firefly.net/OPS/>

Peacefire: <www.peacefire.org>

Platform for Privacy Preferences: <www.w3.org/P3P/>

President's Commission on Critical Infrastructure Protection:
<www.pccip.gov>

Pretty Good Privacy (PGP): <www.nai.com/default_pgp.asp>

PGP freeware: <www.pgp.com:8001/freeware/>

Privacy & American Business: <hudson.idt.net/~pab/>

Prodigy: <www.prodigy.com>

Public Citizen: <www.citizen.org>

Public Interest Research Group credit bureau study:
<www.pirg.org/pirg/consumer/credit/mistakes/>

Qualcomm, Inc.: <www.qualcomm.com>

Quicken: <www.quicken.com>

RSA Data Security: <www.rsa.com>

Saint Paul Pioneer Press: <www.pioneerplanet.com>

Salon: <www.salon1999.com>

Secure Public Networks Act:
<www.senate.gov/~kerrey/inits/encrypt/encrypt1.html>

Securities Exchange Commission (SEC): <www.sec.gov>

Security and Freedom Through Encryption (SAFE):
<www.house.gov/goodlatte/encryption.htm>

Senate Judiciary Committee:
<www.senate.gov/committee/judiciary.html>

Slate: <www.slate.com>

Social Security Administration: <www.ssa.gov>

Solid Oak Software (Cybersitter): <www.cybersitter.com>

STAR TV: <www.startv.com>

State Digital Signature Legislation:
<www.steptoe.com/digsig.htm>

Supreme Court Decisions (FindLaw):
<www.findlaw.com/casecode/supreme.html>

Technorealism: <www.technorealism.org>

Technorealist Conspiracy: <www.technorealist.org>

TED: <www.ted.com>

Thomas: <thomas.loc.gov>

TRUSTe: <www.truste.org>

Trusted Information Systems: <www.tis.com>

United States Constitution: <www.house.gov/Constitution/Constitution.html>

United States Copyright Law: <lcweb.loc.gov/copyright/title17/>

United States Copyright Office: <lcweb.loc.gov/copyright/>

United States Secret Service: <www.ustreas.gov/usss/>

WELL: <www.wenet.net/hooked/services/well.html>

World Intellectual Property Organization (WIPO): <www.wipo.org>

World Wide Web Consortium (W3C): <www.w3.org>

Richard Saul Wurman: <www.ted.com/rsw.html>

X-Stop: <www.xstop.com>

INDEX

A

B

C

D

E

F

G

H

I

J

K

L

M

N

O

P

Q

R

S

T

U

V

W

X

Z

About the Author

After having produced more than twenty computer books and hundreds of articles for various trade publishers, Michael Fraase wrote the first Internet books designed specifically for Macintosh and MS-Windows users (*Internet Tour Guide* series, Ventana Press 1993–1994). Fraase's internationally best selling *Internet Tour Guide* series demystified using the Internet for non-technical readers while predicting the rush to cyberspace. He has appeared as a featured speaker at various conferences and has been a guest on nationally syndicated radio programs.

Poet, Deadhead, former shrimper and tree planter, Michael Fraase left graduate school to co-found Arts & Farces after witnessing his father's personal sacrifices at the hands of the corporate agenda. He makes his home with his wife, Karen, in Saint Paul, Minnesota.

About the Cover Image

Réne Magritte's *Le chef d'œuvre ou Les mystères de l'horizon* (*The Masterpiece or the Mysteries of the Horizon*) is one of the most widely recognizable pieces of fine art in the world. To my eye, it's also one of the most perplexing, disturbing even. Is the horizon to the east or to the west? Is the time of day dawn or dusk? Are the figures malevolent, benevolent, or neither; being merely anonymous? Are the figures three different phases of a single person, or three different people? Is the landscape apocalyptic or maybe even post-apocalyptic?

Magritte painted *Le chef d'œuvre ou Les mystères de l'horizon* (*The Masterpiece or the Mysteries of the Horizon*) the year after I was born, and I've been dumbfounded by these and other questions nearly my entire life.

According to biographer Suzi Gablick, who spent eight months with the artist, Réne Magritte tried to live as anonymously as possible and physically resembled the unexceptional bowler-hatted man portrayed in many of his paintings:

> "His desire to live without history (even his own) and without style, was a calculated choice to render himself invisible...."

> "Magritte's bowler-hatted man is more like a figure in a book than a human being, but a figure with all the inessential elements left out.... [H]e seems to live the history of ideas rather than the history of the world."

About Arts & Farces

Saint Paul, Minnesota-based Arts & Farces is a multifaceted communications and professional services business specializing in information design and architecture, technical writing, publishing (print, electronic, and online), and general business and technology consulting.

In continuous operation since 1979, the firm's clients range from one-person businesses and successful startups to major design firms and Fortune 100 companies.

Vision

A plurality of voices and ideas informing citizens to the point of participation protects and revitalizes democracy. Traditional media have rapidly consolidated, resulting in a handful of international corporate conglomerates with their own agendas predominantly determining what we see, hear, and read. The mainstream media model currently rewards only largess, waste, greed, and the status-quo, resulting in the suppression of diverse voices.

Parallel to the corporate consolidation of media comes the rise of the Internet as a citizens' tool for locating and interacting with information we deem important to ourselves, our values, and our communities.

Arts & Farces subscribes to the economic golden rule set forth by Paul Hawken in *The Ecology of Commerce*: "Leave the world a better place than you found it, take no more than you need, try not to harm life or the environment, make amends if you do." We encourage our stakeholders to follow this creed.

We refuse to believe that largess, waste, and greed are requirements to be a major force in the new millennium and request that you remind us and others of the economic golden rule. Remind all of us that every endeavor—individual, organizational, or commercial—has an obligation to serve the public interest.

Mission

Arts & Farces develops publishing models and business services that work to serve the greatest number. The citizenry's need to know, to participate, and to grow are sometimes eclipsed by the ever-ascending needs of corporate and government bodies.

Arts & Farces presents titles for both time-stressed professionals and everyday people, striving to make complex subjects understandable and accessible.

We are in business to create the highest quality publications—print, electronic, and online—we possibly can while operating the company on a fiscally sound basis centered on steady-state sustainability. We are determined to provide a fair economic return to our principals and to include an overarching concern for the community—both local and global—in our day-to-day decisions.

We actively choose to operate the company in a manner that earnestly recognizes the pivotal role that business plays in our society. We strive to discover and create innovative ways to improve the quality and sustainability of life in our local and global communities.

Recognizing that we have a responsibility to the community that makes the existence of our business possible, we are proud of our progressive, nonpartisan social agenda and integrate that agenda into our day-to-day business activities.

Consultancy Services

Arts & Farces applies creativity and common sense to help you, your products and services, and your organization be more successful. We've found that we're most effective with a small team of dedicated individuals—across the spectrum of the organization chart—who freely involve us in their processes.

We are weary of the way most business is conducted in this culture and are adamant about changing it. We are committed to radically humanize everything we do, including business.

Start by sending a preliminary email describing you, your company, your project, your issues, and your thoughts regarding our involvement. If our strengths and personalities are appropriate for your situation, we will work with you to define the details of our participation, including project scope, budget, time frame, deliverables, and methodology. Upon agreement about these details, our billing cycle begins.

Our fees are US$125 per hour and the minimum contract we will accept is for fifteen hours. We track our time and bill to the nearest half-hour increment. Small activities usually associated with account administration (telephone calls, email, and the like) are aggregated each week to the nearest half-hour. Our invoices include a summary—by day—outlining activity on your account. We send invoices out on the last day of the month and payment in full is due by the fifteenth of the following month.

To begin an engagement, we require an advance payment of US$1,250, which is applied to the first invoice. All expenses incurred by us are billed to you at our actual cost. Your pre-approval is required for any significant expenses. Expenses are invoiced and payable concurrent with our general invoices.

Travel time is billed at the standard hourly rate, and we try to do as much work as possible on your account while en route.

We do not work in exchange for stock and we do not work on a commission basis.

We pride ourselves on minimizing client expenses and working within a budget. We are happy to provide estimates for each phase of a project and are proud of bringing all of our projects in on time and on budget.

Anything we prepare for you becomes your intellectual property upon payment in full, without attribution. We reserve the right to use the material we generate for multiple clients.

The best way to initiate contact with Arts & Farces is via email:

Principal	Email Address
Michael Fraase	mfraase@farces.com
Karen Fraase	kfraase@farces.com

The following functional email addresses are automatically routed to the appropriate human being.

Function	Email Address
Trade book queries	books@farces.com
Publishing queries	publish@farces.com
Editorial queries	editors@farces.com
Technical writing	manuals@farces.com
Information design	design@farces.com
Business/technology reports	reports@farces.com

Function	Email Address
Business/technology research	research@farces.com
Business/technology consultancy	consult@farces.com
Company communications	communications@farces.com

ARTS & FARCES can also be reached by more traditional means:

ARTS & FARCES
2021 Grand Avenue
Saint Paul, MN 55105 USA
+1 (651) 698 0741 (voice)
+1 (651) 698 5106 (fax)

An Invitation

Arts & Farces strives to be mindful of the needs and desires of both its principals and its stakeholders: suppliers, trading partners, collaborators, customers, clients, and readers. With that in mind, please understand that *Information Eclipse* is more than the book you're holding in your hands. *Information Eclipse* is upgradeable and will eventually be interactive.

To learn about options available for participating in this experiment and *Information Eclipse* upgrades, point your favorite Web browser at:

http://www.farces.com/farces/publications/info-eclipse/

With Arts & Farces *internet*—the Arts & Farces Web site—visitors can keep abreast of the politics of information as it unfolds into the new millennium. Continuing the discussion of issues raised in Information Eclipse, visitors will eventually be able to interact with each other, the author, and the Arts & Farces principals. Following associative hypertext links from Arts & Farces *internet* to a richly diverse body of external information sources, visitors are encouraged to think critically as they explore their own mind maps through cyberspace.